THE CLASSICAL ATHENIAN
DEMOCRACY

THE
CLASSICAL ATHENIAN
DEMOCRACY

David Stockton

Oxford   New York
OXFORD UNIVERSITY PRESS

Oxford University Press, Walton Street, Oxford OX2 6DP
Oxford New York Toronto
Delhi Bombay Calcutta Madras Karachi
Petaling Jaya Singapore Hong Kong Tokyo
Nairobi Dar es Salaam Cape Town
Melbourne Auckland
and associated companies in
Berlin Ibadan

Oxford is a trade mark of Oxford University Press

Published in the United States
by Oxford University Press, New York

First published 1990
Reprinted with corrections 1991 (twice)

British Library Cataloguing in Publication Data
Stockton, David
The classical Athenian democracy.
1. Greece. Athens. Democracy, ancient period
I. Title   321.8'0938'5
ISBN 0–19–872136–6 (pbk.)

Library of Congress Cataloging in Publication Data
Stockton, D. L. (David L.)
The classical Athenian democracy / David Stockton.
Includes bibliographical reference.
1. Athens (Greece)—Politics and government.
2. Democracy—History.   I. Title.
JC79.A8S74   1990   321.8'0938'5—dc20   89–23028
ISBN 0–19–872136–6 (pbk.)

Printed in Great Britain by
St Edmundsbury Press
Bury St Edmunds, Suffolk

TO MY GRANDCHILDREN

Harriet, Jack, Jemima, Matthew, and Dickon

in the hope that they may one day enjoy reading this book half as much as
I have enjoyed their company while writing it

ACKNOWLEDGEMENTS

I WISH to express my thanks to those friends and colleagues who have helped me by reading and commenting on some parts or the whole of earlier drafts of this book, or who have been kind enough to discuss individual points with me or to send or lend me offprints of articles, and in particular to: Alan Barrett, Vernon Bogdanor, Peter Brunt, George Forrest, Mogens Hansen, John Kiteley, and Colin Leach. None of them can or should be held to be answerable for any errors or shortcomings in the final version.

D.L.S.

Brasenose College, Oxford
March 1989

CONTENTS

ILLUSTRATIONS

[Plates are between pp. 82 and 83]

ABBREVIATIONS

AA	M. H. Hansen, *The Athenian Assembly in the Age of Demosthenes* (Oxford, 1987)
AB	P. J. Rhodes, *The Athenian Boule* (Oxford, 1972)
AE	M. H. Hansen, *The Athenian Ecclesia* (Copenhagen, 1983)
APF	J. K. Davies, *Athenian Propertied Families 600–300 BC* (Oxford, 1971)
Ath. Pol.	*Athênaiôn Politeia (Constitution of Athens)*, ascribed to Aristotle
CAP	P. J. Rhodes, *A Commentary on the Aristotelian Athenaion Politeia* (Oxford, 1981)
CJ	*Classical Journal*
CP	*Classical Philology*
CQ	*Classical Quarterly*
CR	*Classical Review*
dr.	drachma
FGH	*Die Fragmente der griechischen Historiker*, ed. F. Jacoby (Berlin and Leiden, 1923–57)
fr.	fragment
GHI	R. Meiggs and D. M. Lewis, *A Selection of Greek Historical Inscriptions to the End of the Fifth Century BC* (Oxford, 1969)
GRBS	*Greek, Roman and Byzantine Studies*
HAC	C. Hignett, *A History of the Athenian Constitution to the End of the Fifth Century BC* (Oxford, 1951)
HCT	A. W. Gomme, A. Andrewes, and K. J. Dover, *A Historical Commentary on Thucydides*, 5 vols. (Oxford, 1945–81)
HSCP	*Harvard Studies in Classical Philology*
JHS	*Journal of Hellenic Studies*
JRS	*Journal of Roman Studies*
RÉG	*Revue des études greques*
ZPE	*Zeitschrift für Papyrologie und Epigraphik*

INTRODUCTION

The Greeks had a word for it, and the word was *dêmokratia*, a compound of *dêmos* ('the people') and *kratos* ('power', or 'rule'). But it is significant that the first occurrence of the word in surviving Greek literature is in Herodotus' *History* (6. 43, 131), which he was writing during the third quarter of the fifth century.[1] It was perhaps coined in the period following the reforms of the last decade of the sixth, which later won fame for Cleisthenes as 'the man who gave the Athenians their democracy' (Herodotus 6. 131; *Ath. Pol.* 29. 3)—although in his own day the slogans most favoured may well have been *isonomia* ('equality for all under the law') and *isêgoria* ('the right of everyone to have his say'). In 431 Pericles could claim (Thucydides 2. 37) that the Athenian system of government was unique, and an example to every other society in Greece: 'It is called a "democracy", because it subserves the interests not of a privileged few but of the bulk of its citizens.'

The democracy which existed in Athens for the two hundred years which followed the reforms of Cleisthenes differed in important respects from the democracies under which we live today. It is the object of this book to explain to the modern reader what its institutions were, how they worked, and what assumptions underlay them. The book is principally concerned with the fully developed democracy of the post-Ephialtic period; but a chapter is devoted to tracing the broad development of the Athenian constitution from the reforms of Solon in the early sixth century down to those of Ephialtes in the late 460s, so that the developed democracy can be seen in its proper historical context. A great deal of

---

[1] All the dates in this book are BC, save for a few which the reader will at once recognize as being AD.

work has been done by historians, epigraphists, and archae-
ologists in the past few years to reveal or to clarify much that
was formerly unknown or obscure. This seems a good time
to make the results of their work accessible to a wider
readership.

This book is intended not only for students of ancient
history but also for the educated and interested public. I have
therefore translated or paraphrased the original Greek wherever it occurs in the following pages, and transliterated the
Greek words into Roman lettering. Like most others, I have
not sought total consistency in representing Greek proper
names, but have retained the more familiar Roman or even
English forms for those that are well known ('Thucydides'
rather than 'Thoukydidês', 'Aristotle' rather than 'Aristotelês',
'Corinth' rather than 'Korinthos'). The notes to the text are
intended to direct the reader to the fuller treatments of the
evidence and arguments which can be found set out in
specialized books and articles, especially those written in
English.

I have had perforce to refer frequently to the *Constitution of
Athens* (*Athênaiôn Politeia*), a work ascribed in antiquity to
Aristotle. Some moderns are prepared to accept it as a
genuine work from that master's pen; but I align myself
firmly alongside those who cannot accept it as a product of
Aristotle's rare genius, and attribute it instead to a much less
gifted pupil. It is a valuable document, especially for its
description of the Athenian constitution of the author's own
day, the later fourth century; but it is uneven and in parts
unreliable, and nowhere displays any of that supreme critical
ability and sure grasp of essentials which characterize the
unquestionably genuine works of Aristotle himself. I have
accordingly chosen to refer to this work simply as the '*Ath.
Pol.*', reserving the name 'Aristotle' to those of his works,
and especially his *Politics*, which are indisputably authentic.
The arguments for and against the authenticity of the *Ath.
Pol.* are not new: I have nothing to add to them, and I can see
no advantage in rehearsing them here. Those who are
unfamiliar with them can find them cogently and clearly set
out in Charles Hignett's *A History of the Athenian Constitution*
(pp. 27–30), and in P. J. Rhodes's *A Commentary on the*

Aristotelian Athenaion Politeia (pp. 58–63). So far as I am concerned, it is enough that the reader should be warned that this work cannot be assumed to carry Aristotle's unquestionable authority.

I

FACTS AND FIGURES

One day, during the Cuban missile crisis of 1962, President Kennedy and his advisers were discussing the pros and cons of mounting an invasion of Cuba. They had as good as decided to go ahead, at which point they called into the room a senior officer of military intelligence to ask for his informed appreciation. He had come prepared, and produced a large map of the United States, which he pinned up on a board. 'Mr President, gentlemen,' he said, 'if I were to place the eastern tip of Cuba on New York City, would you like to say how far the island would stretch across this map?'. Various estimates were offered, the most generous reckoning that it might reach about as far as to Philadelphia. The officer said nothing, but took out a cut-out of Cuba to the same scale and placed it over the larger map. It reached from Manhattan Island to Chicago. There were gasps of surprise; but there was more to come. The officer proceeded to place a minute black spot onto the map. 'Is that Havana?', asked the President. 'No, sir, that is Iwo Jima to the same scale. You will recall that Iwo Jima cost us over twenty thousand casualties.' The invasion idea was shelved for further consideration.

Whether that story is true, or true in every detail, is of no great consequence: *se non è vero è ben trovato*, and it serves to underline how important it is to get our sense of scale right. It is easy to misjudge areas and distances if we do not know them well, or to lose a true sense of the passage of time if things happened long ago. So it is necessary to begin an account of the classical Athenian democracy with a discussion of a number of unexciting facts and figures.

Most of the states of classical Greece were tiny by modern standards. Although Athens was one of the largest of them, its superficial area of about 1,000 square miles was only the

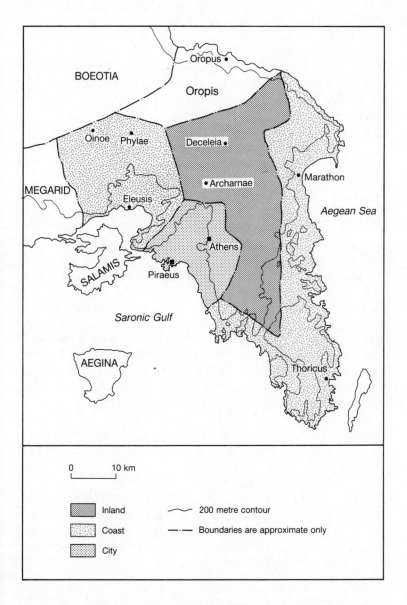

Attica: The Cleisthenenic Divisions (City, Coast, Inland)

same size as modern Oxfordshire, and a mere one-eighth of
that of Massachussetts. From the Athenian Acropolis to
Thoricus in the far south-east of Attica was some 25 miles,
and much the same distance to Oropus on the northern
border and Panactum on the north-western; Eleusis was 12
miles to the west, with the Megarian border 8 miles or so
beyond. All these are distances as the crow flies; but men are
not crows, nor are roads always good or straight or level,
especially in corrugated Attica. Although these distances may
seem short, it was a long and time-consuming haul from a
village or townlet more than a few miles away to get into
Athens itself, the chief market and political and administrative
centre. Lacking modern transport, the ordinary Athenian—
and Thucydides tells us (2. 14. 2) that in 431 most Athenians
were still living in the country districts of Attica, as they had
done since time immemorial—had to walk or drive his cart
or mule over poor roads or tracks in all sorts of weather; and
Attica is not always dry and sunny. Even a fit man in his
prime whose home was only a dozen or so miles away
needed four hours of brisk walking to reach Agora or Pnyx,
the central market and the nearby assembly meeting-place in
Athens itself, and as long again for the return journey; for all
that the ancient Athenian (like our own ancestors) was well
accustomed to walking much longer distances than we are
used to nowadays, he would not make the trip often, and
would need good reason to make it. Thus, while the
Athenian state was only 'pocket-handkerchief' size by our
standards, it was nothing like as small as we may be seduced
into thinking by our modern assumptions about the ease and
speed of travel and communications.

Early in the sixth century Solon had established objective
property qualifications for the different classes of Athens'
citizens. They were expressed in terms of agricultural yields,
for as yet there was no Attic coinage, and indeed coinage
itself was in its earliest infancy.[1] The unit which he used was
the *medimnos* (which was subdivided into 48 *choinikes*): in dry

---

[1] Robinson's article on early coinage in *JHS* 71 (1951), 156–67, superseded all
earlier discussions and assumptions. For early Attic coinage see Kraay, *Archaic and
Classical Greek Coinage*, 55–63.

terms, it equalled about 1½ bushels, some 85 lbs. weight of grain; in liquid terms it was about 50 litres or 88 pints. We can say on good grounds that an adult Athenian male needed about 1 *choinix* of wheat-grain a day, that is, about 8 *medimnoi* a year; and it has been calculated that that represents a calorific value close to the modern recommended standard for an active grown man. Women and children needed less. So we may take it as a rough guide that a family of man and wife and three children needed about 25 *medimnoi* a year. Of course, other items like olive-oil, (watered) wine, some fruit and vegetables, cheese, and a little fish or meat must be added; but the ordinary ancient Athenian (like the ordinary ancient Italian) was predominantly vegetarian in his diet.[2]

Such figures give us a crude yardstick of wealth. The richest Solonian class, the *pentakosiomedimnoi*, as their name implies, owned land which yielded at least 500 *medimnoi* a year, enough to feed perhaps twenty poor families. The next highest, the *hippeis* or 'horsemen', so called because they could furnish a horse for cavalry service, owned land rated at between 300 and 500 *medimnoi*. Next came the zeugites or 'yoke-men', who had enough land to require a plough and a pair of oxen or mules to draw it, with from 200 to 300 *medimnoi*. Citizens with property below that level were classed as thetes, although evidently a man whose holding yielded, say, 150 or so *medimnoi* a year must have had more in common with a zeugite than with another who eked out a bare subsistence on a third that much, or even less.

Modern calculations of Attic landholdings vary; but, allowing for alternate-year fallowing and discounting seed and animal needs, a 500-*medimnoi* holding probably equalled some 70–5 English acres (about 30 hectares), a zeugite holding 25–35 acres.[3] A bare subsistence might be scratched from 3–4 acres of average land, especially if the owner could get occasional work on larger neighbouring holdings. These

---

[2] For a full and properly cautious discussion of such matters see Foxhall and Forbes, 'Σιτμετρεία: The Role of Grain as a Staple Food in Classical Antiquity'. They suggest, tentatively, that cereals and such may have made up as much as 70%–75% of the diet of the poorer Athenian.

[3] See the calculations in Glotz, *Ancient Greece at Work*, 246–7; Finley, *Studies in Land and Credit in Ancient Athens*, 58–60. (The figures favoured by French, *The Growth of the Athenian Economy*, 19 ff., are too high in my opinion.)

figures are only rough guides, for much depended on the quality of the soil and the sort of crops which it could support.[4]

How these asessments were made, and how often they were revised, we just do not know. Yields varied from year to year, and there was no official machinery for regular and precise checks. It must have been chiefly self-assessment, broadly checkable by each local community, and very rough at the edges.

It is both surprising and irritating that we cannot say how long these classifications survived their definition in the early sixth century; hard evidence for the facts or dates of any changes is lacking. As the use of coinage became at first more widespread and later normal, as the Athenian economy grew increasingly diversified and 'international', as a growing number of Athenians came to derive their livelihood or even affluence from non-agricultural activities, so the original Solonian classifications must have become more and more outmoded and hard to justify and maintain, however deeply and innately respectful of real property the ancient world in general was. The author of the Aristotelian *Constitution of Athens* (*Ath. Pol.*), writing with reference to his own day in the late fourth century, says of the ten annual Treasurers of Athena that they were still elected from the class of *pentakosiomedimnoi*, but adds that such a man might be 'quite poor' (*Ath. Pol.* 47. 1); whatever he meant by that, it must surely follow that the qualification for what was still the highest class at Athens must have been lower in comparative terms than it had been in Solon's day. The criteria were probably by now expressed in money terms: an income of 500 drachmai a year or a capital of one talent have been suggested as minimum criteria for a *pentakosiomedimnos*, but it must be insisted that these are simply guesses, and that we do not know what the rules were in the period of the

---

[4] We have hardly any evidence of the size of individual holdings. Two large estates which we do happen to hear of (Plato, *Alcibiades*, 123 c) were round about 70 acres apiece—though there is no reason to suppose that Alcibiades owned only the estate here mentioned, for we know he had property elsewhere (Osborne, *Demos: The Discovery of Classical Attica*, 48 n. 5). The estate of a certain Phainippos was said (Demosthenes 42. 5) to have had a circuit of about 5 miles: but on the questionable accuracy of this evidence see Davies, *APF* 553–4.

developed democracy.[5] It is very plausible to suppose, however, that property-qualifications were given cash equivalents quite early, and that a fall in the purchasing value of the drachma as money became more plentiful did lead to a considerable lowering of the original Solonian levels of qualification for the three higher classes.

That brings us on to prices and incomes. A talent of silver weighed just under 26 kilogrammes, about half a hundredweight. It was subdivided into 60 *minai*, each *mina* into 100 drachmai, each drachma into 6 obols. Some building accounts covering the years 409–406 present us with a standard wage—for citizen, metic (resident alien), and slave workmen alike—of generally 1 drachma, exceptionally 1½ drachmai, a day. Almost a century later both wages and prices had risen, for a similar set of accounts for 326–325 shows unskilled workers getting 1½ dr. a day and skilled men 2–2½ dr.[6] In a speech in 351 Demosthenes (4. 28) reckons a daily ration allowance for soldiers and sailors at 2 obols, but he was pretty certainly deliberately choosing an unrealistically low figure so as to minimize the costs of his proposal; in the Eleusinian accounts twenty years later public slaves are allowed 3 obols a day for food, and at much the same time the ephebes (young Athenians undergoing their statutory military training) had a ration allowance of 4 obols a day (*Ath. Pol.* 42. 3). (It may be that Demosthenes' figure allowed for lower prices outside Attica.) In the late fifth century, during the Peloponnesian War, rowers in the

---

[5] Discussion and refs. in Hignett, *HAC* 225–6. I am not happy with the suggestion of Rhodes in *CAP* 551 that 'the law was only formally observed, and anyone who wished to be a treasurer would claim to be a pentakosiomedimnos and his claim would not be questioned, so that the office might fall to a poor man who was not in fact a pentakosiomedimnos'. These treasurers had to handle substantial sums of public money, and the Athenians would certainly have wanted evidence of private means to distrain on in the event of peculation. 'Quite poor' (*pany penês*) is best taken here in a comparative, rather than in its absolute, sense. So Demosthenes (18. 108) could call all but the richest 300 of the 1,200 well-off citizens who were eligible to share the cost of trierarchies 'poor men' (*penêtes*)! Cf. below, ch. 4 n. 32.

It is to be noted that our evidence indicates that in the fifth and fourth centuries rents were almost universally paid in coin, not in kind. See Davies, *Wealth*, 55.

[6] Paton, *The Erechtheum*, 339, 338, 380, 382, 398, 416; *Inscriptiones Graecae*, ii². 1672–3.

Athenian fleet were payed a drachma a day;[7] hence, a single trireme, with its complement of about 200, cost roughly a talent a month (1 dr. × 200 × 30 = 6,000 dr. = 1 talent) to keep at sea just in pay alone, without counting the costs of construction and maintenance and dockyard facilities etc.

A speech delivered at the turn of the fifth and fourth centuries (Lysias 32. 28) attests a sum of 1,000 dr. a year for the maintenance of three orphan children, a boy and 2 girls, along with a male and a female servant. In 363 Demosthenes (27. 36) regards 700 dr. a year as having been a reasonable allowance to cover the maintenance of his widowed mother, his sister, and himself during his own minority. In these two instances the figures work out at about 3½–4 obols per person per day; and both these families were comfortably off. As for working men or sailors etc., we must remember that they were not on a fixed weekly—let alone yearly—wage, but were paid by the day; work would not be available every day, and to get an annual figure we should multiply by 300 rather than 365 and accept that a skilled man might earn at most about 300 dr. a year in Pericles' time (at a period of extreme financial stringency, the Four Hundred in 411 fixed on 3 obols a day for the subsistence allowance of the archons and the standing committees of the Council: *Ath. Pol.* 29. 5); but, as we have noted already, wages rose above that during the course of the fourth century, evidently to keep pace with rising money prices.

Lysias also lists (19. 46–8) instances of the wealth of some rich Athenians round about 390. They are probably pitched on the low side, for there is here a forensic interest in minimizing the wealth of persons in a comparable position to the defendant. Ischomachus was generally believed to have been worth at least 70 talents, but at his death his sons had found only 10 to share amongst themselves; Stephanus was said to have had more than 50, but when he died his fortune was discovered to be about 11; Nicias, the famous general, was thought to have over 100, mostly in coin, but his son Niceratus had apparently left no cash, and property worth a mere 14 talents; Callias son of Hipponicus had been reckoned

---

[7] Gomme, Andrewes, Dover, *HCT* iv. 293; v. 70–2, 97–9.

the wealthiest Greek of his day when he inherited from his father—his grandfather had valued his property at 200 talents!—but Callias was now rated at a mere 2 talents. The Peloponnesian War, especially in its later years, had, however, had a uniquely devastating effect on personal wealth—a factor Lysias chose to ignore in treating such overestimates as he lists as typical. Some twenty years later, when the rich banker Pasion died (a former slave, he had been manumitted by his masters, the bank's previous owners) he was worth about 66 talents.[8]

Even with public revenues, our information is thin and patchy, though we do have reasonably reliable figures for the period of the Archidamian War (431–421). Thucydides reports (2. 13. 3) that in 431 Athens' external revenues totalled 600 talents a year, a figure that excludes 'her other (domestic) revenues'. (Sadly, he does not tell us what annual expenditure amounted to.) Xenophon (*Anabasis*, 7. 1. 27) gives Athenian revenues in 431 as 'not less than 1,000 talents a year', specifying that that was the total of both internal and external receipts. That would put internal income at some 400 talents a year; and a mere glance at the two passages shows that Xenophon was following Thucydides and taking his external revenue figure as a base. Further confirmation can be found in a passage in Aristophanes' *Wasps* (656–60), which was staged in the spring of 422: here Athens' annual revenue from home and abroad is put at 'getting on for 2,000 talents'. But by now there had been an increase of several hundred talents in the tribute of the Athenian empire (425/4), on top of the introduction of a special wealth tax of 200 talents (428/7), which had produced a large increase over the 431 figures. There may be some exaggeration in Aristophanes' (suspiciously round) total, but it cannot be much, since his figure is too close to what must have been the true one to be funny in itself—the humour of the passage lies, not in the sum of money itself, but in the explanation of how most of this huge sum finishes up in the pockets of the politicians.

It is worth pausing at this point to note the major reason why Athens, for all that her revenues were pitifully small by

[8] Davies, *APF* 431–5.

later Roman—let alone modern—standards, was the richest
state in Greece for most of the fifth and fourth centuries, and
able thereby to afford the relatively expensive system of state
payment for the multitude of public services which under-
pinned the democracy of the period. Leaving aside her
imperial revenues (which ceased after 404, and were often
fully expended on her navy—as we have noted, in the late
fifth century it would have cost all the 600 talents a year from
the empire in 431 to keep 100 triremes in commission for six
months), she drew a considerable income from her publicly
owned silver-mines at Laurium. How much this amounted
to we do not know; *Ath. Pol.* (22. 7) says that there was a return
of 100 talents in the late 480s, but we do not know what
evidence there was for this (suspiciously round) figure, nor
how much it may have varied from year to year.[9] Apart from
that, it was fairly easy for the state to collect simple imposts
on the busy trade which passed through the Agora and the
port of Piraeus by way of market and harbour dues. Quite a
number of public expenses were met by 'liturgies' which had
to be undertaken by well-to-do citizens and went some way
to cover the costs of putting on shows and spectacles,
equipping triremes, etc.[10] The passage in Aristophanes'
Wasps already referred to speaks of taxes in general, 1 per cent
excise duties, fines, leases of mines, market and harbour
dues, public contracts, and public sales.

Ancient states in general suffered from a chronic deficiency
in revenue, much of which is to be explained by the smallness
of the surplus of production over the needs of subsistence in a
world where the level of technology was enormously far
below that to which modern Western countries have become
accustomed. On top of that, revenue was hard to collect.
Land taxes are very old, and tithes of produce could be
exacted, though calculations of amounts due could always
occasion disputes; but sources of wealth other than agricultural
and other real property were more difficult to tap. High
customs dues can constitute an obstacle to trade in so far as
they may discourage it or divert it elsewhere, and hence

[9] Herodotus (7. 144) indicates a yield from the mines of 50 talents, viz. 10
drachmai for every citizen, whose number he took to be about 30,000 (see below).
[10] On liturgies see below, p. 107.

among other things lead to loss by the collecting authority. They are also often not too hard to evade, and effective precautions to prevent evasion can be expensive; they can be collected reasonably efficiently and cheaply only when a substantial volume of trade has to pass through a few easily policed points where the dues can be collected. That advantage was enjoyed by classical Athens, where a relatively large volume of trade passed through a single major port and a few minor ones. Presumably some minor buying and selling went on unsupervised across the land frontiers, and we do hear in the fourth century of a 'Thieves' Harbour' (*phôrôn limên*: Demosthenes 35. 28) where Athenian dues could be evaded; but it is unlikely that much revenue was lost by such smuggling, since otherwise we should expect it to have been firmly suppressed.

There being no concept of an income tax, states had to rely on tithings of produce, and property taxes and indirect taxes, to raise money from individuals. But only what is unconcealable and readily valued gets taxed, and what can be hidden or misreported evades the tax collector. Allegations of deliberate concealment or misreporting in order to escape the burden were probably commonplace (cf. Demosthenes 42. 23). Moreover, valuations can be highly contentious: well-to-do citizens were required to spend their own money on certain public services or 'liturgies', and we may note the disputatious Athenian legal process of *antidosis* or 'mutual exchange' whereby one citizen called on to undertake a liturgy could seek to have the burden shifted to another whom he alleged to be richer than himself by challenging him to an exchange of property.

The concept of a net personal annual income is relatively sophisticated. Many well-to-do people in antiquity did not distinguish clearly between income and capital; the fact that the ancient world never devised a system of double-entry bookkeeping is here very significant indeed.[11] Outside the natural annual cycle of farming, or the regular incidence of sailing seasons, there was no obvious reason why private earnings should be assigned to a particular twelve-month

---

[11] See de Ste Croix, 'Greek and Roman Accounting'.

period, as opposed to calculating the profit on a particular voyage or item of piece-work. Wages were day-wages. Income taxes make their appearance only when there is a fairly large number of people with easily assessable incomes above the level of bare subsistence: landlords with annual money-rents, employees with fixed annual stipends, investors with properly audited and published dividends, regular wage-earners even—though the income-tax-paying wage-earner is a very recent phenomenon and a product of the unique affluence of modern developed nations, and regular weekly and yearly wage-earners are themselves very much a product of the Industrial Revolution and its need for regular as opposed to casual labour to ensure the intensive and at least partially skilled use of costly capital equipment.[12]

All ancient public finances resembled the unsophisticated private finances of Mr Micawber. There was no notion of deficit budgeting or of a national debt (although Rome briefly resorted to 'forced loans' to the state which were to be—and were in fact—repaid when the Hannibalic War was over). Apart from the smallest token coins, money was worth its content of precious metal, so that a government could not 'print money' as it needed it; coinage was occasionally debased, but the advantage gained thereby was short-lived. In brief, budgets had to be balanced; if expenditure exceeded income, then either revenue had to be increased or spending reduced. Prudent provision might build up reserves against rainy days. Athens began her great war with Sparta in 431 with a reserve of about 6,000 talents in coin, equal to some six years' total annual pre-war revenue; but, as the war dragged on and the reserve diminished, and expenditure rose well above peacetime levels, she was compelled to raise further revenue. When times were really hard, all that could be done was to find some way to reduce expenditure and trim the sails to suit the prevailing wind: that was the harsh reality behind the political crisis at Athens in 411.[13]

[12] My debt here to Hicks, *A Theory of Economic History*, will be apparent to all who have read that small masterpiece.
[13] See below, ch. 5. (For Athens' reserve in 431 see Thucydides 2. 13. 3.)

The available evidence for the size of the population of Attica is also much thinner than we should like; and, even where figures survive, scholars may dispute the correctness of those found in our manuscripts and seek to discredit and amend them. What follow are my own 'best guesses', based on recent investigations.[14] Like many other figures in this chapter, they claim to supply no more than a reasonable approximation which will equip the reader with a general sense of scale.

There were some 9,000 hoplites (heavily armed infantrymen) of the zeugite class at the time of the Battle of Marathon in 490. Ten years later, at the Battle of Plataea, Herodotus (9. 28) attests 8,000, probably not the full muster. At the battle of Tanagra in 457 Thucydides (1. 107) reports a 'full turnout' of 14,000, but includes in that figure 1,000 Argives and an unstated number in other allied contingents. The total of all adult male Athenians at about this time, including the thetes (who did not serve as hoplites) and those zeugites too old or too young to serve as hoplites in the field army, was conventionally taken to be 30,000: it was said to be easier in 499 to deceive 30,000 Athenians than a single Spartan, and the same figure recurs in a story at the time of the Battle of Salamis twenty years later. Herodotus, who preserves both these stories (5. 97, 8. 65), was collecting his information round about the mid-fifth century, so the figure of 30,000 Athenians should be reasonably reliable, although we have to bear in mind the possibility that 'thirty thousand' may have been no more than a conventional large round number.

For 431 we have some figures from Thucydides (2. 13. 6–8). Athens now had a field army of 13,000 hoplites. There were a further 16,000 hoplites in the forts of Attica and guarding the sixteen-mile circuit of the Long Walls which girdled and linked Athens and her port of Piraeus, made up of citizen hoplites above or below field-service age together with the metic (resident alien) hoplites; but unfortunately Thucydides does not specify how many of the 16,000 belonged to each of these categories. (The field army figure is confirmed a little later (2. 31. 2) when 10,000 Athenian hoplites invade the

---

[14] See especially Gomme, *The Population of Athens*; Jones, *Athenian Democracy*, 161–80; Hansen, *Demography and Democracy*.

Megarid while 3,000 others are besieging Potidaea.) The hoplites below field-service age were the eighteen- and nineteen-year-old 'ephebes'; but we cannot say whether the over-age hoplites were the over-forties, over-forty-fives, or whatever (the circumstances were abnormal, and 16 miles was a very long circuit of walls to guard), nor how many of the 16,000 'defensive' hoplites were non-citizen metics. As for the thetes, the poorest class of citizens who did not serve as hoplites, Thucydides says nothing at all of their numbers.

To cut a long story short, the figures here suggested are, for all adult citizen males over eighteen in 431, some 22,000 zeugites and about 18,000 thetes, a grand total of about 40,000. As for metics, only the better-off of whom were liable for hoplite service, a census taken at the end of the fourth century is reported by Athenaeus :6, 272 c) as having counted 10,000 of them; a more powerful and prosperous Athens probably counted more in 431, but how many more we cannot say, since they may have constituted a larger proportion of the population a century later—the closing of the citizenship in 451/50 to those of Athenian blood on both sides may have kept citizen numbers fairly stable after the heavy losses in the Peloponnesian War of 431–404.[15] With slave numbers we are really at sea, and there is no reason to suppose that they were ever officially counted. Few accept the figure of 400,000 found in the manuscripts of Athenaeus. Round about 338, Hyperides (fr. 29) talks of over 150,000, which could be much nearer the mark; but the one reliable figure we have comes from Thucydides (7. 27), who tells us that more than 20,000 of Athens' slaves, most of them skilled workmen (*cheirotechnai*) as opposed to unskilled labourers and domestics, ran away to the Spartans at Deceleia during the closing years of the Peloponnesian War. A generation later, Xenophon (*Poroi*, 4. 24–5) assumes 10,000 as a practicable work-force for the silver-mines alone. All in all, there can scarcely have been fewer than 100,000 slaves of both sexes in Periclean Athens, and the total may have been much higher.

[15] The restriction of 451/50 was either ignored or temporarily suspended during the last years of the Peloponnesian War, though reinforced thereafter. (See Rhodes, *CAP* 331 ff., for evidence and discussion.)

A fragmentary inscription dating from 414 which details the proceeds of the sale of the confiscated property of a number of Athenians convicted of sacrilege chances to preserve the sale price of twenty-four slaves. The average price is 170–80 drachmai, the median price 157 drachmai. (The average is considerably weighted by a skilled goldsmith and a—presumably very beautiful—Macedonian woman, who fetched 360 and 310 drachmai respectively.) 'No variation in price between men and women or between nationalities can be detected, except that the two Syrians are high . . . Of the 35 slaves whose origins can be ascertained, 12 are Thracian, 7 Carian, 3 Scythian, 3 'house-born', 2 Syrian, 2 Illyrian, with one each from Colchis, Lydia, Macedonia, Phrygia, Messenia, and Cappadocia.'[16]

Our figures are crude, with the numbers of slaves and metics particularly elusive. Clearly the numbers of all classes and conditions of Attica's inhabitants varied with time and with the fluctuations in Athens' power and prosperity. The Peloponnesian War witnessed a dramatic fall, and not just through heavy battle losses; early in the war the Great Plague carried off about one third of the population, and the privations and final blockade towards the end must have accounted for a lot more, not to mention that between three and four thousand Athenian sailors are reported to have been executed by the Spartans after their victory at Aegospotamoi in 405. Taking a rather untidy plunge, let us posit some 30,000 adult male citizens in the early fifth century, rising to about 40,000 in 431 after half a century of prosperity, and falling to 25,000 at the end of the war in 404, a figure which may have risen to 30,000 again a hundred years later. If we set those figures against our very crude estimates for slaves and metics, then it looks as if probably no more than two in five (and sometimes fewer) adult males living in Attica under the developed democracy were citizens who enjoyed the rights to vote and hold office.

It is important always to keep in mind the enormous extent to which the   Athenian economy depended on slave labour whenever we are tempted to become 'starry-eyed' about her

---

[16] Meiggs and Lewis, *GHI*, No. 79. The quotation is from their commentary, p. 297.

democracy. It was only this large servile work-force which made it possible for even the less well-off free citizens to devote so much time to public business, or for the city itself to call on so many of those citizens to serve in the military and naval operations on which much of her power and prosperity ultimately depended. We should rather compare the situation in the United Kingdom even after the Second Reform Act of 1867, when fewer than two in every five of the adult male population enjoyed the right to vote.

The many thousands of resident aliens or metics (*metoikoi*) were of course free men, but nevertheless they lacked the right to vote or to hold public office. One of the best known is the renowned orator Lysias (who as a metic could not himself plead cases, but wrote speeches for others to deliver in court); his father Cephalus, a Syracusan by birth, was a very rich man, and it was in his fine house in the Piraeus that Plato set the scene of the most famous of all his Socratic dialogues, *The Republic*. As a great trading-centre, Athens naturally attracted to herself large numbers of men from many other communities, especially from the Greek cities of the central and eastern Mediterranean. Some were only occasional or transient visitors, but many settled down more or less permanently. If they did, they could apply to be registered as metics. A metic needed a citizen to be his sponsor (*prostatês*); he had to be registered in the deme where he resided, and pay its local taxes; he had also to pay the state a special tax called the *metoikion*, and (if he was wealthy enough) was required to contribute to any special levies imposed on citizens (*eisphorai*) and take on some liturgies (though never a trierarchy); metics were also liable to serve in the Athenian army and navy, though those well enough off to serve as hoplites did not normally serve in the field army but only in defensive roles. They were not allowed to marry Athenian women, nor to own real property in Attica unless this concession was specially accorded them. For specially meritorious reasons, they were occasionally also granted freedom from taxation. In return, they were accorded a secure and recognized niche in Athenian society, and enjoyed the protection of the law. (Any slave manumitted by a citizen master also enjoyed metic status.)

2

FROM SOLON TO
EPHIALTES

The most authoritative account of Solon's reforms is that
which we are given by Aristotle in a brief paragraph in his
Politics (1273^b–1274^a), which dates from about 330:

Now, as to Solon, there are those who see him as a truly radical
reformer who put an end to an over-extreme oligarchy, released
the body of the people [the *dêmos*] from subjection, and established
the excellent constitutional blend which they call 'the ancestral
democracy'. In the view of these men, the Areopagus Council was
the oligarchic element, the elective magistracies the aristocratic, the
courts the democratic. In fact, however, it looks as if two of the
elements in this blend, the Council and the elective character of
the magistracies, Solon had found already in existence and
continued in being, while himself introducing the *dêmos* as a factor
by throwing participation in the courts open to all. And that is why
some other critics blame him, for they contend that he destroyed
the other two elements by making the courts, whose members
were selected randomly by lot, supreme: after this element had
grown in strength, men truckled to the *dêmos* as if to a despot, and
the constitution was transformed into the present democracy;
Ephialtes and Pericles bridled the Areopagus Council, Pericles
introduced pay for court service, and so one popular leader
followed another in going further in building up to the present
democracy. However, it seems likely that that was not the
deliberate design of Solon, but simply how things happened to fall
out later. The *dêmos* had been responsible at the time of the Persian
Wars [in the early fifth century] for Athens' gaining mastery of the
seas, and so grew cocksure and adopted less worthy men as popular
leaders when the respectable sort opposed their policies. Solon
himself apparently gave the *dêmos* the bare minimum of power, the
right to elect the magistrates and to call them to account for their
conduct while in office—and any people which did not enjoy even

that amount of power would be slaves and enemies to their government. Solon made only the notable and well-to-do eligible to stand for election to public office, the *pentakosiomedimnoi* and the zeugites and the so-called *hippeis* [viz. the top three of the four Solonian census classes]; members of the fourth category of citizens, that of the thetes, were not eligible to hold any public office.

Aristotle is cautious and undogmatic in his treatment of Solon, much more so than the author of the *Ath. Pol.* and many modern scholars, careful to underline the lack of hard evidence even in his own day by using phrases like 'it seems' or 'it is likely'. Nevertheless, if we cut through the tangle of controversy over details, some central facts stand out. Solon, whose legislative activity I prefer to date to the 570s rather than to the 590s.[1] himself tells us that he set down in writing the rules which were to govern the Athenian state (fr. 24. 18–20). To whatever extent he was content merely to restate or add precision to existing rules, however hard or even impossible it is to decide whether this or that regulation later described as 'Solonian' really went back to Solon, however 'liberal' or 'conservative' we may choose to call his achievement, from his day forward the rules were defined and visible and hence capable of being used as an objective check—people 'knew where they were'. In that respect, Solon had a just claim to be regarded as the father of Athenian liberties, and struck a heavy blow at the power of a traditional ruling class which had not hitherto been cabined, cribbed, and confined by published rules. And Solon's rules certainly specified objective criteria to determine who was a citizen, what his public rights were, what level of wealth qualified a man as eligible to hold specific offices. The officers of state were made accountable under the law for any misconduct or wrongdoing in office, and (allied to that) provision was made for reference to the citizenry at large as a court of final instance in cases where magisterial judgements involved penalties above a stated level of severity. In the fragments of his own verses which have survived, Solon attests widespread economic exploitation and discontent,

---

[1] Hignett, *HAC* 316–21 (although I do not allow equal weight to all his arguments for the later date).

grave and justified dissatisfaction with the existing system of justice, unbridled rapacity and widespread corruption and indifference among the powerful, and the danger of civil strife or even tyranny, all of which he declared himself determined to check or restrain or correct. Further, his so-called *seisachtheia* ('shaking-off of burdens') marked the demise of a number of probably archaic obligations or exactions with which the ruling aristocracy had saddled the peasant farmers of Attica.

In themselves, Solon's rules were excellent. When Peisistratus after two abortive earlier attempts finally succeeded in 546 in establishing a secure and lasting personal supremacy at Athens, he left them by and large unchanged—so both Thucydides (6. 54. 5–6) and Herodotus (1. 59. 6) attest—and was content so to manipulate the system as to ensure that he and his sons and his close associates held the most important offices and monopolized the management of state affairs. What Peisistratus and his sons gave Athens was something which Solon had failed to secure, a stable, durable, and effective central direction, free from the tiresome discontinuities of factional politicking, under whose umbrella the Solonian rules could work properly: half the work which a tyrant like Cypselus had had to do for himself to 'bring justice to Corinth' (Herodotus 5. 92) had already been done for Peisistratus by Solon. State-backed loans were advanced to farmers to improve their lands or vary their crops; the Attic 'owls' made their first appearance among Greek coinages; Athens' influence in the Aegean and Hellespontine regions expanded and strengthened; and her exports, especially in olive-oil and pottery, grew in extent and importance. Over a span of a generation and a half, from Peisistratus' final secure seizure of control in 546 down to the expulsion of his son Hippias in 510, the increasingly prosperous inhabitants of Attica became more and more accustomed to look to Athens as the seat of strong central government and national identity; the fissiparous influence and ambitions of the old local ruling families of the Eupatrid nobility were undercut and eroded, while the tyrants understandably and prudently worked to secure and maintain the well-being and goodwill of the mass of the citizenry, and

especially of the zeugite hoplitic class, to underpin their own
controlling position.[2] During those thirty-six years certain
attitudes of mind and certain patterns of expectation were
developing which made it impossible for the reactionaries
who regained power after Hippias had been driven out to
succeed in their attempt to put the clock' back. The bid by the
aristocratic opposition to unseat Hippias had failed miserably
at Leipsydrion: a surviving drinking-song both commemorates
that defeat and attests the aristocratic-oligarchic spirit of the
movement.[3] It was only after they had secured military
assistance from Sparta that Hippias was driven from Athens;
and the subsequent period of control by the 'old gang' was
short-lived and riven by internal squabblings and rivalries.
Two or three years later Cleisthenes came forward with
proposals for reform, and won overwhelming support where
it most mattered, among the zeugites who constituted the
heavy infantry of the army. Despite another appeal by his
opponents for outside military assistance, the Athenian
hoplites turned out to blockade King Cleomenes and his
small Spartan force on the Acropolis and compel their
evacuation of Attic territory; and it is evident that they could
continue to be relied on in the years that followed to present a
united front to the ever-present danger of an invasion by the
full might of Sparta's Peloponnesian League forces to install
an unrepresentative satellite government at Athens.

Cleisthenes, Herodotus reports (5. 66. 2, 69. 2), had
become locked in a struggle for power with Isagoras in the
period following Hippias' expulsion, and was losing ground
to Isagoras as the latter prevailed in their contest for the
support of the aristocratic political associations known as
hetaireiai. He won the commons (*dêmos*) over by advancing
proposals for reform, thereby turning the tables on Isagoras
and his friends and forcing them to what proved this time to
be an ineffectual appeal to Sparta for further help to retain or
regain their ground. According to Herodotus, this turning to

[2] 'Consultation of the assembly by the executive . . . had doubtless become more
frequent since Solon, and especially under the rule of the tyrants, who could rely on
a majority in the ekklesia and had an interest in parading the popular character of
their reign' (*HAC* 152).
[3] *Ath. Pol.* 19. 3—see further below.

the *dêmos* for support was a novelty—the *dêmos* had previously been 'kept at arm's length' (*proteron apôsmenon*). The conventional translation of Herodotus' Greek (*ton dêmon prosetairizetai*) as 'he took the *dêmos* into partnership' is unsatisfactory in that it conceals a paradox in the original, which literally says that Cleisthenes 'enrolled the *dêmos* in his *hetaireia* as additional members' or 'added the *dêmos* to his *hetaireia*'. *Dêmos* and *hetaireia* were as different as chalk and cheese, for *hetaireia* along with its cognate *hetairos* was regularly used in upper-class and aristocratic contexts, of associations for social and political purposes of men from that sort of background, as for example in the Leipsydrion *skolion* already referred to: 'Alas for Leipsydrion, betrayer of *hetairoi*, what fine men you destroyed, brave fighters and of good birth (*eupatridai*), who that day showed their true lineage.' A comparable point was made by Herodotus when he referred to the positions of Cleisthenes and Isagoras in the period immediately following Hippias' downfall as *edynasteuon*, in effect 'standing at the head of an aristocratic pyramid'.[4] We may also notice the part played by the *hetaireiai* in setting up the narrow oligarchy of the Thirty in 404 (*Ath. Pol.* 34. 3); and, though he uses the word *synômosiai*, there is no doubt that Thucydides means to refer to them (8. 54. 4) as organized to apply violence in support of the 'right-wing' extremists in 411. The developed law of the fourth century reportedly made the formation of at least some such associations (*hetairika*) a treasonable offence (Hyperides 4. 8). Thus we can best bring out the meaning of Herodotus' words by rendering him as saying in effect that Cleisthenes 'brought the mass of the people into politics'. Hitherto, politics had been essentially an affair of combinations and manœuvrings among the leading personages of the aristocracy and their associates and supporters, with the *dêmos* left out in the cold except in so far as the commons were expected from

---

[4] Forrest, *The Emergence of Greek Democracy*, 191. Herodotus (6. 33. 1) used the same verb (*edynasteue*) to describe the political eminence of Peisistratus' ally, the elder Militiades. The same language is employed by Thucydides (3. 62. 3) to characterize a tight aristocratic-oligarchic régime at Thebes in the early fifth century: *dynasteia oligôn andrôn*. Hignett (*HAC* 123) concluded that 'the Attica of Solon was not a centralized state governed by democratic institutions and subject to the rule of law, but a confederacy of local dynasts'.

time to time to rally behind this or that leader of group of leading men.

Cleisthenes changed all that, and dramatically. We need not consider here (and in any event we cannot say for certain) whether this was a late and desperate strategy forced on him by Isagoras' predominance, or whether he had all along been alive to the fact that the clock could not be turned back; it could be that it was his insistence that changes were unavoidable that had cost him the loss of much upper-class support to Isagoras, for all that it was he and not Isagoras who had taken the lead in the movement to unseat Hippias in the first place. However that may be, the plain fact that his move won the day and his reforms proved popular and lasting is proof in itself that his judgement was correct, that he moved in the right direction.

Previously, citizenship had been based upon membership of one of four *phylai* (conventionally translated as 'tribes'), which were agglomerations of clans and sub-clans in which the eupatrid families of the nobility played a dominant role both socially and in cult matters. The strengthening of the central cults and festivals of the Athenian state, most notably the Panathenaic festival, which had been fostered by the Peisistratids, had gone some way towards weakening these ties, as too had their institution of circuit judges (*dikastai kata dêmous*) to adjudicate local suits. But Cleisthenes adopted a truly radical approach. He did not abolish the old tribes: he simply left them to wither on the vine. Athenians were allocated to ten new tribes which were based on domicile, a move which must have undercut the hold which the nobles had earlier exercised over the political machinery of the state; and his organization of the demes, the natural 'parishes' or 'boroughs' of Attica, as the basis on which the new system rested gave the ordinary man his first experience of self-government and involvement in administration at the local level. The new system also eased the absorption and consolidation within the citizen body of a considerable number of men whose title to citizenship could be questioned, and whom the restored aristocrats had started to comb out of the citizen register shortly after Hippias' expulsion (*Ath. Pol.* 13. 5). It is a safe guess that these people were most heavily concentrated in the Athens–Piraeus region, having been drawn thither by the burgeoning activity and prosperity which marked the stable and efficient rule of the Peisistratids. Aristotle reports (*Politics*, 1275^b) that Cleisthenes enrolled in his new tribes 'numerous aliens, and metics of servile origin'.

Interwoven with the reform of the tribes was Cleisthenes' creation of a national Council (*boulê*) of Five Hundred, the central and binding element in the developed Athenian democracy. It is not disputed that the special nature of Cleisthenes' arrangement of the citizen body in ten territorial 'tribes' (*phylai*) demands a special explanation. Merely to have moved from a real or supposed kinship grouping to a system based upon a man's place of residence could have been effected simply by dividing Attica into ten (or whatever number it might be) self-contained divisions, like modern English counties. That was what happened at Rome when the 'Servian' reform abandoned a previous kinship system and created new tribes based on territorial divisions. But that was not what Cleisthenes chose to do. Each of his ten new tribes was an amalgam of three separate 'ridings' or 'thirdings' (*trittyes*), each consisting of a cluster of demes. In each tribe one of its three *trittyes* was drawn from each of three distinct regions of Attica: city (which included not only Athens and Piraeus but also an area of the country round about), coast, and inland—*asty*, *paralia*, *mesogeios*. Now, there is no evidence of block voting in the classical Athenian citizen assembly of the *ecclêsia*, that is to say of a procedure whereby the majority vote in each tribe determined the vote of that tribe as a unit, with issues decided by counting the number of tribes voting for or against (as happened, for instance, in the Roman tribal assembly, or as happens in modern British elections when in effect we count the number of constituencies voting for or against the existing government and not the number of individual voters). So what was the point of Cleisthenes' scheme, granted that the Athenians counted heads and not tribes in *ecclêsia* voting? One suggested answer is that it encouraged the cohesion of the Athenian people by ensuring that the ten tribal regiments which constituted the national army each contained infantrymen from different regions, who fought side by side and thereby acquired a wider than local loyalty; but it is hard to suppose that that is the whole story. And even if we allow (although I am not convinced of it) that there could have been some elements of chicanery or 'gerrymandering' in the allocation of particular demes to a *trittys* or a particular *trittys* to a tribe so as to give unfair advantage to Cleisthenes and his associates,[5] the question still has to be asked and answered. And the only satisfying answer to be found lies in the *boulê*, the Council of Five Hundred.

Like any other body of more than minuscule size, the full assembly of Athens' citizens, which might number several thousands on any given occasion, needed to be 'programmed' by some smaller and more effective body. Cleisthenes provided for this by instituting a Council (*boulê*) of Five Hundred which was composed of citizens of at least zeugite standing. It was recruited on an annual basis, fifty from each of the ten tribes, their constituent demes supplying councillors roughly in proportion to the numbers of their registered deme-members. The choice of men to serve as *bouleutai* each year was determined by chance, by a process of random sortition;[6] and no citizen could be a *bouleutês* more than twice in his lifetime. Hence the Council of necessity constituted a random cross-section of citizens of zeugite standing or higher, above all of zeugites themselves, who must have vastly outnumbered the two richer classes of *pentakosio-medimnoi* and *hippeis*. The minimum age for eligibility was thirty. Such a body could evidently never aspire to the sort of influence and power attainable by elected bodies of longer corporate and individual tenure, like the Roman Senate or a modern parliament or local council.

Even so, five hundred men are far too many to be able to function as an effective committee. Plato later took this

[5] Lewis, 'Cleisthenes and Attica'. Given the scantiness of our evidence, I remain unconvinced that the instances listed by Lewis cannot have been either the result of chance or otherwise explicable for reasons which are now beyond recovery. (See further below, p. 60.)

[6] Rhodes, *CAP* 251, very properly observes that 'it is possible that members were elected at first' and that the use of the lot was a later development. He is also inclined to believe that the system of rotating prytanies was later than Cleisthenes (see further below, p. 51). But that seems to me unlikely, since such fundamental later changes ought to have been noted by the *Ath. Pol.*—and, as argued here, the prytany system is closely intertwined with the character of Cleisthenes' tribal organization.

obvious point: in his model constitution (*Laws*, 758 B–D) he accepted that a 'crowd' of councillors could never be capable of performing their duties expeditiously and efficiently, apart from the consideration that most of them were bound to want to devote much of their time to their private affairs; accordingly, his model Council was to be equally divided into subgroups, each functioning in turn as a standing committee of the whole for one month of the year. Aristotle also observed (*Politics*, 1320ª27–9) that 'the well-to-do are unwilling to spend many days away from their own affairs, but are prepared to do so for a short period'. Hence, we find each of the Cleisthenic tribal contingents of fifty councillors, the so-called 'prytanies', serving in rotation for one-tenth of the year.[7] The structure of his tribal organization had a very significant consequence here: given that each prytany contained men drawn from each of the *trittyes* of each tribe, the effect was like cutting slices from a layer-cake, each slice containing men from each of the different regions of Attica city, coast, and inland. That would not have been effected if a straightforward division into self-contained and topographically compact tribes had been adopted.

Thus, just as the whole *boulê* was a random microcosm of the *dêmos*, so too was each of its standing committees, with each of the latter so constituted as to ensure that local interests or issues could not dominate or distort decisions. And that was very important, since the attendance and voting at meetings of the *ecclêsia* must normally have been heavily weighted on the side of those citizens who lived close enough to be able to turn up without undue expenditure of time and effort, especially when we remember that the *ecclêsia* began its meetings early in the morning. But the *boulê* and its prytanies were so organized that that natural

---

[7] The Attic calendar was tiresomely complex: see Rhodes, *AB* 224–30, for a brief summary of the difficulties. Down to the last decade of the fifth century the Council's year followed the solar year of 365 or 366 days. But thereafter it was equated with the 'archontic' year, which ran roughly from midsummer to midsummer (which is why modern books date many events as, e.g., 489/8, or 356/5). The 'archontic' year was a lunar year of about 354 days; hence it had to be intercalated with an extra month of 30 days every three years or so, in order to bring it back into line with the solar year. As a result of that, after the last years of the fifth century in intercalary years each of the prytanies was three days longer than in other years.

imbalance was redressed. That was unquestionably a consequence of Cleisthenes' arrangements, and it may be claimed as an obviously forseeable consequence, and hence as an intention, which helps to explain why this *prima facie* complex scheme was adopted. If we start from the *boulê* as central, the rest follows.[8]

It is not proposed here to argue in detail whether or not Solon had provided for a Council of Four Hundred to operate alongside the Areopagus, the high council of archons and ex-archons. That has long been a disputed question, and it would not still remain contentious if the evidence allowed a decisive answer. Although it is attested by the *Ath. Pol.* (8. 4) and by Plutarch (*Solon*, 19), some scholars will have none of it.[9] Particularly worrying is the fact that a Solonian Council of Four Hundred is nowhere mentioned by Aristotle in his *Politics*, where he speaks only of the Areopagus (1273^b– 1274^a: above). Nevertheless, whatever position we adopt, it can be asserted with confidence that, even granted that such a council was excogitated by Solon, we have no reliable evidence about what the qualifications for membership were, how and by whom its members were selected, what were its powers and functions and tenure and effectiveness, or indeed whether it was effective at all. There is certainly no reason to assume that all that Cleisthenes did was to take an existing council and increase its numbers from four to five hundred: the entirely new system on which his Council of Five Hundred was based guarantees that, apart from any other considerations. Nor should we forget the recent thirty-six years of Peisistratid rule, when whatever system was formally in force was 'worked' by the tyrants themselves.

In such matters, preparation and programming are everything. From Cleisthenes' political victory in 508/7 onwards, the sovereign *ecclêsia*, open to every adult male Athenian, decided on business and draft proposals which were brought

---

[8] How far kinship or clan groupings may have preserved any rough geographical or local cohesion in pre-Cleisthenic Athens it is impossible to determine. Incidentally, I cannot follow Hignett (*HAC* 117ff.) in believing that the thetes were only now admitted to the *ecclêsia*: that is not only implausible, but is specifically denied by Aristotle in *Politics*, 1273–4 (cited above).

[9] Most notably Hignett, *HAC* 321–6. (I must myself confess grave doubts that Solon established a Council of Four Hundred.)

forward for its approval not by a body of elected 'politicians' but by a random and representative cross-section of its own members, and a cross-section so constituted that it could not but reflect the whole spectrum of national interests far better than the *ecclêsia* itself, while precluding the emergence within its own membership of the sort of lastingly powerful corporate influence and expertise which are so commonly found in such bodies at other times and in other places.

It is not to be doubted that after Solon's reforms the Areopagus had continued to constitute Athens' senior (and possibly only, and surely only continuous) council of state. Its members were recruited from the nine annually elected archons, and they held their seats in the Areopagus for life. (Solon had opened the archonship to non-nobles, but only to the wealthiest among them, and the nobility probably continued to predominate.) Apart from *the* (eponymous) archon whose name was employed like those of Rome's consuls to date the year of his office, there were: a king-archon (*archôn basileus*), a 'war-archon' or 'polemarch' (*pole-marchos*), and six *thesmothetai* (law-setters). This college of archons was at some time increased to ten, matching the ten Cleisthenic tribes, by the creation of the office of Secretary to the *thesmothetai*, instituted either by Cleisthenes himself or at some slightly later date unknown to us. Until 487/6 the archons were chosen by direct election.[10] Under Solon's rules only the richest citizens, the *pentakosiomedimnoi*, were eligible; it may be that by Cleisthenes' day the next richest, the *hippeis*, were also eligible, though that is not certain.[11]

Cleisthenes is nowhere reported to have carried any measures which varied the *formal* powers of the Areopagus,

---

[10] The *Ath. Pol.* says that under Solon's rules the archons were chosen by a process of partial sortition (*klêrôsis ek prokritôn*), and that direct election was introduced (or reintroduced) later by the Peisistratids. But Aristotle (*Politics*, 1273ᵇ–1274ᵃ: above) is quite clear that under Solon's rules the archons were elected; and both Herodotus (1. 59. 6) and Thucydides (6. 54. 5–6) assert that Peisistratus left the Solonian rules unchanged. For a detailed demolition of the *Ath. Pol.*'s position see Hignett, *HAC* 321–6.

[11] Hignett (*HAC* 101–2), Rhodes (*CAP* 148, 330), and others incline to believe that the *hippeis* were probably or possibly eligible for the archonship under Solon's rules alongside the richest class of *pentakosiomediomnoi*. (The implication of *Ath. Pol.* 26. 2 is that the *hippeis* were already eligible when the archonship was opened to *zeugitai* not long after 460.) The evidence is not decisive either way.

and there is no compelling argument that he must have. But
that need not mean that the Areopagus was unaffected by his
reforms. It is eminently reasonable to accept that hitherto it
had acted, rather like the Roman Senate, as the great council
of state, advising and influencing the annually changing
officers of state in the exercise of their duties and discretion;
for the Areopagites were themselves all ex-archons of
varying seniority and authority. That aspect of their functions,
leaving aside any formal prerogatives of the Areopagus as a
high court of law, may very well have been a matter of
political realities and conventions rather than of formal
statute-law; but it is not easy to see where else the annual
archons could or would have looked for guidance and
support, or where else active politicians could have found a
secure niche.[12] The tyrants had run Athens for well over
thirty years by ensuring that the archons were their own men
(Augustus shows us how nominally free elections could be
'fixed' at Rome without openly discarding or flouting pre-
existing rules, and there are any number of other and
more modern examples); hence, as year followed year, the
Areopagus had come increasingly to be dominated by their
creatures and collaborators. If we accept this as a reasonably
accurate picture, then the new Council of Five Hundred must
have deprived the Areopagus of a centrally important role,
whatever were the formal powers which Cleisthenes left it in
possession of.

   After Ephialtes' reforms, meetings of the *boulê* or the
ecclêsia were both presided over by that member of the
prytany in office who was selected by lot to take his turn as
that day's chairman. We cannot be sure that that was original
to Cleisthenes. It could be that at first the archons performed
either or both of those offices, and that the rotating
presidency of the prytany members came in later, perhaps
part of the change in 487/6 which abolished direct election to
the archonship, perhaps as one of the Ephialtic reforms:
proof either way is lacking. Of the 487/6 reform we have
only one notice (*Ath. Pol.* 22. 5), and all that is there attested

---

[12] For a suggestion that down to the early fifth century the annual eponymous
archons had regularly, if not invariably, previously held other 'junior' archontal
offices see Forrest and Stockton, 'The Athenian Archons: A Note'.

is a change in the method of choosing the archons with no mention of any variation of their powers or functions; but, again, that is not decisive. [13]

Themistocles' tenure of the eponymous archonship in 493/ 2 has been taken to show that considerable executive or policy-initiating competence still survived in that office. But the argument is far from cogent. It rests on a passage in Thucydides (1. 93. 3) which is assumed to tell us that it was *as archon* that Themistocles had initiated the fortification of the harbour of Piraeus, the completion of which he oversaw more than a dozen years later, after the naval victory at Salamis in 480. However, Thucydides need not be referring to Themistocles' archonship, but rather to another office (the word *archê* could denote any public office) to which Themistocles had been appointed in the late 480s to implement the 'big fleet' policy which he had persuaded the *ecclêsia* to adopt in 483/2. If so (and such a reading suits Thucydides' Greek as well, if not better), we can disregard the archonship and instead suppose that Themistocles was appointed to supervise the consequential work at the Piraeus, just as Pericles was later elected to a special *archê* to superintend the building-works on the Acropolis for which he had secured the approval of the *ecclêsia*. [14]

It is often asserted that the 487/6 reform had as its object, or at any rate its consequence, the elevation of the importance of the *stratêgoi*, the generals who commanded Athens' naval

[13] The introduction of an element of random selection in the early 480s is confirmed by the list of the names of the eponymous archons, which down to 489/8 include those of important men like Hipparchus (496/5), Themistocles (493/2), and Aristides (489/8), but not thereafter—just the sort of pattern which we should expect from such a change as the *Ath. Pol.* attests.

[14] Thucydides 1. 93. 3: 'Themistocles also persuaded the Athenians to complete the construction work at the Piraeus on which a start had been made earlier during the *archê* which he held on an annual basis at Athens.' One would hardly expect Thucydides to waste words telling his readers that the archonship was an annual office, and it is far easier to posit a gap of a year or two in the Piraeus building work caused by the Persian invasion and occupation of Attica than a gap of over twelve years. (I do not regard the observations of D. M. Lewis, *Historia*, 22 (1973), 757–8, as in any way decisive against the interpretation of Thucydides expressed here.) For a vivid description of Pericles and the Acropolis building programme, see Plutarch, *Pericles*, 13. Whatever the formal seniority of the polemarch Callimachus was at Marathon, Herodotus (6. 103 ff.) is clear that he did not operate independently of his nominally subordinate *stratêgoi*.

and military forces. For (so the argument runs), while a man could be directly elected as one of the ten annual *stratêgoi* by popular vote year after year for as long as he could secure enough support, the now chance-determined archonship was depressed in value and influence. The argument is, however, anything but compelling. Far more decisivé in the growth of the predominance of the *stratêgia* must have been Themistocles' 'big fleet' policy of 483/2, which made possible the victory at Salamis in 480 and the subsequent development of the 'Athenian Empire' in the eastern Mediterranean and the Black Sea. That was what made the *stratêgia* the centrally important *archê* which it later became; and that in its turn had been made possible only by the windfall in public revenues provided by the chance discovery of the new silver-lode at Maroneia some four years after 487/6, when this rich new source of income and its possible use to build a powerful fleet could not have been guessed at. The *stratêgia* had obvious attractions and offered rich opportunities to later politicians like Cimon and Pericles and others during the years of Athenian naval and imperial power and warfare. Clearly, none of these men could have made the annually changing archonship a vehicle of continuing power and influence or prestige even if it had remained attainable by direct election.

What lay behind the 487/6 reform we shall probably never be able to say for certain. The *Ath. Pol.* merely records the change in the procedure for appointing the archons, naming no names and proffering no explanation or motive. It may be that the object was to 'depoliticize' the Areopagus; or it may have turned out that Cleisthenes had so diminished the importance of the archons that random selection was all that was needed. There could perhaps have been a connection with the battle of Marathon in 490, when the supreme command was formally in the hands of the polemarch Callimachus, although the victory was won by his nominal subordinate, the *stratêgos* Miltiades; given that a man could be polemarch only once in his lifetime, it must regularly have been true that the *stratêgoi* were men of greater military experience and proven ability than the annual polemarch. But all such suggestions are no more than speculations. We have no solid base to build on.

I incline to believe that the change in the appointment of

archons in 487/6 reflected at least in part an appreciation that the Cleisthenic reforms twenty years earlier had made the archonship a far less important office: its central 'political' functions having disappeared, it was left with judicial and ceremonial ones only. Since its personnel supplied the Areopagus with its members, the change meant that that body gradually became more and more a random selection of the wealthier citizens, educated men who could perform their duties without pay, but who were not 'politicians' *per se* who had stood for and won direct election to their office, as hitherto.

A remarkable feature of the fifth-century democracy, which may have been introduced by Cleisthenes, was ostracism. At a meeting of the *ecclêsia* in the sixth of the ten prytanies of each year (about mid-winter), a vote was taken whether or not to hold an ostracism. If it was affirmative, an ostracism was then held in the eighth. Any citizen who so chose came that day to the Agora and wrote or scratched on a bit of pottery (*ostrakon*) the name of whoever it was he wished to have ostracized. Provided that at least 6,000 valid *ostraka* were handed in, the man with the highest count against him (which apparently did not have to be a majority of the *ostraka* handed in) was compelled to leave Attica and not set foot there again for ten years—although he could still draw the income from his properties there while he was away.[15] Since at least 6,000 *ostraka* had to be cast if an ostracism was to be effective, there had to be a fairly heavy turn-out of voters, which would not happen unless it were widely believed that very important issues were at stake. In 411 the oligarchic plotters claimed (Thucydides 8. 72. 1) that fewer than 5,000 citizens ever turned up at an *ecclêsia*. Despite a justified suspicion that these men had an interest in lying and obfuscation, and for all that wartime conditions must often have led to the absence of many citizens on military or naval service, the figure is probably not all that far from the

---

[15] A variant tradition that at least 6,000 valid *ostraka* had to be cast against any one man is to be rejected—see the refutation by Staveley in his *Greek and Roman Voting and Elections*, 88–93. For other instancs of a quorum of 6,000 where individual rights were involved, see Hignett, *HAC* 153, 166, 216; and Hansen, *AE* 1–23. On ostracism see now Thomsen, *The Origins of Ostracism*.

truth (if at all), for it was produced in an address to an unsympathetic audience of Athenian servicemen who would have spotted a gross lie at once. (What the oligarchs carefully neglected to point out was (*a*) that their proposed body of five thousand citizens who alone would possess full citizen rights was anything but identical with the cross-section of Athenians who normally attended the *ecclêsia*, and (*b*) that they had no intention of creating such a body anyway; it was here, rather than in the actual number given, that the *suppressio veri* and *suggestio falsi* of their argument lay.) In any case, archaeology has revealed that the Pnyx, where the *ecclêsia* regularly met, could at this date accommodate at most some 6,000 or so citizens out of the total number eligible to attend and vote.[16]

Whether ostracism was a Cleisthenic innovation, or introduced only some twenty years later, is hotly disputed. *Ath. Pol.* (22) reports it as Cleisthenic. But some moderns maintain that a later date is attested by the fourth-century writer Androtion in a fragment cited by Harpocration from his (now lost) *History of Athens*, in which he allegedly dated its institution immediately prior to the ostracism of Hipparchus in 488/7. However, good reasons can be adduced to suppose that Harpocration garbled what Androtion had actually written, and that the *Ath. Pol.* (whose text is here so close to that of Harpocration that it is plain that both were following the same source) preserves the correct version of Androtion.[17]

It is beyond dispute that the first *remembered* ostracism was that of Hipparchus in 488/7. If that was in fact the first, how can one account for the long interval between Cleisthenes' legislative activity and Hipparchus' ostracism? It was, when all is said and done, a very curious process. No criminal act had to be proved against its victim, no speeches were allowed at either the preliminary or the actual ostracism meetings, and the penalty was simply an enforced absence from Attica for ten years, with no (other than incidental) financial loss, after which period the *ostracisé* was free to return to Athens

---

[16] See Gomme, Andrewes and Dover, *HCT* v, note on 8. 72. 1; Hansen, *AE* 25–6, 212–13. (Voting on ostracisms took place in the Agora.)

[17] Androtion fr. 5. Against Cleisthenic authorship, Hignett, *HAC* 159–64; for a less committed view, and a summary of the arguments, Rhodes *CAP* 267–71.

and resume his full citizenship there. As Beloch put it in a forceful phrase, 'such a weapon is not forged to be left for twenty years in the sheath'.[18] Other scholars, however, while not challenging the force of Beloch's argument, have sought to counter it by suggesting that Hipparchus was not in fact the first victim of ostracism: conceivably, the only evidence later writers had was the famous amnesty decree of 481/80 which recalled all *ostracisés* during the crisis of the Persian invasion, and that decree would not have named anybody ostracised more than ten years earlier. No doubt that is possible, though it is still not easy to suppose that Athenian fourth-century tradition had completely forgotten the names of any men 'big' enough to have been ostracized before 490. (The story that Cleisthenes had himself been 'hoist with his own potsherd' survives only in an inferior source seven hundred years later than the supposed event, and must be dismissed as at best a garbled fantasy or a misunderstood joke.) Yet, given that no name earlier than that of Hipparchus was remembered, how and why did it ever occur to anyone to invent the story that ostracism was the work of Cleisthenes? The years 490–480 do not lack the names of leading Athenians to whom the institution of ostracism could plausibly have been attributed if good reason to assert Cleisthenes' authorship was lacking.

Whether ostracism was Cleisthenic or not, we still have to ask why it was either invented in the early 480s or why it was then for the first time that it began to be regularly and effectively employed. As so often, we could do with more hard facts than we have. Hipparchus' mother was probably the daughter of the deposed tyrant Hippias; and Hipparchus himself was pretty certainly the Hipparchus who was eponymous archon in 496/5 (although, as Rhodes observes, 'despite much that has been written to the contrary we do not know enough to say whether the fact of his archonship is politically significant'[19]). The *Ath. Pol.* (22) claims that

---

[18] Cited with approval by Hignett, *HAC* 166. (An interesting feature of the process was that apparently, if the preliminary count of all the *ostraka* handed in revealed that fewer than 6,000 had voted, the votes against this or that man were not counted separately: *HAC* 165–6.)

[19] Rhodes, *CAP* 272. Cf. above, p. 31.

Cleisthenes' introduction of ostracism was designedly popular, and a little later asserts that

two years after the victory at Marathon, with the *dêmos* now growing in self-assurance, the Athenians made use of the ostracism law, which had been carried because of the suspicion of those in powerful positions, in that Peisistratus, a demagogue and a general, had set himself up as tyrant. The first man to be ostracised was his kinsman Hipparchus son of Charmus of the deme Collytus, on whose account chiefly Cleisthenes had passed the law, wanting to drive him from Athens. For the Athenian *dêmos* with its customary leniency had allowed those of the tyrants' friends who had not themselves been parties to the crimes committed during the period of troubles to remain in Athens, and of these men Hipparchus was the political leader.

We are then told that Megacles was ostracised the next year (487/6), followed in 486/5 by another (unnamed) victim simply described as 'one of the friends of the tyrants, against whom the law had been devised'. But 'thereafter they began to get rid of any other men who happened to appear too powerful, though unconnected with the tyranny', starting with Xanthippus in 485/4 (father of Pericles, Xanthippus had married Agaristê, an Alcmaeonid and almost certainly Cleisthenes' niece). Two years later, in 483/2, the new silver-lode was found at Maroneia, and this year saw the ostracism of Aristides, apparently in connection with his opposition to Themistocles' ship-building programme. Finally, when Xerxes launched his invasion, all those who had been ostracised were recalled to Athens. Lycurgus (*in Leocratem*, 117) reports that Hipparchus chose not to return; but both Xanthippus and Aristides played leading parts in the fighting against Persia, and continued to be prominent in the years after the Persians had been defeated.

The *Ath. Pol.*'s account here does not carry much conviction, for it looks far too much like a clumsy construction from the fact that Hipparchus was of Peisistratid blood and name; how, if Cleisthenes had aimed the ostracism law against him, did the intended victim manage to escape the trap for nearly twenty years? The explanation of the long delay between the introduction of ostracism and its first effective implementation as due to the Athenians' 'notorious leniency' is not very plausible. Above all, it is hard to believe that men who had been expelled a few years earlier under suspicion of pro-tyrant or pro-Persian leanings would have been not only recalled to Athens but also in some instances promptly entrusted with high military responsibilities in the crisis of a great Persian invasion.

Archaeological discoveries warn us how little we can read the 'small print' of politics at this time. Meiggs and Lewis counted 1,404 surviving legible *ostraka* with a spread of 61 names, and observed that 'for the period 487–480 we appear to have votes for about twenty-five men besides those known to have been ostracized'.[20] Themistocles had the highest count with 568 (of which 191 were unearthed in a single deposit inscribed by only four different hands, suggesting either an attempt at deliberate fraud or the special preparation of *ostraka* by anti-Themistocleans for distribution to illiterate voters).[21] Second to him, however, comes Callixenus son of Aristonymus of the deme Xypete, with no fewer than 263. Yet this Callixenus is otherwise unknown to history, while *ostraka* naming Aristides, ostracized in 483/2, account for no more than 61 of the total. Further, even while 'Meiggs and Lewis' was being printed in 1969, news arrived of a new and large find of 4,463 *ostraka*, comprising nine names, of which three were not previously listed; this find added only 32 to Aristides' total, but enormously increased the number of surviving *ostraka* naming Callias son of Cratias from 3 to over 750. Such finds are random, and new ones may be made at any time which could transform the existing pattern. Moreover, it is impossible to date the *ostraka* which have been found at all precisely. Thus, in the latest find, which produced over 2,000 Megacles *ostraka* and nearly 1,000 Themistocles *ostraka*, three of the former physically join three of the latter, and so clearly came from fragments of the same pieces of pottery, which could show that Themistocles was a candidate for ostracism as early as 487/6, the year when

---

[20] Meiggs and Lewis, *GHI* 40–7.

[21] Plutarch (*Aristides*, 7) tells how Aristides wrote his own name on an *ostrakon* at the request of an illiterate citizen. The story is surely apocryphal; but we need not doubt that quite a few Athenians would have found reading and writing difficult. On the whole question see Harvey 'Literacy in the Athenian Democracy'.

Megacles was ostracized. But another of the Themistocles *ostraka* physically joins one naming Cimon, who was ostracized twenty-five years later at the end of the 460s and was far too young to be a plausible victim as early as 487/6, when he was little over twenty-one years old. Given that there is respectable evidence that Megacles was ostracized twice, a date for this find in the middle or late 470s is a reasonable possibility.[22]

What lay behind this rash of ostracisms in the 480s is very debatable. There had been rumours at the time of Marathon in 490 (Herodotus 6. 115, 121) that some prominent Athenians had been in treacherous communication with the Persian invaders, notable among them the Alcmaeonid family, whose leading member was Megacles. Herodotus vigorously rebutted the allegation that the Alcmaeonids were involved, and almost certainly the colourful story of a flashing-shield signal was a canard—it is impossible to credit that, had there been even a small shred of half-way credible evidence, a formal prosecution would not have been mounted against those allegedly involved once the Persians had been driven off. Nevertheless, allegations were made, either in 490 or in the next few years, that Athens had harboured Persian sympathizers. Given that the invaders had been accompanied by the ageing ex-tyrant Hippias, who in the event of a Persian victory was to be reinstalled as a puppet ruler of Athens, that suggests a belief that some leading Athenians were not unwilling to back him, either through distaste for the democracy or a readiness to join what they thought would turn out to be the winning side. Hipparchus' family relationship with Hippias (who was very likely his maternal grandfather) rendered him particularly exposed to such suspicions; and Megacles and the unknown *ostracisé* of 486/5 may have been tarred with the same brush, justly or unjustly, by their political enemies—for all that no speeches were allowed at the two *ecclêsia* meetings, there were plenty of opportunities for influencing voters at other times and places. Yet (for what it is worth) the *Ath. Pol.* divorces Xanthippus from association with any such group, and nobody suggests

---

[22] Rhodes, *CAP* 275, for the evidence, and for details of the later find.

that Aristides was pro-tyrant or pro-Persian; his ostracism seems to have been the consequence of a conflict with Themistocles over deep issues of naval, financial, and possibly domestic policy.

At least some of the later ostracisms we hear of indicate that ostracism could be an effective way of forcing or allowing a choice between leading politicians with divergent or conflicting policies, rather than a way of getting rid of a man who might threaten the constitution. When Themistocles was ostracized around 470, he was 'soft-pedalling' the war with Persia and advancing the view that Sparta represented Athens' chief worry for the future; Cimon thereafter entered on several years of primacy at Athens, and he was a proponent of vigorous prosecution of the war with Persia, extension and consolidation of Athens' imperial power, and collaboration between Athens and Sparta as the 'twin yoke-fellows of Greece'. (The two men may also, though less certainly, have differed over the question of whether to leave the existing democracy broadly as it was or to advance in a more radical direction.) When in his turn Cimon was ostracized at the end of the 460s, Athens proceeded to renounce her alliance with Sparta and was quickly in alliance with Sparta's inveterate rival Argos and at war with Sparta's allies; more or less simultaneously, the Ephialtic domestic reforms were passed into law. During the 440s Pericles and Thucydides son of Melesias were in strenuous opposition to each other over central issues both imperial and domestic: the ostracism of Thucydides in 444/3 ushered in the long reign of Pericles as the 'uncrowned king of Athens'. The last ostracism ever effected underlines this aspect. In 417 or 416 it was expected by many that either the 'hawk' Alcibiades or the 'dove' Nicias would be packed off, but between them they managed to turn the tables on their common enemy Hyperbolus, and the upshot was that their conflict of policy remained unresolved, leaving Athens awkwardly (perhaps even disastrously) trying to drive two very different horses in tandem. Thereafter, ostracism was never again resorted to (although it was not abolished formally), which indicates that people had lost confidence in its ability to do the job it was meant to do.

These examples make it obvious that ostracism could, and sometimes did, in some ways serve a function not too dissimilar from that of a modern general election, by affording a choice between the leading advocates of conflicting national policies. It might be that Cleisthenes had had something of the sort in his mind, however inchoately, when he introduced ostracism—if he did introduce it—either as a non-violent way of deciding the immediate issue between himself and Isagoras or as generally useful in resolving conflicts under his new system and as a handy weapon with which to threaten anyone who challenged his own position:[23] Isagoras' resort to outside assistance from Sparta, or Cleisthenes' own early death (he does not seem long to have survived his reforms), or the absence over the next twenty years or so of deeply divisive issues or acute personal conflicts, could have left ostracism unresorted to (unless in fact there were ostracisms during this period which have been lost to the record). Why it began to be used so regularly in the 480s (or why it was only then first introduced) remains to be explained. But once again we are reduced to speculating on the basis of inadequate evidence about what issues, domestic or international, may have been uppermost and divisive at the time—although plausible guesses can be offered. Nevertheless, whether or not the original purpose of introducing ostracism can safely be inferred from some of its later functions, and despite the fact that after the 480s there were some ostracisms which less evidently involved issues of the magnitude of those already singled out, that later aspect is not seriously contestable: considerably larger numbers of citizens than regularly attended the *ecclêsia* sometimes took the time and trouble to turn out and express a decisive view about which of the current leading politicians they would like to be rid of for ten years; and that view, clearly and strongly expressed in an effective vote, could provide a sort of political bench-mark, even a sort of national referendum. Above all, ostracism underlines the highly personal nature of Athenian politics, and the importance of individual leaders

---

[23] Rhodes, *CAP* 269–70.

(as opposed to 'parties', as we nowadays understand that term).[24]

Ephialtes' sudden and mysterious death[25] may have led some ancient writers to discount his importance and to portray him as a subordinate collaborator of Pericles. But modern opinion prefers to see him as the leading figure and Pericles as a considerably younger man, still in his early thirties, with some way to make to the top. That is borne out by a passage in the *Ath. Pol.* (35. 2) where Ephialtes and (the otherwise obscure) Archestratus are named as the authors of the reform legislation which the Thirty destroyed during their brief oligarchic rule in 404. And, given that Ephialtes is attested (Plutarch, *Cimon*, 13. 4) as a *stratêgos* in command of a fleet of thirty warships at some time in the 460s, he was probably of good family and somewhat older than Pericles.

Our only reasonably full account of the Ephialtic reforms is that in the *Ath. Pol.* (25–8). It runs roughly as follows:

'The Athenian political system (*politeia*) remained by and large stable from the period of the Persian Wars down to the middle to late 460s. The numbers of the poorer citizens (*plêthos*) increased, and Ephialtes emerged as the political leader of the *dêmos*. Generally reputed a just and incorruptible man, he assailed numerous individual Areopagites. The prestige and influence of the Areopagus as a body in and over state policy had been enhanced by its splendid leadership at the time of Salamis. [It is described as 'running Athens' (23. 1) and 'being pre-eminent' (25. 1).] Then, in the archonship of Conon (462/1), Ephialtes pounced, stripping the Areopagus of all its "acquired" (*epitheta*) powers which gave it its

[24] Those who find it surprising that 6,000 could be seen as a large turnout from a citizen body of 30,000–40,000 should remind themselves that in modern Britain the average turn-out for general elections is about 75% and for local elections only 40%–50%. Yet these occasions are far less frequent than the meetings of the *ecclêsia*; and a modern voter has to travel only a short distance to his local polling-station at whichever time of day suits him best, the whole business of voting being over in a few minutes. (In the USA turn-outs are a lot lower, currently averaging just over 50% even in a Presidential election.)

[25] That Ephialtes was murdered, as is pretty well universally stated or assumed, is in my view improbable on the evidence as we have it: see my brief discussion in 'The Death of Ephialtes'.

"guardianship of the state" (*phylakê tês politeias*), and re-distributing those powers, some to the Council of Five Hundred, and some to the *dêmos* and the courts (*dikastêria*). [Ephialtes is said to have been working in collaboration with Themistocles, himself an Areopagite and threatened with a charge of treachery with Persia. That is nonsense as it stands, since Themistocles had by now been in exile and settled in Persia for several years. If there is anything in it, it is probably a garbled tradition that Ephialtes was in some sense following in Themistocles' footsteps, having first come to prominence as one of his collaborators.] Not long afterwards, Ephialtes was murdered through the agency of Aristodicus of Tanagra.

'The "better sort" (*epieikesteroi*) of the citizenry of Athens had suffered very severe losses in fighting, two to three thousand in every campaign [clearly a ridiculously exaggerated figure], thanks to incompetent commanders appointed for high birth rather than ability. Energetic demagogues ensured that the political system became "slacker"; they left the archonship alone, but five years after Ephialtes' death the zeugites were made eligible to hold this office, the first archon from this class being Mnesitheides (457/6).[26] Four years later, in the archonship of Lysicrates (453/2), the thirty local or circuit judges, the so-called *dikastai kata dêmous*, were reinstituted; and two years after that, in the archonship of Antidotus (451/50), Pericles carried a law that citizenship should henceforth be confined to those whose parents were both Athenian—previously it had been sufficient if only one parent, presumably the father, was of citizen standing.

'Pericles now emerged as the leading populist politician. He took away some powers from the Areopagus,[27] and he was a great champion of Athenian naval power, which gave the poorer citizens the confidence to seek to control the body politic. He was also the first to provide pay for court service, that being his way of using public moneys to fight back

[26] Mnesitheides may simply have been the first zeugite to be picked as eponymous archon; the archonship may have been opened to zeugites a year or two earlier, perhaps as part of Ephialtes' reforms.

[27] What these were is not specified. It may be no more than a clumsy reference to some share which Pericles had had in the work of Ephialtes.

against the private philanthropy of Cimon, whose personal wealth is described as being "on the tyrant scale".[28] Pericles was working closely with Damonides of the deme Oa, who was later ostracized on that account.[29] The consequent change from "respectable" jurors to courts composed of "any Tom, Dick, and Harry" gave rise to bribery, as was first instanced at the trial of Anytus, who bought an acquittal when indicted on a charge in connection with the loss of Pylos.[30] Nevertheless, so long as Pericles was alive things were not too bad; but with his death the traditional role of respectable men as political leaders was taken over by the low-bred, raucous, and theatrical Cleon, followed by Cleophon, and so on. By now, hardly any decent politicians remained.' [At this point the *Ath. Pol.* moves on to the story of the attempted oligarchic revolution of 411.]

Plainly, that does not tell us very much, and our other sources of information add little. Aristotle (*Politics*, 1274^a) merely notes briefly that Ephialtes and Pericles 'cut down' or 'debased' the Areopagus and introduced court pay and demagogy: but that is only an aside while discussing Solon and dissociating him from the more radical developments at Athens which Aristotle saw as the result of Athens' fifth-century naval power, and is not part of a direct treatment of Ephialtes. Plutarch adds some colour in his biographies of Cimon (10, 15) and Pericles (7, 9): Ephialtes matched Aristides in his reputation for personal incorruptibility, and at last under his leadership 'the many' jumbled up the existing political order, deprived the Areopagus of all jurisdiction save in a few matters,[31] and making themselves masters of the law-courts turned Athens into a pure and unadultered democracy.[32] Diodorus Siculus (11. 77. 6)

---

[28] Whether this means that we are to date the introduction of court pay before Cimon's ostracism in the late 460s or after his return is questionable. The thought-connection here seems very loose.

[29] The ostracism may belong to the late 440s, and the man's true name may have been Damon son of Damonides. See Rhodes, *CAP* 341-2.

[30] This trial cannot have been earlier than 409, when Pylos was lost; which deprives the argument of much of its force if the courts had really remained untainted for forty years or so after court pay was first introduced!

[31] For Plutarch, this jurisdiction was part of 'the ancestral rules' (*ta patria nomima*).

[32] Plutarch's image of a society intoxicated by too heady draughts of freedom is explicitly borrowed from Plato's *Republic*: 'a democratic state may fall under the

reports, in his usual cheerfully slipshod manner, that 'roughly about the time of the Athenian operations in Egypt' (i.e. 459–454!), the Athenian commons (*plêthos*) were inflamed against the Areopagus by Ephialtes and persuaded to humble it and to rescind Athens' 'ancestral and renowned practices' (*ta patria kai periboêta nomima*). What else remains is mostly scrappy, derivative, and at times silly, though it may occasionally throw up the odd useful hint. Demosthenes (22. 55–6) and Lysias (7. 22) testify that in the fourth century the Areopagus still had competence as the court which tried cases of deliberate homicide and damage to the sacred olive-trees.

It would be helpful if we could know for sure when the *graphê paranomôn* was first introduced, and how it related in time to the Ephialtic reforms. This *graphê* was an indictment which could be brought against anyone alleged to be responsible for introducing to the *ecclêsia* a proposal that was either invalid in form or substantially in conflict with an existing law: the proposal was held in abeyance until a court had decided the question; or, if the proposal had already been voted on and carried by the *ecclêsia*, it could be declared invalid by the court and its proposer fined. The earliest securely datable instance of a *graphê paranomôn* comes in a speech (*De mysteriis*, 17) delivered by Andocides in 399, where he says that his father had brought such a charge successfully against Speusippus in 415. The *Life of Antiphon* (20) mentions a speech composed by Antiphon involving a *graphê paranomôn* brought against the Demosthenes who sailed as a *stratêgos* to Sicily in 414, where he met his death the following year; the date and circumstances of this speech are not given, but it can be no later than 414, and could well be a few years earlier. Thucydides (8. 67. 2) shows that this *graphê* was an established and very important feature of the Athenian system in 411, when the earliest formal move made by the oligarchs to replace the democracy was to suspend or rescind the *graphê* to clear the way for their own proposed reforms.

influence of unprincipled leaders ready to minister to its thirst for liberty with too deep draughts of that heady wine; and then, if its governors are not complaisant enough to give it unstinted licence, they will be arraigned and punished as being accursed oligarchs,' (*Republic*, 8, 562 C–D).

Given that it is not explicitly attested earlier than a few years before 414 at most, it has been maintained that the *graphê paranomôn* may have come on the scene only many years later than the Ephialtic reforms, after a long period of practical experience of the dangers that might be involved in the unfettered legislative competence of the *ecclêsia* had awoken people to the need for a constitutional 'brake' on hasty and ill-considered enactments. But this argument from silence is a weak one, given the nature and paucity of the surviving sources, especially our lack of any forensic speeches from these years. The *graphê* could in fact date from Ephialtes' day, or thereabouts, and be closely connected with the loss by the Areopagus of its so-called 'guardianship of the laws', *nomophylakia* or *phylakê tôn nomôn* or *phylakê tês politeias*. A much later lexicographer cited Philochorus (fr. 64b: he wrote his work on Athenian institutions early in the third century, having been born some time before 340) in connection with an entry on the Athenian officials called *nomophylakes* or 'law-guardians': 'the *nomophylakes* compelled the officers of state to abide by the laws, and sitting with the presidents (*proedroi*) at meetings of the *ecclêsia* and the Council they prevented them doing anything to the state's disadvantage. They were seven in number, and, according to Philochorus, they had been instituted at the time when Ephialtes left the Areopagus with jurisdiction only in cases of homicide.' We hear nothing directly of these *nomophylakes* earlier than 322, which could indicate, as Hignett suggested,[33] that the lexicographer's account is seriously flawed; but, even if that is so, behind this garbled account could well lie sound information in the original text of Philochorus which connected Ephialtes with a concern to institute some sort of watch over legislation to replace that which the Areopagus had previously exercised.

All in all, our surviving accounts of the reforms of Ephialtes leave a lot to be desired. It looks as if their authors had no clearly articulated idea of what Ephialtes had done, and had to be content with generalizations. The explanation

---

[33] *HAC* 209–13. *Nomophylakes* are nowhere mentioned in the text of the *Ath. Pol.* Jacoby, however (*FGH* iii b. ii, p. 243 n. 11), accepted Philochorus' evidence. See now Cawkwell, '*Nomophylakia* and the Areopagus'.

of this vagueness is almost certainly the fact that the official
text of Ephialtes' laws was physically destroyed in 404 by the
short-lived Spartan puppet oligarchy of the Thirty (*Ath. Pol.*
35. 2). The text even of Cleisthenes' laws may well not have
survived intact to the end of the fifth century: there is a
suspicious lack of detail and precision in the *Ath. Pol.*'s
account of Cleisthenes' measures, which shows no sign of
having been based on a study of their actual wording;
elsewhere, the *Ath. Pol.* records (29. 3) the proposal by an
oligarchic activist in 411 that 'a search should also be made
(*prosanazêtêsai*) for the laws of Cleisthenes', wording which
indicates that by 411 the full text was not readily accessible;
and it is not without significance that no Cleisthenic law
is ever cited by any fourth-century orator. As Rhodes
observed:[34] 'The events of 411–10 showed that the laws of
Athens were confused and uncertain, and in 410/9 a process
of revision and republication was begun which proved to be a
lengthy one' (it was still uncompleted when the Thirty came
to power in 404). Hence it is easy to see how hard it must
have been for later investigators to discover precisely which
elements in the revised code were specifically attributable to
Ephialtes.

There was evidently a tradition that the prestige and
influence of the Areopagus had revived during the crisis of
Xerxes' invasion and the evacuation of Attica prior to the
victory at Salamis, and that thereafter it had continued to be
prominent and influential for the next two decades. A
resolute sceptic like Hignett could discount that as a
simplicistic and erroneous reconstruction.[35] However, it
does not strain common sense to believe that the massive
disruption occasioned in 480 by the Persian attack and the
evacuation of Attica by its inhabitants, together with the
breath-taking rapid expansion of Athens' external activities
in the years immediately following—the complex and urgent
military, naval, diplomatic, and financial arrangements and

---

[34] *CAP* 376.
[35] *HAC* 147–8. Against that, Aristotle clearly accepted the tradition when he
wrote (*Politics*, 1304[a]20–2): 'It seems that the Areopagus having acquired an
excellent reputation in the fighting against the Persians tightened up the constitution'
(*syntomôteran poiêsai tên politeian*).

innovations involved in the prosecution of an offensive against Persia and the foundation, organization, and extension of the Confederacy of Delos under Athenian leadership and direction—could have brought the Areopagus to the fore and won it public confidence and esteem. After all, for a dozen or more years after 487/6 a majority of its members continued to be men who had won direct election to the archonship, and were hence a substantially more authoritative and politically activated collection of senior Areopagites than the later-comers who owed their seats to the accident of the lot. It could also have happened that at this period special powers or discretion had been conferred on or assumed by the Areopagus, some of which could in due course be characterized by Ephialtes as 'acquired' (*epitheta*) and in a sense improper in a body the great majority of whose members were by the late 460s men selected from the richest or two richest classes by a random procedure which none the less gave them membership of the Areopagus for the rest of their lives. Still, whatever view we take about that, it is plain that a large part of the thrust of Ephialtes' attack on the Areopagus was that it possessed or exercised powers which could at least plausibly be described as 'acquired', and not original to it, and separable from its 'proper' and more circumscribed competence and functions.

Since there is little or no force or evidence to sustain the view that Ephialtes extended the overall competence of popular jurisdiction in legal matters in general, there is much to be said for the conclusion that Ephialtes was chiefly concerned with the procedures (*euthynai*) whereby public officers were called to account for their conduct in office, and those major political impeachments which went under the name of *eisangeliai*.[36] As has already been emphasized, control of the executive is everywhere the vital element in the control of the state itself. It is eminently probable that, from pre-Solonian times, the Areopagus had been the body which by tradition and convention, perhaps even to some extent by specific enactments, had exercised control and corrective powers over the transient annual officers of state; that it had

---

[36] *HAC* 193 ff.; Sealey, 'Ephialtes'. On *eisangeliai* see further below, p. 101.

been tamed and directed by the tyrants; that Cleisthenes had been content to leave it as he found it; and that nearly fifty years' experience of the Cleisthenic democracy, and the 'sea-change' in attitudes and habits of mind associated with the rise of the 'naval commons' (*nautikos ochlos*), had made such an institution seem anachronistic and hence led to growing pressure for at least some of its powers to be transferred to more representative and less entrenched bodies like the Council of Five Hundred, the popular courts, and the *ecclêsia* itself. This view receives some support from the tradition that for several years before he carried his reforms Ephialtes had been notable for his persistent and successful harrying of officers of state for alleged shortcomings and misdemeanours. And he may also have been responsible for introducing a greater publicity into the affairs of state, since it is probably more than a coincidence that from this time on we have increasingly richer remains of public decisions and documents incised durably on stone for all to see and read.[37] That greater publicity accords well with something which the lexicographer Harpocration (s.v. *ho katôthen nomos*) records that the fourth-century historian Anaximenes had stated in his *Philippica*: 'Ephialtes had the *axones* and *kyrbeis* [that is, the Athenian written codes] removed from the Acropolis and set up instead in the Council House and Agora.'

Wade-Gery argued[38] from the language of a surviving public document, the Phaselis decree (*GHI*, No. 31), and especially from the use of the verb *katadikazein* in lines 18–19, that at the time when this decree was carried into law the archons, and particularly here the polemarch, were still passing judgements themselves rather than simply announcing the verdicts of the courts over which they presided. Believing that Ephialtes was the man who deprived the archons of this power, Wade-Gery dated the Phaselis decree to the early or middle 460s. Hignett, however, inclined to follow Tod in his argument that the formulae of the decree point to a date in

---

[37] Meritt, *Epigraphica Attica*, 89 ff.; Davies, *Democracy and Classical Greece* 63 ff. Jacoby (*Atthis*, 207) pertinently obverved that in the collection of Athenian decrees made by Craterus in the third century those dating from before 454/3 filled only two books, while those dating from 454/3 to 411/10 filled six.

[38] *Essays in Greek History*, 180–92.

the later 450s;[39] so he suggested that 'the reform which deprived the magistrates of independent jurisdiction may seem to us the logical consequence of the affirmation of popular sovereignty implicit in the Ephialtic revolution, but the Athenian radicals may have been slower to react against the jurisdiction of magistrates, holding office for one year only and responsible at the end of it for their official actions, than against the jurisdiction of an irresponsible council whose members held office for life. Hence the law which made *ephesis* [roughly = 'referral'] obligatory in all cases brought before a magistrate may perhaps be dated several years after 462.' But Sealey has argued powerfully[40] that the verb *katadikazein* can simply denote a verdict reached by a vote of the jurors (*dikastai*) and formally announced by the presiding magistrate. Meiggs and Lewis reject that in their note on the decree, but it could be correct all the same.

It is manifestly improper to assert any one conclusion on the basis of a decree the date of which is uncertain and of a Greek verb the precise nuance of which is debatable. Indeed, as Sealey suggested, the whole process whereby this change came about could have been the result, not of a single legislative act, but of a gradual and piecemeal yet fundamentally comprehensible development over a considerable period of time, a possibility which is not incompatible with the tradition that Ephialtes did carry legislation of a consolidating and mandatory nature. In the developed Athenian democracy the magistrates retained the authority to deliver judgement themselves only where relatively trivial penalties or issues were in question, while for the rest disputes or charges had to be forwarded to one of the popular courts for decision. It is hard to believe that Ephialtes did not have a significant hand in this outcome.

It has been maintained that we can learn something useful about what Ephialtes did from the *Eumenides*, which was written by Aeschylus and presented in 458. However, my own negative but far from idiosyncratic position is that all such arguments lack a really solid basis. Admittedly, this tragedy does to some degree echo or reflect the tensions and

---

[39] Hignett, *HAC*, 397; Tod, *Greek Historical Inscriptions*, No. 32 and nn.
[40] 'Ephialtes', 16 ff.

controversies which had attended Ephialtes' legislation two
or three years earlier—indeed, given the central part assigned
by Aeschylus to the Areopagus in this play, it can scarcely
not have. But this great climax to the *Oresteia* trilogy was
anything but a partisan political credo; and the most
discussed passages in it (681–790, 861–6) could have been
taken by different members of the audience in different ways,
as they can still be taken differently by different modern
readers. The *Eumenides* is above all else a hymn to justice and
social order and the rule of law, and gives us no secure
assistance in reconstructing the detail of Ephialtes' reforms
nor any reliable guidance either to the specific nature of the
arguments of the opposed groups or to Aeschylus' own
attitude.[41]

Ephialtes was later seen as the man who had put the final
coping-stone on Athens' democracy. Whatever the precise
details of his measures (which must, in default of new
evidence, remain obscure), few would quarrel with Hignett's
assertion that 'the essence of the reform was a transference of
jurisdiction'.[42] The Areopagus was stripped of its supervisory
and disciplinary and revisionary powers, which thereafter fell
to be exercised by the *boulê*, the *ecclêsia*, and the *dikastêria*. It
was evidently a momentous achievement: whether or not the
story was true, it was at least plausible to allege that he had
been done away with by his enemies. For one hundred and
fifty years after his death Athens represented the realization
of one of the most open societies known to history, a political
entity in which the totality of the free-born citizenry
exercised a tighter control over legislature, judicature, and
executive than any other in the ancient or modern worlds.

The nature of the evidence available to us for the period
down to (and even, although to a lesser extent, after) the
reforms of Ephialtes is such as to leave many questions

---

[41] See Rhodes, *CAP* 312, for reference to recent discussions. For the most recent
full discussion of Ephialtes' reforms see Ostwald, *From Popular Sovereignty to the
Sovereignty of Law*, esp. pp. 34–6, 41–50, 70–8, 175–9. Cf. also Cawkwell,
'Nomophylakia and the Areopagus'.

[42] *HAC* 199.

debatable, or even unanswerable. The orators, historians, and antiquarians of the fourth and later centuries appear to have found very little to build on in the way of hard facts. Our only full account is that contained in the Aristotelian *Athenaion Politeia*, a work which is not without serious defects and which certainly shows none of the intellectual power which shines out in every one of the genuine works of Aristotle. It is, nevertheless, of great value; but its historical survey (1–41) goes down only to the end of the fifth century, and has very little to say of any changes in the period which followed Ephialtes, apart from the two short-lived intermissions of the Four Hundred and the Thirty. The final twenty-eight chapters (42–69) consist of an invaluable (but, again, far from impeccable) description of the political organization of the Athenian state as it was at the time when the *Ath. Pol.* was written, round about 330. Other literary sources, and inscriptions and other material remains, are insufficient to fill more than a few of the gaps.[43]

Hence, as has already been occasionally noted, we cannot be one hundred per cent sure of a number of things: were the division of the *boulê* into ten tribal 'standing committees', the entrusting of the presidency of *boulê* and *ecclêsia* to the Chairman of the current 'standing committee', even the selection of the members of the *boulê* by lot and the rule against serving more than twice in one's lifetime, all part of Cleisthenes' original reforms, or were any or all of them later refinements? Did the Cleisthenic *ecclêsia* meet forty times a year, or less frequently to begin with? When was ostracism introduced, and in what circumstances, and with what intention? Was there more to the reform of the archonship in 487/6 than just a change in the selection process? What exactly were the reforms of Ephialtes? How far is it safe to extrapolate backwards from the detailed features of the arrangements as they were in post-Ephialtic times?

Nevertheless, our overall picture of the Athenian democracy as it was after Cleisthenes' reforms, and subsequently those

---

[43] See above, p. 2. On the work of the local historians of Attica (the so-called 'Atthidographers'), and how little of what they wrote has survived for us to evaluate, see Pearson, *The Local Historians of Attica*; Jacoby, *Atthis*; and (so far as concerns Ephialtes) Hignett, *HAC* 198.

of Ephialtes, is not seriously affected by these patches of
ignorance or controversy. Its broad shape remained the same
from the middle of the fifth century to the final quarter of the
fourth. Admittedly, a number of changes in detail were
introduced during that long period. These will be noted in
their appropriate contexts in the following chapters; but it is
convenient to list some of them here succinctly, if only to
demonstrate that they were not of a kind or of a magnitude to
alter the overall pattern significantly or substantially.[44]

A codification of the laws was begun in 410, and was
completed not long after the fall of the Thirty in 403.
Thereafter there emerged a formalized distinction between
decrees (*psêphismata*) approved by the *ecclêsia* and laws
(*nomoi*) enacted by boards of 'legislators' (*nomothetai*); the
broad distinction between the two was that *psêphismata* were
particular and specific, *nomoi* general in their application.
(But that *is* no more than a broad distinction, and in truth a
nomos seems to have been essentially a decision which could
not be changed except by the special procedure of *nomothesia*,
nomoi being the rules which had been given that status in the
revised code and any others subsequently enacted by the
nomothetai.) *Psêphismata* were carried by a simple majority
vote of the *ecclêsia*. The establishing of new *nomoi* and the
annulment of old ones was decided—less expeditiously—by
a special body of *nomothetai*, recruited from those Athenians
over thirty years old who had taken the oath to serve as
jurors. That has been represented as a serious erosion of the
power of the *dêmos* as a whole,[45] but such a position is too
extreme. The *ecclêsia* alone could authorize the process of
revision to be set in motion; any proposed changes had to be
given wide advance publicity; and quite clearly the large
number of citizens who functioned as *nomothetai* were
regarded as a random cross-section of the *dêmos* which was

---

[44] For a convenient review of these changes see Rhodes, 'Athenian Democracy
after 403 BC'. Like many others, I cannot share the view of M. H. Hansen (most
recently reaffirmed in *AA* 4) that the changes introduced in and after 403/2 affected
the essential character of the democracy. We may note that the author of the *Ath.
Pol.* closed his historical account of the development of the democracy at the end of
the fifth century, and then proceeded to conclude his work with his account of 'the
democracy as it now is' (i.e. round about 330).

[45] Most notably by Hansen in *Eisangelia* and *AE* 161–76.

entrusted with a task which was far too detailed, complex, and lengthy to be conveniently or efficiently performed by the *ecclêsia* itself. (The frequent use of the legal process of challenging the validity of individual *psephismata* in the courts (*graphê paranomôn*) broadly reflects the same approach.)

In the first quarter of the fourth century the presidency of meetings of *boule* and *ecclêsia* was entrusted to a new board of nine *proedroi*, chosen one from each of the nine tribal tenths of the *boulê* other than that which was the prytany at the time. (Why that was done is obscure.) And the Secretary of the *boulê*, originally chosen from among its own members and serving for one-tenth of the year, came in and after the 360s to be chosen to serve for a whole year and did not have to be himself a *bouleutês*. That was most probably a move towards greater efficiency and some degree of professionalism. A similar trend can be discerned in a greater centralization of financial control from the 350s onwards under the overall supervision and direction of a single officer, who was elected (instead of being appointed by lot) and was eligible for repeated re-election. A number of details requiring professional expertise involving matters like public building were left to permanent salaried experts; and individual *stratêgoi* began to be assigned to specific tasks and responsibilities. More stringent precautions were taken to avoid corruption of, or improper influence on, the courts; and the powers and influence of the Areopagus increased somewhat beyond the narrow limits within which Ephialtes had confined that body. But there are no good grounds for seeing any of these developments as even beginning to undercut the central importance of the *boulê* or the ultimate sovereignty of the citizenry in the *ecclêsia*. One of the essential features of the developed Athenian democracy was the provision of pay for public service, which opened public office to a far wider circle than just those who could afford to serve without remuneration. The latter half of the fifth century saw extensions of the principle of payment for office, and at the very end of that century a modest payment was instituted for attending the *ecclêsia* itself, though it was restricted to a set number of those who were the first to arrive and claim it.

In his *Politics* (1317ᵃ–1318ᵇ) Aristotle defines and enumerates what he sees as the essential features of full democracy as follows:

> If all citizens are to be equal, the mass of the people must be sovereign; and the will of the whole people as determined by the majority vote in a popular assembly open to all citizens regardless of wealth or rank must be decisive.
>
> There should be no 'governing class', and all citizens should take turns in holding office; officers of state should be appointed randomly, by the use of the lot, save where it is clear that some exceptional quality or expertise is essential; there should be no property qualification for holding office, or at any rate it should be no more than minimal; tenure of office should be for short periods only, and repeated tenure for the most part (save in military appointments, for example) avoided, or resorted to only very infrequently.
>
> All the most important judicial decisions, including the review of the conduct in office of the officers of state, should be taken by courts which are drawn from, and representative of, all the citizens.
>
> There should be state payment for the execution of as many public duties as possible: the holding of magistracies, service as a member of a law-court or council, attendance at assemblies.

Those were indeed the features of the developed democracy of Athens. But why did the Athenians want democracy, why did they prefer it to alternative systems of government? The answer to that question will be discerned, sometimes explicitly, sometimes implicitly, in the chapters which follow, which set out the details of the Athenian system; the ways in which they worked; what their objects or effects were; what lay behind the two major attempts to overthrow the democracy, and why they failed; what theoretical and practical criticisms there were of the system, and what defence was made, or can be made, against such criticisms. However, two points may appropriately be stressed here.

First and foremost, without doubt the greatest benefit which the ordinary Athenian derived from the democracy was that it secured for him the most effective protection before and under the law. The chief guarantee of this was that the laws themselves were approved and enacted by the whole citizen body and not by some small and privileged section of it, and that all decisions in legal actions were reached by broadly based courts and not by upper-class magistrates operating to safeguard the interests of their own class. (It may be argued that the ordinary citizen could not afford to employ the expensive services of a professional lawyer or speech-writer, and could not make his case so well; but, as we shall see, he would seldom if ever be involved in cases which required such special talents.) The poorer citizens got some benefits from public pay, but they were not large, and the pay earned by those who served in the fleet was earned at the cost of exposing themselves to a hard life and to great personal dangers. (Every decision of war and peace and on military expeditions lay with the very men whose lives would be at risk in war and fighting—a most significant feature of the Athenian system.) We must note too that the Athenian citizenry did not embark on a systematic policy of 'soaking the rich'. After Solon's day in the early sixth century, we can discern none of those moves to redistribute property or cancel debts which were so common elsewhere in other ancient states which were controlled by non-democratic governments. That was due both to the strength and importance of the large middle group of Athenians who were neither rich nor indigent, and to the absence of disparities of wealth and influence sufficiently large and widespread and resented as to fuel political agitation to moderate or remove them. In our modern societies we are much preoccupied with a fairer division of a very large and rich cake. But ancient Athens was a stranger to the vast material surpluses of modern Western countries—there was only a tiny cake to divide. At Athens we should look chiefly, not to the material benefits of modern democracies in the shape of unemployment pay or old-age pensions, free education and health care, subsidized housing or transport, and so on, but to the ordinary man's natural desire for freedom and power (which come to much the same thing in the final analysis), and hence for political equality and that freedom from exploitation and injustice which only democratic institutions can engender and preserve.

It is worth remarking that, whereas at other times and in other places we encounter phenomena like the secessions of the Roman *plebs*, or peasant revolts, or Peterloo riots, which give rise to learned books about violence and mobs and social conflicts in this or that society, such phenomena were conspicuous at Athens only by their absence. That is in itself an excellent indication of how effective the democracy was in giving its citizenry as a whole a sense of being in charge of their own affairs, masters in their own house. There was no potentially dangerous mass of oppressed and underprivileged citizens to worry a 'governing class' and compel the privileged and comfortably off to have recourse either to 'bread and circuses' or to bloody acts of repression. The sort of violence which characterized the later Roman Republic, for instance, was essentially the product of a society which repressed the full and free exercise of the common will of its nominally equal citizens by effectively restricting initiative and control of decision-taking to a small élite; it is to be looked for in vain in classical Athens.[46] Or, to take more up-to-date examples, the idea of some Trades Union Congress or Confédération Générale du Travail or AFL/CIO deciding on an open conflict with 'the government' is ridiculous in an Athenian context: the citizens of Athens were themselves 'the government' of Athens, took their own decisions by open and free individual vote, and kept their executive on a very short and tight rein.

---

[46] So far as concerns Rome, see Brunt, *Social Conflicts in the Roman Republic*, and Sherwin-White, 'Violence in Roman Politics'.

3

LOCAL AND CENTRAL GOVERNMENT

The Demes[1]

Early in 424 Aristophanes staged his comedy *The Knights* (*Hippeis*) at the Lenaean Festival. It won the first prize. It exploited the amusing fancy of presenting the Athenian people (the *dêmos*) as a householder, with politicians as his slave-servants. The name he gave his householder was 'Dêmos Pyknitês', 'Mr Demos of the Pnyx'. (The *ecclêsia* regularly met in the Pnyx, in the shadow of the Acropolis of Athens.) Aristophanes' choice of the adjective *Pyknitês* is significant: it is a made-up 'demotic'. An Athenian might be addressed or referred to either simply by his personal name, or by his personal name plus that of his father, or by his personal name plus that of his deme; but the full 'official' form of his name was 'A, son of B, of deme C', the deme element (his 'demotic') being either adjectival or adverbial, for example 'Acharnian' or 'of or from Alôpekê'. Thus, the name 'Mr Demos of the Pnyx' underlines the central importance which his deme had for every Athenian both in his private life and in his standing as a citizen.

In the final decade of the sixth century Cleisthenes' reforms had divided Attica into 139 demes (*dêmoi*). They varied very widely both in their area and in their population, as can be deduced most clearly from their quotas of representatives on the *boulê*, the central Council of Five Hundred.[2] If all had

---

[1] For full citation of the evidence on points of detail or dispute, and references to modern work, see D. Whitehead's excellent book *The Demes of Attica 508/7–ca. 250 B.C.* (1986), which has made it possible to reduce the number of notes to this section very considerably.

[2] Above, p. 24. Until recently the number of the Cleisthenic demes was regularly

been more or less the same size, each deme should have provided either three or four Councillors (*bouletai*); but some thirty or so of the smaller demes provided no more than one *bouleutês* apiece every year, while eight demes each sent ten or more, and the largest (Acharnai) twenty-two. There can be no doubt that the demes had already existed for a long time as the townlets or larger villages which constituted the natural local centres of Attica, although hitherto they had not played any formal role in the political and constitutional organization of the state, which had been based on the four so-called 'Ionic' tribes with their subdivisions of real or supposed kinship or clan groupings. Hence it is very reasonable to suppose that Cleisthenes simply took them over as the 'building-bricks' of his new system.[3] A list of demes was accordingly produced and published, and the free inhabitants of Attica were then required each to register at whichever he regarded as his local centre—or perhaps in cases of doubt instructed by the registering officers to go and register 'next door'. Some scholars have supposed that the five demes which were physically located within the city walls of Athens itself must have been new, and in some sense 'artificial', creations; but there is no compelling reason why we should accept that. Not only did they vary widely in size (their quotas of *bouleutai* ranged from three to twelve, which would seem to tell against any obvious artificiality), there are many examples which we can adduce of other cities which in the course of their growth have absorbed pre-existing townlets or villages which none the less retain some identity of their own. (Archaeology indicates that as late as Solon's day Athens was made up of several villages separated by open areas in which the dead were buried.) The resultant 'map' may thus have been somewhat ragged at the edges, and it seems that clearly marked physical boundaries between one deme and its neighbours seldom existed; but again that is not

given (following Strabo 9. 1. 16) as 170 or 174. It is now clear that the correct figure is 139. See Traill, *The Political Organization of Attica*; Whitehead, *Demes*, 19–21. The number of its members which each deme contributed to the Council of Five Hundred is tabulated on pp. 369–73 of Whitehead's book (following Traill).

[3] Andrewes, 'Kleisthenes' Reform Bill'. (Small villages or hamlets, *kômai*, existed which did not constitute deme centres.)

uncommon elsewhere before the development of modern mapping techniques and cadastral surveys.

Cleisthenes divided Attica into three subdivisions, coast, inland, and city (the latter including a considerable area outside Athens itself), each of which was made up of ten 'ridings' (*trittyes*). From each of these three subdivisions one of its ten constituent *trittyes* was selected and assigned to one of the ten new tribes (*phylai*), so that each consisted of three *trittyes*, each drawn from a different area of Attica. A *trittys* was made up of a group of demes, which varied in number, save that very large demes like Acharnai and Aphidna constituted a *trittys* in themselves. Like the demes, the *trittyes* also display considerable differences in area and population. On a straight average, each of a tribe's three *trittyes* should have supplied one third of its tribe's quota of 50 *bouleutai* = 16 or 17 each: but the city *trittys* of the tribe Aiantis supplied only nine *bouleutai*, and the inland *trittys* of Hippothontis only one or two more, while the coast *trittys* of Aiantis supplied at least twenty-seven and the inland *trittyes* of Aegeis and Oeneis over twenty apiece. There was also an imbalance between the three major subdivisions of coast, inland, and city as a whole: city supplied a quota of 130 (or 129) of the total of 500 *bouleutai*, inland 174 (or 175), and coast 196. Why so wide a divergence between city and the other two existed we simply do not know (although modern Britain tolerates considerable variations in the numbers of voters in individual Parliamentary constituencies, and both Scotland and Wales have a significantly more generous proportion of Parliamentary seats to registered voters than England has);[4] we must simply accept that the Athenians evidently did not worry about it, for they left the Cleisthenic system unchanged for getting on for two hundred years.[5]

[4] This must not be taken to imply that Athens had a system of delegated representative government like that of modern states: it did not. The analogy is meant simply to underline the fact that perfectly symmetrical systems are seldom if ever found in the real world, which tolerates a good deal of unevenness in such matters, for which there are good practical explanations. The fact that we do not know the reasons for the (sometimes considerable) Athenian deviations from a neater pattern should not be allowed to worry us overmuch.

[5] Hansen's suggestion in 'Political Activity and the Organization of Attica in the Fourth Century BC', 230 ff., that the bouleutic quotas were revised about 403/2 is

The function of the *trittyes*, apart from acting as a cross-regional link between demes and tribes, is obscure. According to Hignett, 'in themselves the trittyes had little importance and were apparently named after the principal demes in each . . . but apart from [some] minor functions [they] had no importance except as determining the allocation of the demes to the ten new tribes'.[6] A few irregularities have been discerned in the assigning of demes to *prima-facie* unexpected or 'unnatural' *trittyes*. Some scholars have suggested that this could point to 'gerrymandering' by Cleisthenes so as to increase his own influence and that of his supporters or decrease that of their opponents; but, if so, why were these 'irregularities' allowed to stand for so long? A study of the Attic road system indicates that at least some of these apparent irregularities may be explained by the location of the demes concerned along the line of certain muster routes for Athens' military levy.[7] But, leaving that issue on one side, it is I think hard to deny that the most important function of the *trittyes* was to ensure that each of the ten tribal prytanies of fifty *bouleutai* which served for a tenth of each year as the standing or working committees of the full Council of Five Hundred should contain men drawn not just from one part of Attica but from a cross-section of its whole territory and interests; that was surely a foreseeable consequence of the system which was originally introduced, whatever other purposes it may have been expected or planned to subserve.[8]

Another at first sight odd feature of the system was that every citizen was registered as belonging to that deme in which his direct male ancestor had been registered as resident in the last decade of the sixth century, regardless of where he himself was now domiciled.[9] (A modern citizen of the

supported by no direct evidence, and need not be taken seriously. I cannot believe that the *Ath. Pol.* could have been ignorant of so important a change.

[6] Hignett, *HAC* 137.

[7] Siewert, *Die Trittyen Attikas*, the most recent full treatment. On the suggestion of 'gerrymandering' see above, p. 26.

[8] Above, p. 27.

[9] There were two (obvious) exceptions to this rule: (*a*) adopted sons were registered in the demes of their adoptive fathers, and hence might belong to demes other than those of their natural fathers; (*b*) any non-Athenian granted citizenship

United Kingdom would certainly find it odd to be registered in the constituency in which his great-great-grandfather happened to have been domiciled!) Obviously, in the long period from the end of the sixth century to the end of the fourth quite a number of Athenians must have moved, not only to other parts of Attica but also to the citizen settlements ('cleruchies') which were sometimes established outside Attica within the sphere of Athenian imperial influence; and there was certainly a very considerable increase in the population of the conurbation of Athens/Piraeus (though a lot of that must have been the result of an influx of non-citizens, slaves, and metics—as Thucydides noted (2. 14), in 431 most Athenians were still living in the country districts of Attica, and had been doing so 'since time immemorial'). Nevertheless, such migration cannot have affected the large majority of Athenians, for, if it had, there would surely have developed an increasingly urgent need to overhaul the system to prevent its breaking down; but we never hear of that happening or even being mooted. Moreover, given the small size of Attica, if men came to live only a few miles away from the demes in which they were registered as members, the inconvenience of attending meetings or festivals in those demes, or even holding deme offices there, would not have been serious.

Thus, in the developed democracy the citizens actually living in deme X were (a) those who paternal ancestors had been registered as living there at the time of the Cleisthenic reforms, and (b) those who had moved there since. Membership of the deme assembly, however, and eligibility to hold deme offices, were restricted to those in category (a), together with those in the same category who were now living in other demes. Some Athenians might own property, and even (if they were well-to-do) private houses, in more than one deme; but, if so they were registered simply as members of their original Cleisthenic 'family' deme. Women

had to be assigned to a deme. (Zimmern observed that it was not until 1835 that a local qualification generally replaced a birth qualification for the 'freedom' of English boroughs, and that 'membership of the seventeen parishes of Siena is still hereditary' with the families constantly moving from one to another: *The Greek Commonwealth*, 158.)

'belonged' to their fathers', and after marriage to their husbands', demes.

(The districts of Oropos and Eleutherai, on Attica's northern frontier with Boeotia, and the island of Salamis, were not included in the system. Those Athenians who were living in these 'annexed' areas at the time of Cleisthenes' reforms were registered in one or other of the demes of Attica proper, but on what criteria we cannot say. The original 'Cleisthenic' non-citizen inhabitants of those districts were required to serve in the Athenian forces, and probably enjoyed the private rights of citizenship; their status was surely somewhat analogous to that of the Roman *cives sine suffragio*.)

The resident aliens (metics) were not members of any deme, and what part they were allowed to play in the affairs of the demes in which they lived probably varied considerably from one deme to another—the known facts are very thin and scattered. They certainly could not vote in the deme assembly or hold public office, although they were liable to pay local taxes and might make voluntary donations to local funds or needs. Again, our evidence is sparse. Of the many tens of thousands of metics who lived in Attica during the period under review, we know the deme of residence of a mere 366, of whom 223 (61 per cent) lived in or just outside Athens itself, and a further 69 (almost 19 per cent) in the Piraeus; but, although 366 is a very small sample, these figures confirm the natural presumption that the heaviest concentrations of metics were to be found in or near the 'business centre' rather than in the country districts.

An Athenian's title to Athenian citizenship rested on his enrolment as a member of one of the 139 demes of Attica; from that his membership of the *trittys* and the tribe to which he belonged followed automatically, as did his right to attend and vote and speak in the *ecclêsia* and his eligibility to hold 'national' office. A male Athenian had his name duly entered in the Deme Register (*lêxiarchikon grammateion*) when he reached the age of eighteen; he was then presented to the demesmen, who had to decide under oath whether he had reached the prescribed age and whether he was otherwise qualified. Until Pericles' law on citizenship in 451/50, he had to be the legitimate offspring of an Athenian father and a free-born mother, who might herself be a non-Athenian by birth (the mother of the illustrious Cimon, for example, was a non-Athenian); but thereafter, apart from a temporary reversion to this less restrictive criterion during the last years of the Peloponnesian War,[10] both father and mother had to be of citizen birth. An applicant who was rejected by the demesmen could appeal to the courts (but at the risk of being sold as a slave if his appeal failed); they were empowered to reverse the deme's decision if they so decided, and order the appellant's enrolment in the Deme Register. Finally, the Council of Five Hundred reviewed and confirmed the enrolments, but had the power to disqualify anyone they deemed unqualified and to fine the demesmen who had enrolled him.

Each deme selected its own officers, probably by sortition (at least from the mid-fifth century), and probably only from those of its members who were aged thirty or more. Like the officers of the Athenian state, they were subject to a preliminary scrutiny (*dokimasia*) before entering office, and to an examination of their conduct in office (*euthynai*) after laying it down. (No doubt steps were taken to ensure that anyone who was formally eligible, but in practice incapable of holding office, was excluded from the selection procedure.) The most important officer was the Demarch (*dêmarchos*)— we might appropriately call him the Mayor—who held his office for one year. We do not know whether that office could be held more than once; all we can say is that our evidence, such as it is, reveals no example of a man who was Demarch more than once. Some demes certainly appointed other deme officers like treasurers, secretaries, accountants, examiners, advocates, heralds, and so on to lighten the Demarch's work-load or keep an eye on what he was up to; but, so far as our evidence goes, there was no standard pattern laid down by the central government, and practices varied from deme to deme, probably depending on its size and the complexity of its business. The one officer common to every deme was the Demarch.

[10] Above, p. 16.

The Demarch was the link between local and central government. He presided over the deme assembly, and was responsibile for the Deme Register. In addition, he kept the register of any property forfeit to the state; acted as collector of special taxes (*eisphorai*) down to the reform of the collection system in 378/7; collected the first-fruits for the Eleusinian Festival, and organized and marshalled his deme's contingent to the Panathenaic Festival; enforced certain debt recoveries or distrainments; ensured that corpses were given a proper funeral, with power to charge the cost to the relatives where appropriate; was ultimately responsible for keeping proper records of deme decisions, and income and expenditure and cash balances; executed certain duties in connection with local cults and festivals; acted as his deme's spokesman in cases involving the deme corporately; and carried out various *ad hoc* tasks. Any particular Demarch's duties fell into two categories: those laid down by the central government (which were uniform in all demes), and those determined by the deme itself for its own purposes and needs. Whether he received any remuneration for his office is unknown.

The number of citizens eligible to attend any deme assembly varied widely, from well under a hundred in the very smallest to well over a thousand in the very largest. It is plausible to suppose that a quorum was required for some or all assembly meetings; if so, it must have been different in different demes. The assembly normally met in the deme itself, but it could be summoned elsewhere, notably in Athens; and its decisions would be taken by ballot, or less formally if the business was routine and uncontentious. Every demesman was entitled to speak, but details of actual proposals are obscure, dependent as they are on the chance of scattered epigraphic finds—and a great many decisions would not have merited the expense of inscribing them on stone. Something over one hundred decrees have turned up, but they come from only about a quarter of the total of 139 demes, with most of them dating from the fourth century and especially from the years after 350; fewer than one third of these surviving hundred or so decrees are concerned with deme administration (and mostly sacral matters at that), the rest being honorific, recording gratitude for individual services or benefactions.

We can safely take it that the volume and complexity of deme business and the formality with which it was conducted, and even the frequency of assembly meetings, were by no means the same in both tiny Sybridai and massive Acharnai, which had over twenty times Sybridai's population and covered a far more extensive territory.[11] But all had business to conduct, apart from that of vetting and registering new members. They raised and spent revenues, from both their own members and those members of other demes who held property in their area; the demes themselves owned property which was rented or leased to bring in income, and buildings (especially local shrines or temples) which had to be maintained; they could lend out deme moneys at interest, usually at 12 per cent; they received and spent or administered benefactions, either of cash or in material form; oversaw local cults and festivals (some had permanent theatres built of stone); spent money on having important or honorific records cut on stone; levied fines; appointed local priests and priestesses. At any rate, in a middle-sized or large deme a Demarch must have been kept reasonably busy. We know that a certain Euboulides was Demarch of Halimous in the same year (346/5) as he was a member of the Council of Five Hundred; but such a combination of duties was probably very unusual. Halimous was a smallish deme (its bouleutic quota was only three) and it lay only five or six miles from Athens, which must have made the double duties more manageable than they would have been had Euboulides come from a larger or more distant deme.

The deme system thus ensured that fairly homogeneous groups of people, most of whom lived near each other and knew each other pretty well, would share in running their own local affairs as well as playing their part in the affairs of the state as a whole. Young boys must have early become accustomed to hearing about, or watching, their local deme

---

[11] The text of Thucydides (2. 20. 4) reports that Acharnai supplied 3,000 hoplites to the Athenian army in 431. Despite attempts by some moderns to justify that figure, it is far too high and must be rejected as a copying error; but the actual figure which Thucydides wrote is beyond secure recovery.

meetings, and listening to their elders discussing deme business. The demesmen as a whole would find the idea of attending and voting on proposals at meetings of the 'national' *ecclêsia* in Athens more natural and less formidable than would have been the case without this background of local experience, and would have been less daunted by having to serve as members of the central Council of Five Hundred. The demes were each a 'city in miniature' (*mikra polis*).

They were scarcely, at any rate in the developed democracy, local 'power-bases' for politicians operating on the central Athenian stage; and local politics were not, as they sometimes are nowadays, an 'apprenticeship' for a career at a higher level. But they demonstrate how the principles of equality and participation, the freedom of all citizens to debate and decide matters which affected their own well-being, their sense of independence and shared responsibility, went right to the roots of the Athenian democracy.

As in any human system, there could be abuses: funds misapplied or mismanaged, officials corrupted, seats on the Council of Five Hundred in any particular year 'fixed'. Enrolment on a Deme Register was the prerequisite of Athenian citizenship; hence, not surprisingly, men tried to get registered by fraud, or get their illegitimate sons slipped in. In the large demes, especially as the numbers of *dêmotai* living outside their original 'family' demes increased, such deceptions were less difficult to contrive. But, when all is said and done, the system offered far more secure safeguards against individual corruption and abuse than can be assured in more hierarchical societies. [12]

---

[12] Antiphilos, the father of Euboulides, himself an earlier Demarch of Halimous, had one day announced that the Deme Register had been 'lost'; and a formal exercise had to be begun to reconstruct the Register. Ten men whose names were not included in the new Register appealed to the courts, and nine of them were ordered by the courts to be reinstated. It was alleged that the original Register had not been lost accidentally, but deliberately destroyed or hidden by Antiphilos for his own nefarious purposes, to exclude enemies or insert frauds. The scandal was resurrected in 346/5, when his son Euboulides was Demarch of Halimous, in connection with a more widespread concern, when the *ecclêsia*, allegedly with the whole of Athens incensed about widespread malpractices, decreed that every Register be examined and a vote taken on oath on every name which was listed therein. However, this Attica-wide revision of Deme Registers was probably unique, at any rate in the fourth century, for had there been other instances we should expect to have heard of

'Since the middle ages,' wrote Keith Thomas, 'England has possessed a bewildering mass of local institutions—parish vestries, courts baron, courts leet, village communities—each accustomed to making bylaws, appointing officers, and levying rates. They dealt with a variety of matters of local concern and they were composed in many different ways. But they frequently afforded even the humblest members of the community some experience of self-government and the opportunity to participate in matters closest to their own interests. "Anyone who reads the manorial records . . . cannot fail to be astonished at the extensive participation of nearly every adult male in local affairs".'[13] Sadly, for ancient Athens we lack that rich harvest of information which can be reaped from the far more abundant and multifarious local records of medieval and early modern England. But what Thomas wrote of England was quite evidently much truer of Athens, where every freeborn citizen stood on an equal footing with his neighbours and could take his turn in holding local office in communities which were all of them ordered in the same way, while at the same time (quite unlike the ordinary English villager) he was able to play a full part in the workings and decisions of the central government as well. It is to the latter that we shall now turn.

The Ecclêsia[14]

The two best surviving pictures of a meeting of the *ecclêsia* stand in stark contrast with each other.

Aristophanes' *Acharnians* was produced in 425, when, like *The Knights* a year later, it won the first prize at the Lenaea. The play opens with Dicaeopolis, a typically Aristophanic ordinary, independent-minded, and slightly 'bolshy' Athenian,

---

them somewhere. On the whole episode see Whitehead, *The Demes of Attica*, 105–9; Demosthenes, *Against Euboulides*.

[13] Keith Thomas, 'The United Kingdom', in Grew (ed.), *Crises of Political Development in Europe and the U.S.*, 67–8.

[14] For full citation of the detailed evidence, and a summary of modern arguments, see Hansen, *AE*, *AA*.

sitting all by himself in the Pnyx. He is bored, restless, and irreverent. Nearby, in the central market-place, the Agora, people are chattering away, showing no inclination to move into the Pnyx, and dodging the policemen who are trying to herd them in. 'Even the *prytaneis* aren't here yet,' moans Dicaeopolis, who is impatient for the proceedings to begin and looking forward to interrupting any speakers of whom he disapproves with shouts and boos and abuse. At last the 'noon-day *prytaneis*' arrive, and the public Crier comes forward and pronounces the customary formula 'Does anybody wish to address the meeting?' The *ecclêsia* is in session. A certain Amphitheos ('Semi-divine') gets up to announce that he has been charged by the gods to make peace between Athens and Sparta, and is promptly and forcibly removed, despite Dicaeopolis' protests, by order of the *prytaneis*. Next, an embassy which had been sent to Persia a dozen years earlier, and has spent its time living well on its expense allowance, produces a Persian 'King's Eye', who gabbles away in pidgin Greek and is soon seen through and seen off by Dicaeopolis. Next appears another envoy with a gang of barbarian mercenaries, who steal our hero's packed lunch. The *ecclêsia* is then adjourned after Dicaeopolis has announced that a drop of rain has fallen, and got that deemed inauspicious; and he goes off and gets Amphitheos to conclude a private peace with Sparta in his (Dicaeopolis') name only—thereafter the fun gets even faster and more furious!

Demosthenes (*De corona*, 169–81) is grimmer, but not essentially different, with his account of what happened after Elatea in Boeotia had fallen to Philip of Macedon in 339.

Evening had come, when a messenger reached the *prytaneis* with the news that Elatea had been taken. They were in the middle of their supper. At once, they all got up, and while some of them set to clearing stall-holders out of the Agora and burning the wattle screens there, the others sent to fetch the generals and summoned the public trumpeter. The whole city was full of noise and confusion. Next morning at daybreak the *prytaneis* summoned the full Council, while you citizens began making your way to the *ecclêsia*. Before the Council had finished its discussions or framed any draft proposals, all Athens was sitting there waiting.

The Council appeared, and the *prytaneis* announced the news they had been given, the messenger himself being introduced to give his own report to the *ecclêsia*. Then the public Crier made the announcement, 'Who wishes to speak?' Nobody volunteered. The Crier repeated the invitation over and over, but still nobody came forward . . . At last I got up and addressed you . . . Everybody applauded what I had to say, and nobody said anything against my proposal. Nor did I just make a speech, I drafted the decree; not only did I draft the decree, I served personally as one of the ambassadors . . . I was there from the start, and I went through right to the finish of the whole business . . . Bring me the decree which was carried that day . . . and read it out: 'Nausicles archon, prytany of the tribe Aiantis, seventeenth day of the month Skirophorion: proposed by Demosthenes, son of Demosthenes, of the deme Paiania' . . .

That occasion was very unusual, given that only one man got up and addressed the *ecclêsia*. On such an important issue there would usually be a keen debate. So, in 431, Thucydides tells us (1. 139–45) how the final Spartan ultimatum was put to the *ecclêsia*, in effect amounting to an undertaking that war could be avoided if Athens rescinded the decree which banned Megara from access to markets and harbours in Athens and her empire: 'A lot of people came forward and addressed the assembly with arguments on both sides, either advocating war or urging that the decree should not be allowed to be an impediment to peace but should be repealed. One of those who spoke was Pericles, son of Xanthippus, the foremost Athenian of his day . . . who gave the following advice . . .' Then, having summarized Pericles' arguments against giving in to the Spartan demands, Thucydides resumes: 'That was what Pericles had to say, and the Athenians, judging that his was the best advice, voted accordingly.' There are, of course, many other examples one could give of comparable debates, most notably that on the question of what penalty should be imposed on Mytilene after the suppression of her rebellion from Athens in 428/7, when Thucydides (3. 37–48) summarizes the two chief speeches, each of which advocated a widely divergent penalty.

Meetings of the *ecclêsia* were summoned, and their agendas prescribed, by the *prytaneis*, the standing committee of the *boulê*, the Council of Five Hundred. In the fully developed democracy of the later fourth century there were four meetings in each prytany, that is to say forty in every year. One of these four was termed the 'principal meeting' (*kyria ekklêsia*), whose business it was to vote on whether the officers of state were performing their duties properly, to deal with matters concerning the food supply and national defence and security, to receive notice of any proposed indictments for serious public offences (*eisangeliai*), to listen to inventories of confiscated property being read out and any claims to inheritances or the right to claim heiresses in marriage. In addition, at the *kyria ekklêsia* in the sixth prytany of each year a vote was taken on whether an ostracism should be held that year.

That is what we are told at *Ath. Pol.* 43, where it is also reported that the *kyria ekklêsia* in the sixth prytany was the only occasion in each year for receiving complaints against 'sycophants' (viz. individuals who had deliberately and dishonestly deceived or misled the *dêmos*), a statement which may well be muddled and incorrect. [15] We are also told here that at one of the other three meetings in each prytany formal private petitions were received when people might address the assembly on matters of public or personal interest, while the remaining two meetings dealt with religious business and foreign policy. But *Ath. Pol.* omits to mention that during the fourth century the *ecclêsia* met regularly on the eleventh day of the first prytany of each year to consider the annual revision of the laws (*nomoi*).

When this pattern of meetings was first established we do not know; and it may well be that there were fewer in the pre-Ephialtic period. The pattern of business was also surely different in the fifth century, when matters concerning the 'Athenian empire' bulked large in importance. But it is reasonable to suppose that some programme of regular meetings in each prytany and some allocation of different categories of business to specified meetings was already the rule from about 460 at the latest. In an emergency, it was sometimes necessary to summon a meeting without the usual

---

[15] See Rhodes, *CAP*, note on 43. 5.

notice (that which Demosthenes addressed after the fall of Elatea is an obvious instance), and such meetings could be additional to the regular quota.[16]

From about 460 onwards, although the *ecclêsia* did sometimes meet elsewhere, notably in the Peiraeus to deal with naval matters, the Pnyx was its almost invariably regular meeting-place. This natural auditorium in the heart of Athens, about 300 yards from the foot of the Acropolis and the edge of the Agora, could accommodate about six thousand down to the end of the fifth century; at that point further work increased that number by about five hundred, and considerable enlargement round about 340 may have almost doubled its capacity, if those present were ready to tolerate dense and uncomfortable packing.[17] It is significant that 6,000 was the quorum required for ostracisms, grants of citizenship, and certain cases of deprivation of civic rights, and by the second half of the fifth century the courts were drawn from a pool of 6,000 jurors. A full Pnyx could thus be assumed to constitute a full quorum of citizens, although at an ostracism, when the voting took place in the Agora, the number of *ostraka* handed in was counted to ensure that the required number of citizens had voted.

In the developed democracy of the fourth century the agenda for any meeting of the *ecclêsia* had to be posted for all to see four days in advance (although in an emergency such notice had to be dispensed with). Evidently, similar practices must have been observed in the earlier period. Meetings were normally arranged by the *prytaneis*; but the Council of Five Hundred or the *ecclêsia* itself could order that one should be summoned. Only citizens could attend and vote, although spectators were allowed to watch and listen from outside the assembly area. How many citizens turned up we cannot say (although a few decisions, as has already been noted, were valid only if at least 6,000 had voted); obviously, much would depend on how important and interesting the business was. We know that in the late fifth century people were sometimes herded in from the Agora by the police using red-

[16] On this last point see Harris, 'How Often did the Athenian Assembly Meet?', controverting Hansen's view.
[17] Above, p. 34.

dyed ropes to drive them towards the Pnyx;[18] whether that was done to enforce attendance or diminish the noise and distraction of the market-place we cannot say, but more probably the latter, since no attempt was made to compel attendance from further away. Pay for attending meetings of the *ecclêsia* was first introduced at some time not long after the overthrow of the Thirty in 403 (it could well be that their traumatic experience of the oligarchic 'take-overs' in 411 and 404 led the Athenians to take this step to ensure fuller and hence less easily manipulable turn-outs). Originally fixed at one obol, the payment had risen to three obols by 390 at the latest; and before the last thirty or so years of the century had been fixed at one drachma (six obols) for 'ordinary' meetings and one-and-a-half for the *kyriai ekklêsiai*. Down to the considerable expansion of the capacity of the Pnyx in the 340s, those who arrived too late to find a place were turned away without payment.[19]

[Hansen has argued that, since most meetings were over by noon or shortly after, the attendance payment should be seen as recompense for the loss not of a whole day's 'wages' but only half a day's, since a man who attended the assembly would be free to work for the rest of the day. That can have been true only for those citizens who lived or had their work within a reasonable distance from the Pnyx; but, all the same, three obols, and later one drachma (one-and-a-half for *kyriai ekklêsiai*) must have seemed a very reasonable *douceur* for attendance. It was certainly not cheap, for the cost of meeting the attendance bill could have reached, at the later rates, 45 to 50 talents a year.[20]]

How efficient the checks were to ensure that only properly qualified voters were admitted to the *ecclêsia* is obscure. Officials were appointed to control admission; but with several thousand coming in, and in the absence of anything like identity-cards, it must have rested very much with the citizens themselves to spot and denounce a 'stranger'; but we hear nothing to suggest that there was ever a problem about this. Some scholars believe that the members of the ten tribes

---

[18] Aristophanes, *Acharnians*, 21–2.
[19] Aristophanes, *Ecclesiazusae*, 183–8, 289–310, 383–95.
[20] Hansen, *AA* 47–8.

sat each in their separately designated enclaves; but the evidence seems rather to point very much to people sitting or standing wherever they chose.[21]

With only one or two exceptions, there were no fixed meeting-days. But meetings could not be summoned on festival-days and such (which made getting on for half the days in any year unavailable); and, for obvious reasons, the *ecclêsia* and the popular courts could not be summoned for the same day. Meetings began very early in the morning, with certain solemn religious preliminaries. They would normally be over by midday or thereabouts—a *kyria ekklêsia* could well go on longer, and that may be why it came to be remunerated at a higher rate than other meetings. During that time (and its length would vary with the season of the year) there were a considerable number of items to deal with (at least nine, and quite often more than that); but often many of the items would be routine and uncontroversial, and 'nodded through' without debate. Speeches again would mostly be brief, except on the most momentous occasions when vitally important issues were at stake; unwanted or wordy or uninstructed speakers could be shouted down or removed. Voting was normally by a show of hands (save that in those instances when a quorum of 6,000 was required by statute, or when the *ecclêsia* was acting as a court, the vote was by ballot to ensure that all was in order). There was no precise count, which would have protracted business intolerably; the result of the show of hands was roughly assessed by the presiding officers, but anyone present might lodge a formal objection and call for a recount. Early in the proceedings concerning the trial of the generals after Arginusae, we are told that a vote was postponed because the failing light made it too dark to count the hands (that was an unusually protracted meeting); and when subsequently a vote was taken to decide whether the accused generals should be tried individually and separately or *en bloc*, the *prytaneis* at first reported that the former proposal had been carried, but a certain Menecles lodged a sworn objection and a fresh show of hands was called for, which this time was judged to reveal

---

[21] Hansen, *AE* 134–6.

a majority in favour of a trial *en bloc* (Xenophon, *Hellenica*, I.
7. 7 & 21). Aeschines (3. 3) indicates that the 'tellers' might
sometimes be alleged to have misreported the count, and that
to do so was an indictable offence. That the balance of voting
could be quite close is *a priori* to be expected; and Thucydides
(3. 49. 1) reports that the decision in favour of the less
stringent of the penalties proposed for Mytilene in 427 was 'a
narrow one'. It could be that on occasion a politician might in
effect have challenged a narrowly approved decree by
inventing grounds for bringing a *graphê paranomôn* against its
proposer, in the hope that the courts would annul the decree
in question.

As already noted, to have carried out a precise count of
thousands of hands would have been very time-consuming,
and would certainly have protracted proceedings in the
ecclêsia beyond tolerable limits. Hansen has set out the
evidence fully, and has argued (in my view conclusively) that
the count was always an estimate except in the rare cases
when a ballot was employed.[22] He very pertinently compares
the procedures and practices in the 'direct democracy' of
some of the small cantons in modern Switzerland which still
retain a People's Assembly (*Landsgemeinde*) in which all the
adult citizens of the canton have the right to vote. These
cantons do have popularly elected 'parliaments', but these
bodies (rather like the Athenian Council) are mainly charged
with preparing the agenda for the meetings of the *Landsgemeinde*, their competence otherwise being restricted to minor
matters; it is the People's Assembly itself which makes all
cantonal statutes and other important decisions, and elects
not only its cantonal officials and judges but also the canton's
representatives in the Swiss Federal Senate.

The largest of these units is the canton of Glarus, with an
area of some 700 square kilometers (rather over a quarter the
size of Attica) and a population of some 40,000; the smallest
is only a quarter the size of Glarus, its population only a
third. The attendance figures range from about 3,000 to as
high as about 11,000 (regular meetings are summoned only
once a year, and extraordinary meetings are extremely rare).

[22] Hansen, *AE* 103–17.

Apart from elections, the agendas can comprise up to twenty items. All the items have been sent in well in advance, and have been 'predigested' by the cantonal officials; most are quickly approved without debate, but with disputed matters no vote is taken until after a debate, and sometimes amendments are permissible. But most of those attending do not exercise their right to speak, and those who do keep what they have to say short and to the point. The results of 'divisions' are by a show of hands, assessed quite quickly by the officials on a rough estimate, and never precisely counted. A meeting often lasts no more than four hours.[23]

One might also point to the practices of the University of Oxford, at any rate until the fairly recent introduction of the possibility of a 'postal ballot'. The '*ecclêsia*' of the University is Congregation, which is composed of the resident senior members of the University, numbering well over one thousand. They meet one afternoon a fortnight in term with provision for extra meetings if the Vice-Chancellor so orders. The agenda is published in advance by a Council which is elected by the members of Congregation; but individual members can give notice of matters to be included on the agenda. Most items go through without any discussion; but controversial items can generate fierce debates. Attendances vary in size in accordance with the nature of the business. Members soon learn to keep their speeches as short and pertinent as possible; but only a very small proportion of those present do make speeches. Most decisions are only roughly assessed by the Vice-Chancellor (who presides at the meetings); but he may direct that a division be held and a precise count be taken, and he is required to do so if six members rise in their places to call for one.

These examples can serve to show that it was in practice possible for the Athenian *ecclêsia* to function perfectly adequately in a broadly similar manner, especially given the arrangements whereby the Council of Five Hundred, and its constituent standing committees of *prytaneis*, who were charged with preparing and publishing its agenda, were so effectively representative of the whole spectrum of Athens'

---

[23] Ibid. 207–26.

citizens and incapable of developing into a separate 'estate of the realm'.

In this connection it is worth giving here a list of rules concerning speakers in both the *boulê* and the *ecclêsia* which can be found in the text of Aeschines' speech *Against Timarchus* (1. 35). Although this section is agreed to be an (irrelevant) insertion by a later editor, there is no reason to doubt that the rules are genuine:

Anyone addressing the *boulê* or the *ecclêsia* must keep to the matter in hand, must not deal with two separate matters together, and must not speak twice on the same matter at any one meeting; he must not engage in slanders or scurrility, or interrupt others; must speak only from the platform, and must not assault the presiding officer, on pain of a fine of up to 50 drachmai for each offence to be imposed by the *proedroi*, who may, if they think the offence merits a heavier penalty, refer the case to the *boulê* or to the *ecclêsia* at its next meeting for decision by secret ballot.

Down to the very end of the fifth century the *prytaneis*, the monthly-changing standing committee of the Council, presided at meetings of the *ecclêsia* under the chairmanship of that one amongst them who had been selected by lot to serve for the day in question. There was then a change, at a date which must lie between 403/2 and 378/7. Henceforth, early in the morning before the *ecclêsia* met, the *prytaneis* handed over the agenda etc. to a board of nine *proedroi* who were chosen by lot, one from each of the other nine tribal contingents of the Council, and from these nine one was chosen (again by lot) to act as chairman. (Whether the object was to relieve the *prytaneis* from some of the pressure of their duties, or to ensure an added safeguard against possible corruption, is unclear.) The *prytaneis*, and with them (after 403) the *proedroi*, were seated by the platform (*bêma*) in the centre of the base of the natural amphitheatre of the Pnyx. To assist them in maintaining order they could call on members of a 300-strong official police force of archers, who were public slaves and were known as 'the Scythians' after the region from which they had originally been acquired. After the late 340s, the members of one of the ten tribes who were present at any meeting were charged with this task as well, and presumably accommodated in a specially marked-off area facing the central platform.

No business could be put to the *ecclêsia* which had not come via the Council. (Even in an extreme emergency, as when the news about Elatea reached the *prytaneis* in the evening, they sent out to summon the rest of the Council, which was still deliberating before the *ecclêsia* met next morning.) The items on the agenda, the probouleumata, could take one of two forms. The Council could draft a specific proposal to be put to the *ecclêsia* to assent to or reject, although very often the assembly accepted riders or amendments 'from the floor', so that the original *probouleuma* might be carried in a highly modified form. Alternatively, the Council might simply put a topic or issue on the agenda for discussion and decision without any positive proposal of its own, leaving it to individuals to suggest what form a decision should take. (The available evidence suggests that 'specific' and 'open' *probouleumata* were roughly equal in number.[24]) The *ecclêsia* itself could instruct the Council to introduce a *probouleuma* on a given topic at a future meeting. Otherwise, to get an item on to the agenda a man had either to be a Councillor himself and persuade the others to accept it, or he had to know someone on the Council and get him to push it. Of course, the officers of state, and most notably the *stratêgoi*, were regularly in a position to ensure that items in their fields of responsibility were put to the Council to be added to the agenda. (There were also, as has already been noted, a number of regular items which were automatically on the agenda for certain meetings.)

It was only after 403/2 that a formal procedural distinction was made between 'decrees' approved by the *ecclêsia* (*psêphismata*) and 'laws' (*nomoi*). But there must surely have been some distinction between decrees and laws before then, at least from the date of the institution of the *graphê paranomôn*, if not earlier.[25] Plainly, it was regularly within the power of the *ecclêsia* to reverse its own decrees, as in 427 the first decree on Mytilene was overridden by a second and more lenient

---

[24] Rhodes, *AB*, 78–9. For examples of *probouleumata* see below, p. 88.
[25] Above, p. 44.

one (Thucydides 3. 49). Some decrees were of a general character, and established lasting rules, like the decree promoted by Pericles in 451/50 which restricted citizen status to those born of both an Athenian father and an Athenian mother. Most were simply 'one-off' decisions—to expend a stated sum, say, on a building project, or to send a squadron of triremes on a given mission. How that distinction was observed in practice is opaque to us, for apparently even the major reforms of Cleisthenes and of Ephialtes were simply effected by securing the *ecclêsia*'s assent. It seems best to suppose that an urgent need to sharpen the distinction had become apparent through the experience of the oligarchic 'take-overs' in 411 and 404, when fundamental changes in the constitution had been carried by decrees of the *ecclêsia*, albeit in a violent and irregular fashion, although it is important to note that in 411 care was taken to rescind or suspend the *graphê paranomôn* as a preliminary step.[26]

The *graphê paranomôn* (in its fourth-century form, which was probably substantially the same as it had been in the fifth) made it possible for any citizen to object to a proposal in the *ecclêsia* by making a formal statement under oath that he purposed to institute a *graphê paranomôn* against the proposer on the grounds (*a*) that his proposal was incorrect in its form; or (*b*) that there was a fault in the procedure; or (*c*) that the substance of the proposal was in conflict with an existing law. Voting on the proposal had then to be postponed, or if it had been carried the *psêphisma* itself was suspended, until the case had been decided by a court. If the court decided in favour of the accuser, the proposal lapsed or the *psêphisma* was annulled; the proposer himself was fined, and three convictions led to the loss of his civic rights, although it appears that if a *graphê* was brought more than a year after a *psêphisma* had been carried the proposer was not liable to any personal penalty.

How often such cases were brought in the fifth century, we have no idea; but they were clearly very frequent occurrences in the fourth. A certain Aristophon is said to have boasted that he had been charged on seventy-five

---

[26] Below, p. 148.

occasions (although that is likely to have been a perhaps conventionally exaggerated figure) and acquitted every time; Cephalus, however, took much pride in the fact that he had proposed more decrees than any other man and had never once been charged under a *graphê paranomôn* (Aeschines 3. 194). Given that the time allowed for speeches in the *ecclêsia* was generally very short, and far too short to allow any really full development and examination of wider themes, a *graphê paranomôn* gave the orator-politicians the chance to develop their arguments and explain and justify their policies at greater length and in fuller detail than was otherwise possible. We find a similar situation obtaining in late Republican Rome, where 'political' trials gave politicians the chance to do precisely that, as is clear from many of the forensic speeches of that era, often paying scant regard to the actual details of the indictment—it is quite understandable that they had to seize such opportunities as came their way in a society which, like Athens, knew nothing of general elections or organized 'national' political parties with articulated 'programmes' and manifestos. We have an exceptionally good example of this in a case which was heard in 330, for the main speeches for the prosecution and for the defence both survive for us to read.[27] Ctesiphon, a friend and admirer of Demosthenes, had several years earlier proposed that the city should award Demosthenes a symbolic crown to mark his great services to Athens. Demosthenes' old enemy and persistent opponent Aeschines now brought a *graphê paranomôn* against Ctesiphon; his grounds were partly technical (and essentially trivial, though probably valid), but also, and most importantly, that the inclusion in the decree of the statement that Demosthenes had always been a patriot who had served Athens splendidly was an untruth. Aeschines, in his speech

---

[27] Aeschines, *Against Ctesiphon*; Demosthenes, *De corona*. It is worth noting that, for all the Athenians' efforts to avoid or remove clashes or conflicts in their public rules, both Aeschines (32 ff.) and Demosthenes (120–1) were each able to cite a different and conflicting law on the granting of crowns (or perhaps each the same law, which was however so loosely worded as to admit of two different interpretations of it). Fifty years earlier, in 380, Isocrates (*Panathenaicus*, 144) could have been heard lamenting that the laws of Athens were full of confusion and muddle.

for the prosecution, and Demosthenes, who was the real
target of the attack and who spoke in defence of Ctesiphon,
both seized the opportunity to review the city's policies over
many past years, each defending his own record and
attacking his rival's, in a wealth of detail and at a length
which would not have been possible elsewhere than in a
court. (It is, incidentally, worth noting that Aeschines had
waited six years before bringing his charge—presumably
judging that the political climate was now more favourable
to his chances of success.)

The task of codifying the Athenian laws was begun after
the restoration of the democracy in 410 and brought to
completion during the period immediately following the
overthrow of the Thirty in 403. The exercise inevitably
involved sifting the general from the particular, the durable
from the temporary, the current and relevant from the
obsolete and superseded, among the great mass of prior
enactments which fell to be reviewed in order to determine
what should and what should not be included in the code; it
must therefore have sharpened awareness of that basic and
fundamental distinction between *nomos* and *psêphisma* which
now secured formal recognition in the new procedural
arrangements. Henceforth, the *ecclêsia* could not itself create
new general and permanent rules (*nomoi*) by a simple
majority vote taken after proper notice and debate: *nomoi*
(which, incidentally, did not include treaties with foreign
states, whatever their duration) could be annulled or created
only by a legislative body called *nomothetai*.

This procedure is set out in a law which is cited verbatim in
a speech delivered by Demosthenes in 355 (24. 20–3):

In the first prytany of each year, and on the eleventh day thereof,
after the Crier has read out the prayers, there shall be a vote on the
laws: first on those which concern the Council of Five Hundred,
next on those which are of general application, then on those
governing the nine archons, and finally on those which govern the
other offices of state. The voting shall be as follows, viz. those who
are in favour of the laws concerning the Council shall hold up their
hands first, and then those who are against; and so on with the rest.
. . . If any of the laws already in force shall be rejected on a show of
hands, the *prytaneis* in whose term of office the vote is held shall

designate the last of the three meetings of the *ecclêsia*[28] for the consideration of those laws which have been so rejected. The *proedroi*, who shall have been appointed by lot to preside at the said assembly, are required to put, as the first item of business after the religious preliminaries have been completed, the question concerning the sessions of the *nomothetai* and the source from which their fees are to be met. The *nomothetai* shall be selected from among those who have taken the oath to serve as jurors. . . . Before the meeting of the *ecclêsia*, any citizen who so wishes shall write out any laws he purposes to propose and post them up in front of the statues of the Eponymous Heroes [which occupied a prominent position in the Agora and stood on a long base which was eminently suitable for posting public notices], so that the *dêmos* may be able to vote on how much time is to be allowed for the sessions of the *nomothetai* in proportion to the number of laws proposed. Whoever proposes a new law must write it on a whitened board and exhibit it in front of the Eponymous Heroes every day until the meeting of the *ecclêsia*. On the eleventh day of the month Hecatombaion [simply another way of saying 'on the eleventh day of the first prytany'] the *dêmos* shall elect from the whole citizen body five men whose duty it shall be to speak in defence of those laws which have been proposed for prospective repeal by the *nomothetai*.

A citizen who proposed a new law ran the risk of being indicted on a charge of having 'proposed an inexpedient law' (*graphê nomon mê epitêdeion theinai*), analogous to the *graphê paranomôn*. *Nomoi* were superior to *psêphismata*, and accordingly any *psêphisma* which was alleged to be in conflict with a *nomos* could be challenged by a *graphê paranomôn*; and, at least in some instances, a new *nomos* could have the effect of invalidating any *psêphisma* which had been carried earlier— but pretty certainly only when that was explicitly stated by,

---

[28] Hansen (*AA* 23) interprets this to show that down to about 355 there were only three meetings of the *ecclêsia* in each prytany of the year and that the programme of four per prytany must have been introduced later. (Cf. ibid. 145 for reference to a suggestion by D. M. Lewis that the first prytany in each year may have had only three meetings, but the other nine prytanies four each.) Personally, I can see no serious objection to the view that this passage of the law simply means 'the last of the three [remaining] meetings of the *ecclêsia* [following the first meeting in the prytany]'. The inscribed *nomoi* surviving from the fourth century reveal *nomoi* enacted at times other than this special procedure attests (Rhodes, *AB* 51). Presumably the first prytany was the one occasion when such business was an *obligatory* agenda item.

or an inescapable corollary of, the *nomos* in question.[29] The
nomothetai themselves were selected at random from among
the total of 6,000 who were registered each year as jurors in
the public courts. Nevertheless, it is highly unlikely that the
Athenians regarded that as constituting any serious derogation
from the *ecclêsia*'s sovereignty; far more probably, the
procedure was seen as taking a lengthy and complex
set of questions off *ecclêsia* agenda, after due preliminary
consideration and a preliminary vote about which items
should go forward to the *nomothetai* for final decision, and
entrusting that final decision to what they saw as simply a
large, random, and representative cross-section of themselves.

Down to about 360, the *ecclêsia* sometimes itself functioned
as a court for the hearing and decision of *eisangeliai*, broadly
speaking impeachments brought against any citizen alleged
to be guilty of a grave offence such as treason or serious
corruption in a public office, especially the military office of
the *stratêgia*, although such cases could alternatively be heard
in the courts. (Such judicial meetings of the *ecclêsia* were
probably additional to the regular meetings.) But after 362 all
twenty-seven *eisangeliai* of which we have any evidence were
heard in a court, none by the *ecclêsia* itself. *Inter alia*, that will
have produced a considerable saving in public expenditure,
since court sessions cost far less than meetings of the *ecclêsia*;
and that may have been the reason for this apparent change.[30]
But, once again, the *ecclêsia* always itself took the initiative by

[29] *Pace* Hansen (*AE* 170–1), who takes Demosthenes 20. 44 to demonstrate that a
new *nomos* abolishing any form of *ateleia* (tax exemption) would, if enacted,
automatically repeal all previous grants of *ateleia* made by earlier *psêphismata*. I am
not convinced, since I find the suggestion that all *nomoi* were invariably retrospective
as well as prospective in force difficult to stomach. I share the view of those who
take it that Demosthenes is rhetorically and dramatically claiming that many people
who would have benefited from such grants in future will be deprived of their *ateleia*
if the *nomos* is enacted. Hansen cites a recently discovered *nomos* on silver coinage
(Stroud, *Hesperia*, 43 (1974), 157–88) as support for his contention. But the text of
this law specifically invalidates all previous *psêphismata* which are in conflict with it
and orders the destruction of any posted copies of such *psêphismata*. It certainly does
not follow that every other *nomos* did the same, unless it contained a similar specific
retroactive provision. In any case, the *nomos* in question did not invalidate all past
transactions under the earlier rules, but merely altered the rules for all future
transactions. (At *AA* 98 Hansen puts his case more cautiously.)

[30] Hansen, *AE* 60–2. On *eisangeliai* see Hansen, *Eisangelia*; Rhodes, 'Eisangelia in
Athens'; Hansen, 'Eisangelia in Athens. A Reply'; Ostwald, *From Popular Sovereignty
to the Sovereignty of the Law*, index, s.v.; below, p. 101.

Plate 1. The surviving left-hand section of the Decree of Kleinias (*GHI* no. 46: ?447 *BC*). An example of a decision of the Athenian Assembly inscribed on a block of marble for public view. It is prefaced by the formula: 'Resolved by the *Boule* and the *Demos: Edochsen tei bo[lei kai] toi demoi*'. Epigraphical Museum, Athens.

Plate 2. The local Deme Theatre at Thoricus. Its construction dates from about 500, not long after Cleisthenes' reforms. It was probably also used as the venue for meetings of the Deme Assembly. (Photo Comite voor Belgische opgravingen in Griekenland)

Plate 3. The Temple of Hephaestus (also referred to as the Theseum) which dominated the Agora. It was built in the third quarter of the fifth century. (Photo Michael Holford [Gerry Clyde]).

Plate 4. The Acropolis seen from the north-west, showing the monumental entrance gate, the Propylaea, constructed during the Periclean period. (Photo Ken Lambert, Camera Press).

Plate 5. The Erechtheum (Temple of Erechtheus, a legendary early King of Athens) on the Acropolis, constructed in the last quarter of the fifth century. (Photo Hirmer Fotoarchiv).

Plate 6. 'The Mourning Athena', a beautiful relief, found on the Acropolis, and dating from about the middle of the fifth century. It represents the goddess leaning sadly on her spear as she reads an inscribed list of the names of citizens who had been killed fighting for Athens. Acropolis Museum. (Photo Museum).

Plate 7. School scenes, from an early fifth century Attic cup. Berlin Museum.

Plate 8. Athenian silver tetradrachm (four-drachma piece), minted in the third quarter of the fifth century. The obverse face shows the head of Athena: the reverse Athena's owl, a sprig of olive, and the letters ΑΘΕ (ATHE). This was the standard format employed by the Athenian mint from the late sixth century onward, whence the common description of Attic silver coins as 'owls'. Private collection. (Photo Hirmer Fotoarchiv).

Plate 9. A Roman copy of the celebrated bust of Pericles executed by his contemporary, the sculptor Cresilas. British Museum. (Photo Michael Holford).

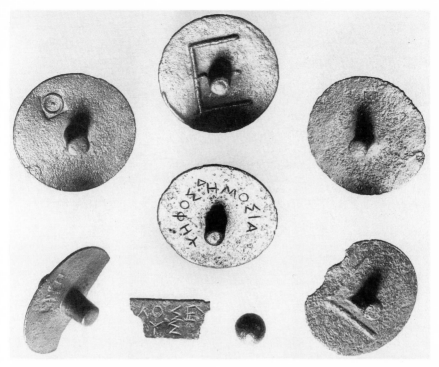

Plate 10. Voting by ballot. (a) Bronze disks which could be slotted into a sort of 'cribbage-board' to facilitate the counting of votes cast by the dicasts in a court case. Those with solid axles were for acquittal, those with hollow axles for conviction. When counting, the former would be slotted into the rows of holes at one end of the board, the latter into those at the other end. The disk in the centre bears the words *Psêphos Dêmosia* (Official Ballot); (b) the (damaged) bronze tablet at the bottom was a dicast's identity token; (c) the bronze sphere next to it was used in a machine which allotted jurors at random to the various courts sitting that day. Athens, Agora Excavations. (Photo American School of Classical Studies at Athens).

Plate 11. Bits of broken pottery (*ostraka*) on which voters wrote the name of the man they wanted to see ostracized. The names on these are: Aristeides (son) of Lysimachos; Themistokles (son) of Neokles (of the deme) Phrearrhioi; Kimon (son) of Miltiades; and Perikles (son) of Xanthippos. Athens. Agora Museum. (Photo American School of Classical Studies at Athens).

Plate 12. A general view of the Athenian Agora, looking westward, with the Temple of Hephaestus (the Theseum) dominating the far end. (Photo American School of Classical Studies at Athens).

passing a decree to the effect that there was a *prima-facie* case to answer before referring it to a court.

So it was, then, that all the important decisions (and a great many minor decisions too) which were made by the Athenian state were determined, or at the very least had to be initiated, by a show of hands from as many free adult male Athenians as had chosen to attend the meetings of the *ecclêsia*, which were held in the centre of Athens. Except in rare emergencies, those meetings were advertised several days in advance, and a vote was taken only after those present had heard the proposed decrees and any amendments or riders to them read out in full, and after they had first listened to any debate which a given proposal had generated; and in these discussions every citizen who attended was entitled to speak. It was the *ecclêsia* alone which took the final decisions on declaring war or making peace or concluding alliances and treaties; on despatching particular expeditions, specifying the number of men and ships to be employed, and who was to be in command; it appointed overseers of public projects, architects, shipwrights; elected those officers of state who were not selected by random sortition; imposed or varied taxes and imposts, and authorized expenditures; ordered public buildings to be erected, or impeachments to be instituted; decided just about everything that affected the state in matters both large and small. The system would have broken down unless routine proposals had been carried 'on the nod', and that was only possible because the citizenry could trust the *boulê* to act as its watch-dog. Forty meetings a year for regular business are a lot of meetings (and the fact that extraordinary meetings could be summoned at short notice is also important); the *ecclêsia* was thus able to direct the affairs of Athens to a remarkable extent and in extra-ordinary detail, and these frequent meetings enabled ordinary citizens to gain a wide experience of government, while a high proportion of them acquired further experience by serving their year as *bouleutai* and as holders of public offices. The publication of decrees and accounts and so on (regardless of how many or how few citizens actually studied what was posted for all to read) reflects the openness of the Athenian government, which was essential if the power of the *dêmos* was to be effective. Indeed, an important reason why we know so much about the Athenian system is just because it was so open, and so much of the information inscribed on stone for public display has survived the centuries for us to read. The simple fact that no other Greek state of the fifth and fourth centuries has bequeathed us anything remotely comparable to this rich store of detail about its affairs underlines the uniqueness of the Athenian concept of democracy.

The number of citizens who bothered or were able to exercise their right to attend meetings of the *ecclêsia* often or regularly was for much of the time only at most somewhere between one-seventh and one-fifth of the total number eligible to attend; there must have been a higher proportionate turn-out from those who lived within reasonable walking-distance from the Pnyx than from those who lived much further away.[31] But the nature and composition of the *boulê*, the co-ordinating Council of Five Hundred which 'programmed' the *ecclêsia* and oversaw the execution of its decisions, were such as to ensure that the voice and interests of the whole *dêmos* were in fact heard and represented in the *ecclêsia*. It is to that Council that we now turn.

The Boulê[32]

Each year five hundred citizens over the age of thirty were selected to serve for a year as the members of the *boulê*, fifty of them from each of the ten tribes. They were drawn from the 139 demes which constituted the *trittyes* and tribes in proportion to the numbers registered on the lists of deme-members in each.[33] Certainly from the mid-fifth century, and in my view pretty certainly under Cleisthenes' original dispositions, they were chosen by lot. By the late fourth century (*Ath. Pol.* 62. 3) no citizen could serve as a *bouleutês* (councillor) more than twice in a lifetime, and never in

---

[31] Above, p. 6. (This was bound to be even more true of emergency meetings.)
[32] For full citation of the evidence and references to recent discussions see Rhodes, *AB*.
[33] Above, p. 58.

successive years (it may be that at first only one term was allowed).[34] It is to be presumed that the qualifications of the prospective *bouleutai* were scrutinized at deme level; certainly those selected were subjected to an examination (*dokimasia*) by the *boulê* in office to check their credentials—were they citizens, were they over thirty, were they subject to any disqualification, etc.? A certain number of deputies (*epilachontes*) were selected also, presumably to take the places of any who were rejected at the *dokimasia* or who died or were seriously incapacitated after their original selection.[35]

Strictly speaking, no citizen was eligible to serve as a *bouleutês* unless he was registered as possessing the minimum property or income to qualify him as a zeugite. By the late fourth century, although that rule was still *de jure* in force, *de facto* a certain number of thetes, at least in certain circumstances, did come forward and were allowed to serve (*Ath. Pol.* 7. 4). (How many thetes actually served as *bouleutai*, and when first a blind eye had begun to be turned to their ineligibility, we simply do not know.) *Bouleutai* were certainly receiving state pay by 411, and the institution of such payment is best dated to the period of, or just following, the Ephialtic reforms of the late 460s, one consequence of which was a considerable increase in the work of the *boulê*. We do not know what the rate was then, but a hundred years later (*Ath. Pol.* 62. 2) it stood at 5 obols a day for ordinary *bouleutai* and 6 (one drachma) for the *prytaneis* or standing committee of the *boulê*. How far there was any undue weighting in the *boulê* of better-off citizens (in that they were readier or more easily able to give up their time) we cannot say; there is no fifth-century evidence, but some scholars have claimed to discern some evidence for such a bias in the fourth. If so, it cannot have been much. Every year 500 new *bouleutai* had to be found; so even if, *per impossibile*, every *bouleutês* served twice in a lifetime, over any twenty-five-year period 6,250 men would be needed—in reality, the number

---

[34] It could be that the sharp decline in citizen numbers during the Peloponnesian War of 431–404 (above, p. 17) had impelled the Athenians to relax a previous limit to a single term once in a lifetime, if the rule allowing two terms was not original to Cleisthenes.

[35] Rhodes, *AB* 7–8.

required must have been more like 10,000 at least. The broadly representative character of the *boulê* is therefore not in doubt.[36]

The new *boulê* began its year of office in midsummer, with certain religious ceremonies including the taking of the Bouleutic Oath (the exact terms of which were modified with the passage of time), which bound its members to observe the laws and faithfully and conscientiously perform the duties of their office. Like other officers of state, the *bouleutai* wore a crown of myrtle as a badge of office; and they were entitled to special places on public occasions. During their year, they were exempted from military service, and (except in special circumstances) they were required to stay in Attica. The *boulê* met every day except on festival days and days of ill omen, normally in the *bouleutêrion*, the Council House on the western side of the Agora, but occasionally elsewhere. How fully attended the meetings were we have no idea (presumably the daily payment was made only to those who turned up or were otherwise engaged on Council business); it seems probable that those who lived fairly near turned up more often than those who lived any considerable distance away, who may frequently have limited their attendances (except during their month as *prytaneis*) to the more important meetings. Certainly, Demosthenes in his speech in 355 *Against Androtion* (22. 36) talks both of *bouleutai* who attended but took no active part in the *boulê*'s proceedings and also of those 'who for the most part did not even come to the *bouleutêrion*'.[37] It was normally possible for a certain number of non-members to listen to the discussions, or even by invitation address the *boulê*. Office-holders had, of course, regular opportunities to be present and to speak. Occasionally 'secret sessions' were held, but given the large numbers involved anything done at these could have been kept confidential for only a limited period.

[36] Ibid. 4–6. Of the 3,000 or so *bouleutai* whose names have survived, fewer than 3% are identifiable as having served two terms: Rhodes, 'Ephebai, Bouleutai, and the Population of Athens'.

[37] Cf. above, p. 27. For occasional absence from Attica (I believe only on official business or urgent personal grounds) see Rhodes, *AB* 13.

Each tribal contingent of fifty *bouleutai* took it in turns to serve as the *prytaneis* or standing committee of the *boulê* for one-tenth of the year, the order in which each tribe served being determined by lot month by month.[38] Being on more permanent duty than the rest of the *bouleutai*, they were specially housed and fed in their own quarters (the *tholos* or *skias*) adjacent to the *bouleutêrion* itself. Each day one of their number was chosen by lot to act as their chairman (*epistatês tôn prytaneôn*) and given charge of the state seal and of the keys to the public treasuries. (No man could hold this office more than once in his lifetime.) He was required to be physically present in the *tholos* the whole twenty-four hours, and could direct some of the other *prytaneis* to stay with him, probably fellow members of his own *trittys*.[39] The *epistatês* presided over any council meeting held on his day, and down to the early fourth century also over any meeting of the *ecclêsia* if it fell on that day; thereafter, the duty of presiding at *ecclêsia* devolved on to the *proedroi*, who were members of the *boulê* belonging to the nine tribes other than the tribe of the *prytaneis* themselves, and who took over the agenda for the *ecclêsia* which the *prytaneis* had previously prepared and published.[40] It was the *prytaneis* to whom envoys and messengers[41] and others who wished to bring matters before the *boulê* (and through it before the *ecclêsia*) first presented or addressed themselves. In the developed democracy both the *boulê* and its individual standing committees could be voted honorific crowns as a mark of good service.

As has already been noted, our grave uncertainties about the details of the Ephialtic reforms and the large absence of surviving inscriptions from the years between Cleisthenes and Ephialtes leave us in considerable doubt about the precise powers and functions of the *boulê* before about 460.[42] Its work was, however, pretty certainly specifically 'probouleutic': that is to say that its prime function was (as it always remained) that of preparing the business which had to go to

---

[38] On the 'bouleutic year' see above, p. 27, n. 7. For a possible exception to the normal random determination of prytany order in 408/7 see Rhodes, *AB* 20.

[39] Ibid. 23–5.   [40] Above, p. 76.

[41] As at the 'Elatea' *ecclêsia* described by Demosthenes: above, p. 68.

[42] Above, p. 51.

the *ecclêsia* for a final decision. Leaving aside purely routine
business, matters could be brought before the *boulê* for
referral to the *ecclêsia* by all officers of state as well as by
individual *bouleutai*; so too by any citizen who could manage
somehow or other to get a proposal or issue brought to the
attention of the *boulê*. There was always a class of more or
less active and articulate 'politicians' who were ready to set
the machinery in motion, and they did not themselves need
to hold any office to be able to so. In the fifth century
Pericles, so it was said (Plutarch, *Pericles*, 7. 4), 'was to be
seen walking along only one road in Athens, that leading to
the Agora and the *bouleutêrion*' (although he was a *stratêgos*
many years in succession, Pericles certainly did not confine
his political activities to military business); a century later
Demosthenes (according to Aeschines: 3. 125) on one
occasion 'entered the *bouleutêrion*, had all the non-*bouleutai*
removed, and took advantage of the inexperience of one of
the *bouleutai* to get him to propose the motion which he
wanted put'.

The *boulê* formulated draft proposals (*proboulemata*) for
submission to the *ecclêsia*, which voted on them either after or
without a preliminary debate. A *probouleuma* could take the
form of a specific recommendation (many of which must
have been uncontroversial, and approved with little or no
demur), or it might simply formulate an open question,
leaving it to individual members of the *ecclêsia* to propose a
specific course of action. As far as we can tell, both types
were common. It is worth giving an example of each.

The first is a decree inscribed in the early fourth century
which records that the *boulê* had proposed to the *ecclêsia* that a
certain non-Athenian named Heraclides should be given the
title of '*proxenos* [which carried certain significant privileges]
and benefactor', and that the grant should be publicly
recorded by the Secretary of the *boulê*, in recognition of
Heraclides' assistance to Athenian diplomatic representatives
and of his general support of the Athenian *dêmos*. The
proposal was approved by the *ecclêsia*, together with a rider
proposed in the *ecclêsia* by a certain Thucydides, who
persuaded the *ecclêsia* to add to the rewards proposed by the
boulê ('in other respects as the *boulê* has proposed, but also

. . .') the right (normally confined to Athenian citizens) to acquire and own real property in Attica, together with freedom from taxes and imposts (*ateleia*).

The second is an inscribed decree dating from 333, which tells how some metic merchants hailing from Citium in Cyprus had approached the *boulê* for permission to establish a shrine of their patron goddess, Aphrodite, in Athens. The *boulê* resolved that they should put their request to the *ecclêsia* for the *ecclêsia* to decide what should be done 'after giving a hearing to the Citians and to any Athenian who might wish to speak on the matter'. Lycurgus, a prominent politician, did choose to address the *ecclêsia* and he secured its assent to the Citians' request.

(Neither of these decrees is of any great consequence; they are cited simply to exemplify the two basic types of *probouleumata*.[43])

In the fifth century, for our knowledge of the activities of the *boulê* we have to rely almost exclusively on modern epigraphists and their patient and meticulous work in deciphering and supplementing, interpreting and dating, the often badly damaged physical remains of the decrees and such which were inscribed on stone. (The Athenians did, of course, keep records on less cumbersome material, but lacking the durability of stone these have not survived for us to study.) Although Thucydides' *History* is very much a political as well as a military work, it tells us very little about the detail of Athenian politics; apart from his account of the short-lived take-over of control by the Four Hundred in 411 (which nevertheless makes it plain how vital it was for the anti-democrats to replace the *boulê* with their own substitute)[44] he mentions the *boulê* only once, in connection with a trick which Alcibiades played on a Spartan delegation in 420 (Thucydides 5. 44–5). For Thucydides, the *ecclêsia* itself, and the men like Pericles and Cleon, Nicias and Alcibiades, who

---

[43] Meiggs and Lewis, *GHI*, No. 70; Tod, *Greek Historical Inscriptions*, ii, No. 189 (and cf. the 'Elatea' *ecclêsia*, above, p. 68). For a selection of more important decrees (with commentary) in the original Greek see these two works. For a selection in an English translation see Fornara, *Archaic Times to the End of the Peloponnesian War*, and Harding, *From the End of the Peloponnesian War to the Battle of Ipsus*, vol. i and ii in the series: *Translated Documents of Greece and Rome*.

[44] Below, p. 148.

achieved varying degrees of influence over its sovereign decisions, occupy the centre of the stage. Nor do we get much help from the fifth-century comedies of Aristophanes. For the fourth century, however, not only is the epigraphic material increasingly more abundant, but we have the further bonus of the considerable number of political speeches of Athenian orators which have survived and which enable us to read much more of the 'fine print'. There is also the *Ath. Pol.*'s account of the constitutional rules of the later fourth century.

After the repulse of the Persian invasion of Greece, Athens emerged as the leading member of a confederacy of Greek states which were prepared to concert their resources and efforts towards freeing the Aegean from Persian control. This 'Confederacy of Delos', which first took shape in the winter of 478/7, developed (perhaps inevitably) during the next quarter of a century or so into what became in effect an 'Athenian Empire'.[45] It is clear that the *boulê* came to be much involved in the financial and diplomatic aspects of Athens' new role; the *ecclêsia* necessarily, and no doubt readily, accepted that the *boulê* was its agent in such matters, and while retaining ultimate control relied on this cross-section of itself to dot the i's and cross the t's, so that the *boulê* was charged with the oversight and control of the implementation of the *ecclêsia*'s decisions by the individuals and boards which executed them. The *boulê* came also to exercise a similar sort of oversight of internal revenues and expenditures, although here too of course ultimate control remained with the *ecclêsia*: it kept a vigilant eye on the treasurers of the various religious funds which in effect constituted national reserves, on the officers responsible for raising domestic revenues through the sale of leases of mines or lands etc. or of the right to collect a wide range of state taxes and imposts, and on the spending of public moneys. The widespread use of random selection of public officers by means of the lot, and of boards rather than individuals, together with the practice of annual and generally non-consecutive or even repeatable tenure of executive responsibility, meant that only

---

[45] On all this see Meiggs, *The Athenian Empire*.

the *boulê*—and those who kept in close touch with it—had a comprehensive grasp of the overall state of the public finances. In brief, it was the body to which all the multifarious agents of the Athenian *dêmos* were, in the first instance at least, answerable and accountable.

Down to the end of the fifth century expenditures of public moneys seem to have been authorized piecemeal; but thereafter there developed a system of allocations or apportionments (*merismoi*) of stated sums to the various spending agencies. These *merismoi* were made by the state 'Receivers' (*apodektai*), who were the officers charged with receiving domestic revenues, a duty they discharged under the eyes of the *boulê*, to which fell the task of enforcing debts to the state in the event of failure to pay; the *boulê* was likewise the body to whom the Receivers submitted their *merismoi* for approval and correction. The *boulê* also appointed ten of its own members by lot each prytany as Auditors (*logistai*) to examine the accounts of all public officers.[46] Somewhere about the middle of the fourth century there was a move to a greater 'professionalism', which saw the election of individual citizens (who may have been preceded by special boards) as officers with responsibility for major funds, military and civil alike.[47] While the *boulê* retained its oversight of financial matters (and the *ecclêsia* itself, of course, its ultimate authority), these new officials, who could be re-elected to their posts for a number of years in succession, acquired an expertise and authority in financial matters which could never be matched by the haphazardly selected and annually changing *bouleutai*. However, even before this development it was manifestly the case *de facto* that there had always been men (Pericles and Cleon are obvious examples from the fifth century) who over the years acquired a comparable detailed knowledge and mastery of financial matters far exceeding that of the *boulê*, a mastery which they put to use in influencing the direction of public finance—and indeed their influence was exercised in other aspects of public policy too.[48] Hence the later appointments of these new

---

[46] *Ath. Pol.* 48. 2–3. [47] Rhodes, *AB* 106 ff.
[48] Compare Pericles' review of Athens' financial and military resources in 431: Thucydides 2. 13.

financial officers made little substantial difference, but
essentially only gave formal recognition to a situation which
already existed, and was inevitably bound to exist, given the
way the Athenians organized their affairs. The prominence of
Lycurgus during the twelve years when he held his important
financial office (the precise definition of which is obscure) in
the 330s and 320s was more than matched by that dominance
which Pericles had enjoyed for the dozen years or so before
his death in 429, a shaping of his city's policies which was so
secure and unchallengeable that Thucydides (2. 65. 9) could
characterize him as 'the uncrowned King of Athens'.

It is not clear how far the financial system, in some ways
ramshackle and in general 'penny-packet', encouraged or
permitted malpractice on the part of any members of the
boulê. As early as the 430s or 420s the 'Old Oligarch' (3. 3)
reports an assertion that the way to get things done by the
boulê is to approach it with money in hand;[49] in Aristophanes'
Wasps (655 ff.) Bdelycleon has it that corruption is widespread,
and in the same comedian's *Thesmophoriazusae* (936–9)
Mnesilochus refers to the habit of *prytaneis* of 'holding out an
empty hand to have money pressed into it' in return for
favours. In general, allegations of corruption are commonplace in the orators; and it is significant that it had to be noted
of certain politicians (or claimed by themselves) that their
hands were incorruptibly clean. Nevertheless, given the
system of public checks involving so many people, it would
be over-cynical to suppose that any serious direct peculation
or embezzelement of public moneys (as opposed to the
acceptance of bribes or other inducements in return for
'services rendered') would have gone undetected.[50]

---

[49] On the 'Old Oligarch' see further below, p. 168.

[50] Aeschines I. 110–12 reports a public allegation of an attempted theft in 361/60
of 1,000 drachmai of public money by a *bouleutês*, Timarchus, working in collusion
with one of the Treasurers of the Goddess (i.e. Athene)—coupled with a claim that
both were scandalously active homosexuals. The *boulê* suspended or expelled
Timarchus on a 'straw vote', but reinstated him on a second and final vote. How
well founded the charge was, and whether any trial took place in the courts (though
that seems unlikely) we do not know. The *boulê* was not voted a crown that year for
good service, but that may have had no connection with this incident; even though
the speaker wants to imply that there was such a connection, he may well have been
relying on the *post hoc ergo propter hoc* style of argument. In 355 Demosthenes (22. 17)

Although not closely involved with army matters, apart from certain responsibilities in connection with the cavalry, the *boulê* was intimately concerned with Athens' navy: the construction and maintenance of its ships and dockyard facilities, oars and other necessary equipment, and the general oversight of the trierarchs who fitted out and commanded her warships. It had also wide responsibilities in the supervision of public buildings both sacred and secular and public works in general; in the sphere of religious rites and festivals, either in co-operation with the relevant priests and hierarchs or on its own authority; in the selection of the judges who awarded the prizes at the great theatrical or musical festivals. In brief, as the body which in a sense encapsulated the sovereign Athenian *dêmos*, and which formulated the agenda for the meetings of its *ecclêsia*, the *boulê* became the representative instrument by which the *dêmos* exercised its oversight and control of the execution of its expressed will; and to it the *dêmos* entrusted many of the minor but necessary consequential decisions required to implement the larger directives of the *ecclêsia*, which thus found formal expression as decrees of the *boulê* itself.[51]

Understandably, the *boulê* possessed the judicial authority to enforce its own decisions and to initiate proceedings against *prima-facie* offences brought to light in the course of its wide supervision of other public officers and agencies. (Thus, it could order the imprisonment of those who defaulted on their debts to the state, or require sureties for such debts.) In many instances, it could itself impose fines up to a limit of 500 drachmai, although for heavier penalties it could only refer the charges to the *ecclêsia* or the courts. It could also act as the channel through which allegations of serious public offences (*eisangeliai*) were transmitted to the *ecclêsia* or the courts.[52]

Until the early 360s one of the members of the *boulê* drawn from one of the tribes which were not serving as the standing

refers to a Treasurer of the Warship Constructors who had absconded with two and a half talents of public money; the theft did not escape detection although the culprit got away.

[51] On these see Rhodes, *AB* 52 ff.
[52] On the judicial competence of the *boulê* see ibid. 144–207. On *eisangeliai* see further below, p. 101.

committee was selected to serve for one month as the Secretary of the Council. Thereafter, this Secretaryship became an annual office, its holder chosen by lot (from a pool of applicants judged capable of the duties) from non-members of the *boulê*; and a number of other secretaries, drawn from the same source, are attested with responsibilities for records and inventories and bouleutic accounts. The *boulê* could also call on the services of a number of public slaves (*dêmosioi*) for various tasks requiring some considerable degree of literacy and numeracy, as well as humbler jobs.[53]

This, necessarily far from full, account of the Athenian *boulê* makes it plain that what A. W. Gomme once wrote in a masterly essay was a central truth: 'the council . . . is the lynch-pin of the democracy . . . By its activity, its effective execution of its many duties, it secured the predominance of the assembly and so its own subordination: government of the people, for the people, *and* by the people.'[54] Gomme also observed that the *boulê* was 'not powerful', by which he meant simply to emphasize the point that this random and annually changing microcosm of the Athenian *dêmos* could never acquire anything like the corporate identity of comparable but more permanent bodies. Yet, from a different but not opposed viewpoint, the *boulê* was indeed a very powerful body. 'Certainly', writes Rhodes,

the boule was a selection of citizens taking their turn in office, not a powerful governing class with vested interests to protect, but I would say that for this very reason it could be trusted to be powerful. When the sovereign body was a large assembly, unable to hold frequent meetings, a council with executive and judicial powers in so wide a field was bound to become powerful, not least because it was the city's centre of information; but because all citizens could take their turn in exercising this power the assembly had nothing to fear.[55]

On several occasions both in this section and elsewhere I have described the *boulê* (and some other institutions of the Athenian state) as 'representative' of the Athenian *dêmos*.

---

[53] On secretaries and attendants see Rhodes, *AB* 134–43.

[54] Gomme, 'The Working of the Athenian Democracy' in his *More Essays in Greek History and Literature*, 177–93 (the quotation is from p. 186).

[55] Rhodes, *AB* 214–15.

Some moderns take exception to this use of the word. Well over fifty years ago, Zimmern could write: 'We often hear it laid down as an axiom that Greek democracy differs from modern because it did not use the representative system.' But he went on to add, quite rightly: 'This is of course a complete mistake, and it could never have won acceptance but for the foolish idea . . . that the only public work that a democracy requires of its citizens is an occasional vote either in or for Parliament. The Greeks were not so short-sighted'.[56] The view with which Zimmern took issue still finds its exponents; but, with him, I decline to accept so narrow a reading of the term, which effectively confines its use within far too parochial limits. In any year the *boulê* contained between one-eightieth and one-sixtieth of the adult male citizens of Athens, and over any twenty-five-year period something between a quarter and a third of those citizens served a year as *bouleutai*. If we can nowadays regard the twelve randomly chosen members of a jury as in some sense representative of the community at large, or accept the claims of opinion-pollsters that one thousand potential voters questioned constitute a significant and reasonably accurate representative sample of a United Kingdom electorate of getting on for forty-five million, we surely cannot deny the epithet 're-presentative' to the Athenian *boulê*, or to the Athenian courts (which could number up to a thousand, or even several thousand, jurymen for really major trials). Indeed, the some six hundred and fifty members of the modern British House of Commons, who sit there for up to five years between elections and are frequently re-elected for further terms, compare very badly as a representative body with the five hundred *bouleutai* of ancient Athents chosen at random each year from a citizen body of at most about one-thousandth the size of that of the United Kingdom in the 1980s.[57]

---

[56] Zimmern, *The Greek Commonwealth*, 158.

[57] Put differently, and as a *reductio ad absurdum*, in 1989 the UK would need a House of Commons numbering from 500,000 to 700,000 members (changing every year) to match the ratio of *bouleutai* to 'registered voters' in fifth- and fourth-century Athens! Among recent scholars who think it erroneous to call the Athenian system 'representative' are Finley (*Politics in the Ancient World*, 74) and Hansen (*AA* 2).

Courts of Law: The Dikastêria[58]

In Aristophanes' *Clouds* (202–8), which was staged in 423, Strepsiades pays a visit to Socrates' 'School of Thinkology', and while there he is shown a map of the world. 'Look, here's Athens.' 'Get away with you,' says Strepsiades, 'that's not Athens! I can't see any jurymen sitting there.' In 414, in his *Birds* (108–9), the Hoopoe asks two Athenians where they hail from. 'The land of fine triremes,' they reply. 'So you're jurymen, then?' At a more serious level, Thucydides (1. 77) attests that in the opinion of many other Greeks the Athenians were over-fond of litigation (*philodikoi*). And it is surely significant that the *Ath. Pol.*'s review of Athens' constitution assigns what might seem at first sight an inordinately disproportionate amount of space to the courts of law.[59] But the mere fact that every year 6,000 citizens, between one-seventh and one-fifth of the total citizen body, were registered for service as *dikastai* should alert the modern reader to the truth that the lawcourts played a much more immediate part in the Athenians' lives than they do in most of ours.

Our modern doctrine that politics and the courts are two different worlds reflects a view which is not merely often wrong-headed, but also historically speaking myopic. Throughout most of human history, those members of any society who have lacked both wealth and influence (terms which have frequently been virtually synonymous) have regularly found it difficult, if not impossible, to secure justice, or redress for private wrongs; and not simply because the legal processes were difficult for the ordinary man to avail himself of, or the laws themselves failed to safeguard his true interests, but also because those who interpreted and administered the laws and handed down the decisions were

---

[58] See Harrison, *The Law of Athens*, and MacDowell *The Law in Classical Athens*, for full discussions of Athenian law and jurisprudence. For the *dikastêria* see also especially Rhodes, *CAP*, notes and commentary on *Ath. Pol.* 45, 52–3, 63–9.

[59] In the review of the Athenian *politeia* as it was in the late fourth century, *Ath. Pol.* allots seven sections (43–9) to the *boulê*, and seven (63–9) to the *dikastêria*; only five sections apiece are given to the archons (55–9) and to the other annual officers of state chosen by lot (50–4), and three (60–2) to other officers.

safeguarding (consciously or instinctively) the interests of their own kind. And that is true both of what we may term private law and also of the law in so far as it governs criminal and public offences.

The Athenian democracy placed the administration of justice firmly in the hands of its citizenry. There were no highly paid professional judges, no Directors of Public Prosecutions or Attorneys-General or District Attorneys or Juges d'Instruction (save that certain officers of state, and especially the members of the *boulê* individually or corporately, might in fact initiate proceedings in areas which came within their oversight). Both judges and juries were amateurs. Indeed, the very words 'judge' and 'jury' are misleading, for the 'judges' in all important cases were simply responsible for 'managing' the courts, and did no more than preside over 'jurymen' (*dikastai*) who were themselves the judges of both fact and law, and who themselves determined both verdicts and penalties. To avoid any misconceptions, I shall hereafter refer to these latter as 'dicasts'.

In Athens the distinction between what we call civil and criminal cases or private and public law was different from ours. There were those suits, roughly termed *dikai*, which could be instituted only by the injured party or his or her guardian (*kyrios*), or in the case of a deceased party by his relatives, in a strictly prescribed order. From the middle of the fifth century thirty 'deme-judges' (*dikastai kata dêmous*) were available to hear such cases all over Attica. They may have been chosen one from each of the thirty *trittyes*, but at this time we have evidence only of their existence, not of how they were appointed or of their procedure or of the limits of their competence. Not long after the fall of the Thirty in 403, the number of these 'deme-judges' became forty, four from each tribe; they no longer 'went on circuit', and were generally simply called 'the Forty'. They were responsible for most *dikai*, except those which were specifically assigned to other magistrates, like the archon for inheritance suits or the *thesmothetai* for mercantile. If the claim was for a sum up to 10 drachmai, the four 'deme-judges' appointed to act for the tribe in question were competent to decide it themselves. If it involved a larger amount, it went to a

publicly appointed Arbitrator (*diaitêtês*). These Arbitrators
were instituted in 399,[60] and they worked in combination
with the 'deme-judges'; every citizen was required to be
available to serve as an Arbitrator during his sixtieth year
(unless he was holding a public office), which meant that
Arbitrators, to whom cases were allocated by lot, were
simply ordinary men with considerable experience of life.
They received a fee (paid by the plaintiff) of one drachma for
each arbitration which they handled. Their decisions were
final if both parties accepted them. If, however, one or other
declined to do so, the four deme-judges from the defendant's
tribe arranged for the case to come before a *dikastêrion*, where
it was decided by a body of dicasts drawn from the pool of
6,000, who numbered 201 for suits up to 1,000 drachmai and
401 for larger sums. The case was brought to the dicasts by
the four 'deme-judges', but the evidence and pleadings of the
hearing before the Arbitrator were first deposited in sealed
containers, and no further material could be presented to the
dicasts when they decided the issue. Strangely, to our minds,
a number of charges which we should unhesitatingly call
'criminal' or 'public', most notably cases of murder, fell
under the heading of *dikai* in that they could be instituted
only by interested parties—though charges of wilful murder
(along with some other crimes held to involve religion, like
the pollution traditionally associated with murder) continued
to be heard by the ancient and august court of the Areopagus, which despite the less representative and life-tenured
character of its ex-archon members was never attacked for
having misused its authority in these matters. Again, in the
case of theft (*klopê*) the aggrieved party might, if he chose,
simply pursue a private action before an Arbitrator to recover
what he had lost; in this instance, and in a range of other
actions, there was in practice a choice between different
available procedures involving different penalties for both
plaintiff and defendant, so that for a number of reasons an

---

[60] What happened before 399 is unknown. It may be that all suits over 10
drachmai went straight to a *dikastêrion*, or it may be that the 'deme-judges' had a
wider competence which was now transferred to the Arbitrators. (Private
arbitration was of course always available to such as preferred to 'settle out of court':
on this see MacDowell, *The Law in Classical Athens*, 203–6.)

aggrieved party might choose to proceed by a simple *dikê*, which entailed lighter penalties for a convicted defendant, but none at all for a man who brought a case and lost it, rather than by a *graphê* (the generic term for a charge which could be brought by anybody and not just the injured party), which if successful would result in more severe penalties but which exposed the man who brought the charge to the danger of being penalized himself if he failed to secure the votes of a given proportion of the dicasts who heard the case.[61]

Broadly speaking, *graphai* were cases which were held to involve matters of public concern, a category which the Athenians interpreted very widely. Such cases could be initiated by anybody who so chose (*ho boulomenos*). Not only did the convicted defendant pay a penalty to the state, anything from a fine to loss of civic rights (*atimia*) or even death and confiscation of property depending on the gravity of the offence, the successful prosecutor was entitled to a reward, which might be substantial. However, if the prosecutor abandoned his prosecution before it came to court, or if he failed to secure the votes of at least one-fifth of the dicasts who decided the case, he was himself liable to a fine of 1,000 drachmai and the loss of civic rights; these risks were plainly intended to deter frivolous or opportunistic prosecutions, for there arose a number of 'professional' prosecutors, the so-called 'sycophants', who were out to make money and who might even plan to extort money from others by threatening to institute a *graphê* unless it was made worth their while not to. The sycophants were seen as an abuse, but it was not easy to devise means of checking their activities without deterring the genuinely disinterested voluntary prosecutor.[62]

A 'pool' of 6,000 dicasts was appointed every year from citizens aged thirty or over. (If too many applicants came forward the lot was probably used to select the number needed, but it may have been a case of 'first come, first

---

[61] On this aspect of Athenian thinking in such matters see the important and perceptive article 'Law in Action in Classical Athens' by Osborne.

[62] On sycophants (and the difficulty of disciplining them) see MacDowell, *The Law in Classical Athens*, 62–6.

served'.) We cannot say how often any individual dicast might be empanelled to hear a case, since the number required on any given day must inevitably have varied with the number and the nature of the cases due to be heard. To ensure that service as a dicast need not be confined to those who could afford to give their time free, on Pericles' initiative public payment was introduced, evidently in consequence of the reforms of Ephialtes which gave the *dikastêria* a lot more (and more important) work to do.[63] Originally fixed at two obols a day, it was increased on Cleon's initiative to three in the 420s. There, somewhat surprisingly, it stuck, and three obols was still the figure a century later, although other rates of state pay had risen to match inflation. Probably the expense involved in paying so many dicasts on so many days had a deterrent effect; but the result must have been that as time passed the ordinary Athenian could not afford to commit himself to being available so frequently for such a low rate of pay, and in consequence the dicasts were either those who could afford to take less or the more elderly citizens who had passed active working age.[64] In any case, the impracticability of having any large number of citizens of an age for active military service (in a world where war was so common) tied up in work as a dicast is self-evident.

What all this amounts to is that, leaving aside very minor and (for the Athenians) essentially 'private' suits, pretty well every case of any consequence was heard and decided by a *dikastêrion*, which was presided over by one or other of the nine archons (or his appointed deputy) or by some other officer specifically entrusted with such responsibilities. *Dikai* where one or other party declined for whatever reason to accept the ruling of an Arbitrator were decided by a *dikastêrion* manned by either 201 or 401 dicasts; *graphai* (with the occasional exception of the special category of *eisangeliai*, of which more later) went straight to a *dikastêrion*. The

---

[63] Above, p. 43.

[64] Sinclair (*Democracy and Participation in Athens*, 124–5) adduces evidence and arguments which suggest that the richest stratum of the citizens, those liable to pay the property tax (*eisphora*), did not constitute a significant element among the dicasts in the early fourth century, at any rate.

number of dicasts in any *dikastêrion* could be as low as the 201 who decided a *dikê* of less than 1,000 drachmai or up to 1,000 or even more for an important *graphê*. Despite the apparent safety which such huge numbers provided against bribery and corruption and other improper influences, from the early fourth century highly elaborate and complicated precautions were taken to ensure last-minute random selection of both dicasts and court presidents so that nobody could know in advance which among those available would be allocated to hear and decide which cases.[65] A *dikastêrion* could deal with a number of *dikai* on any single day, but the hearing of a *graphê* was always allocated a whole day to itself. (The courts could not sit on days when the *ecclêsia* was meeting, nor on a considerable number of other days excluded for religious reasons.) Having heard the evidence and arguments on both sides, the dicasts at once proceeded to cast their votes by a secret ballot in favour of one side or the other, and (where appropriate) for a particular penalty, without any summing up from the court president or further discussion.[66] Their decision was final, and no appeal lay from a *dikastêrion* to any higher authority. Like the Romans of Cicero's day, the Athenians evidently took the view that courts established by a decision of the people exercised the authority of the sovereign body by which they had been established: however warmly modern theorists may argue that the *dêmos* by so doing surrendered an important element of its own sovereignty to a body other than itself,[67] that was a nicety which did not disturb them. But individual officers of state or other bodies were in quite a different category, and whenever they had the power to inflict penalties on their own authority, such penalties were purely pecuniary and could not exceed a relatively low limit.

We come now to *eisangeliai*. An *eisangelia* (we might translate it as an 'impeachment') was a process directed against crimes which were considered as serious threats to the

---

[65] For the details of these arrangements see *Ath. Pol.* 63–6, with Rhodes's notes in *CAP*; MacDowell, *The Law in Classical Athens*, 35–48.

[66] For the detail of voting in the *dikastêria* see Staveley, *Greek and Roman Voting and Elections*, 95–100.

[67] Most notably Hansen, *AE* 139–58.

social or public order and were thought to demand prompt action. For a long time the prosecutor was not subject to the risk of a penalty of 1,000 drachmai and loss of civic rights should he desist from his prosecution or fail to secure a fifth of the votes of the dicasts; but that privilege evidently came to be so seriously abused by sycophants thàt in the latter half of the fourth century it was abolished, although only in respect of exemption from the fine, for the exemption from *atimia* continued. Arbitrators (*diaitêtai*) did not hold an office which was classed as an *archê*, and so were not liable to a formal examination of the discharge of their duties (*euthynai*); but they were exposed to *eisangelia* if accused of misconduct. The procedure was also available against anybody alleged to have done wrong to orphans or heiresses (reflecting the central importance to Athenian society of the family and hence also of the property of the family). But the most important category of *eisangeliai* concerned those alleged to have committed 'crimes against the state', viz. attempts to overthrow or subvert the constitution, and other acts of what anybody would call 'treason'; serious misconduct by anyone in the performance of a public duty (the *boulê* could deal with such cases only up to its maximum permitted penalty of 500 drachmai); the taking of bribes by a speaker to promote measures against the interest of the state; and what was in general called 'deception of the *dêmos*'. Indeed, *eisangelia* threatened to become something of a 'catch-all' process, rather like the Roman law of *maiestas*, since the definition of what can be construed as a crime against the state is always bound to be somewhat nebulous.[68]

The right to hear and decide these most serious *eisangeliai* was probably one of the powers which Ephialtes got transferred from the Areopagus to the *boulê* and the *ecclêsia*.[69] Thenceforth, a would-be prosecutor had to approach the *boulê* with a request to place the matter on the *ecclêsia*'s agenda, or he could it raise it first at a *kyria ekklêsia*.[70] To begin with, the final hearing may always have been in the *ecclêsia* itself; but at some point the *dikastêria* came to be employed at first as an alternative, and later after about 360;

---

[68] Hyperides, *Pro Euxenippo*, 1–3. Cf. Rhodes, *AB* 163–4.
[69] Above, p. 47.   [70] Above, p. 70.

probably as the exclusive, forum for these hearings.[71] Nevertheless, every trial of an *eisangelia* had always to be authorized by a decree (*psêphisma*) of the *ecclêsia*, which sometimes specified the penalty to be imposed if the case were found to be proven.

As we have already seen, it was the *dikastêria* which decided the issue if ever a *psêphisma* was alleged to be invalid or improper (*graphê paranomôn*) or a new law challenged as inexpedient (*graphê nomon mê epitêdeion theinai*).[72] And it was from the pool of dicasts that were drawn the 500 or more *nomothetai* to whom the *dêmos* entrusted the final decisions whether or not to ratify a proposed new law or to annul an existing one. Of the central political importance of the dicasts there can then be no shadow of a doubt. In his speech in his own defence in 411, Antiphon, the first in the long line of the 'Attic Orators', claimed that his practice of composing speeches for others to deliver in court, and his powers as a speaker in general, were bound to count for nothing under an oligarchy but guaranteed him great power and influence under the democracy.[73] Is it any wonder that Strepsiades refused to believe that any place could be the Athens which he knew if large numbers of dicasts were not immediately visible to the naked eye?

The Offices of State

The Athenian word for a public office was *archê*. Such offices fell into two broad categories: they were filled either by the random operation of the lot (*klêros*), or by election. The former category consisted of those *archai* the duties of which the Athenians believed could be performed satisfactorily by any citizen of average competence and intelligence, since they called for no special talent or expertise, and (with the exception of membership of the *boulê*) they were regularly tenable only once in a man's lifetime; the latter, however, were judged to require particular skills or qualities or experience possessed by only a limited number of individuals,

[71] Above, p. 82.   [72] Above, pp. 78, 81.
[73] Antiphon fr. B. 1.

and accordingly there was usually no restriction on repeated tenure of such an *archê*.

The most obvious sphere where it was assumed that an ordinary 'Mr Demos of the Pnyx' was not to be entrusted with serious responsibility was that of the command of military and naval operations. The Spartan Demaratus once observed to King Xerxes (Herodotus 7. 102) that 'Poverty has always been a foster-sister to Greece'. The same could have been said with no less truth of war. From 480 Athens was at war with Persia, and from time to time with some of the Greek states which had joined the Athenian-led (and increasingly Athenian-dominated) Confederacy of Delos but later sought to secede and had to be coerced. From about 460 she was also at war with the Peloponnesian League. These conflicts involved much fighting on both land and sea in Greece, the Aegean, the Levant, and Egypt. We chance to have an inscription which records the names of the members of just one of the ten tribes (Erechtheis) who died in a single year, either 460 or 459, while engaged in operations in Cyprus, Egypt, Phoenicia, Halieis, Aegina, and Megara: there are 177 names on the list.[74] Both these wars ended in the early to middle 440s, but a few years later Athens had to suppress the revolts of Samos and Byzantium, with an attendant risk that both the Peloponnesian League and the Persians might intervene against her. From the mid-430s the cloud of war loomed up again with the mounting tensions caused by Athens' alliance with Corcyra and the revolt of Potidaea; and the Peloponnesian War which finally broke out in 431 ended only with Athens' capitulation in 404 and the loss of her empire. The same sad tale continues in the fourth century: the 'Corinthian War' of 395–386; war with Sparta 379–371, and with Thebes in the 360s, as Athens strove to re-establish her dominance in the Aegean and recover Amphipolis; the 'Social War' in the early 350s; and the debilitating wars with Philip of Macedon from 357 to 346 and again from 340 to Philip's decisive victory at Chaeronea in 338. Athens did make some use of foreign mercenaries, and in the fifth century in particular many of the rowers in her fleets were

---

[74] Meiggs and Lewis, *GHI*, No. 33. (Such heavy casualties from a single tribe in a single year must have been exceptional.)

non-Athenians;[75] but her main human strength lay, and had to lie, in her own citizens. Given that there was no standing army or navy, that every adult male citizen could be called on (and frequently was called on) to fight in her land-battles and man her triremes, no Athenian was ever so foolish as to be prepared to risk his life under the command of any chance-selected man in the street; he wanted to be free to choose the men he judged best fitted for that task.

From the end of the sixth century ten *stratêgoi* were elected each year from among citizens aged over thirty to command Athens' military and naval forces. For a few years one of the nine archons, the polemarch, remained the nominal supreme commander; but Callimachus, who fell in the fighting at Marathon in 490, is the last polemarch known to have so acted. (Down to 487 the archonships were still filled by direct election, but thereafter all nine archons were selected by lot.)[76] To begin with, one *stratêgos* was elected by the *ecclêsia* from each of the ten tribes, but later in the fifth century it became possible for more than one *stratêgos* to be chosen from one tribe. How often that happened, why it happened, and what the procedure was, we are not told; the likeliest explanation is that the Athenians did not want to deprive themselves of the services of one of two men of high qualities just because both happened to belong to the same tribe, or felt that the continued occupation of one of the ten *stratêgiai* by particularly outstanding men like a Cimon or a Pericles was unfair to other aspirants from their tribes.[77] By the latter part of the fourth century the connection with the tribes seems to have been abandoned altogether. The *stratêgoi* were originally no doubt the actual commanders of their tribal contingents, but that duty soon fell to other elected officers, leaving the *stratêgoi* free if needed for wider responsibilities. By the third quarter of the fourth century five of the ten were elected for specific tasks (one to command the army if it operated outside Attica, one charged with home defence, two responsible for the Peiraeus harbours, and one with the oversight of the arrangements for outfitting the fleet), leaving

[75] Below, p. 174, n. 10.
[76] Above, p. 30.
[77] Rhodes, *CAP* 264–6.

the remaining five available for *ad hoc* duties or assignments
(*Ath. Pol.* 61. 1).

[The fact that the *stratêgia* was not only an elective office
with important responsibilities, affording considerable independence of action, ready access to both *boulê* and *ecclêsia*,
and the opportunity for winning renown, but also an *archê*
which could be held as often as a man was able to command
sufficient support from the citizen-voters each year, meant
that during the period when Athens was a great imperial
power the *stratêgoi* were not merely competent generals and
admirals but included among their number some who were
also among the leading political figures of Athens. But that
aspect of the office will be left on one side until we come to
consider the whole question of 'politics' and political
leadership.]

Each year the *dêmos* also elected the ten commanders of the
ten tribal regiments (*taxiarchoi*), two cavalry-commanders
(*hipparchoi*), and under them ten commanders of the tribal
cavalry squadrons (*phylarchoi*). There was no structured
system of lower commissioned or non-commissioned ranks,
but in practice the more experienced and intelligent of the
hoplites were appointed by the commanders to act as section-
leaders or occasionally put in charge of special detachments.

At some date between 403 and 370 a period of two years of
compulsory full-time military training was introduced for
citizens aged from eighteen to twenty, almost certainly only
for those of zeugite family or higher, for thetes were not liable
for hoplite service but only as light-armed troops and in the
fleet.[78] These *ephêbai* were under the authority of a Super-
intendent of Training (*kosmêtês*), elected by and from all the
citizens, and under him were ten Controllers (*sôphronistai*),
one for the ephebes of each tribe, elected by the *dêmos* from
four candidates aged over forty put forward by each tribe.

Naval forces were also under the command of the *stratêgoi*
(which makes the common translation of *stratêgos* as 'general'
somewhat misleading). No formally elected subordinate
posts existed here; but Athens was never short of highly
competent and experienced skippers and seamen who might

---

[78] Rhodes, *CAP* 502–10.

be deputed to command a small squadron or carry out some other special task. Each trireme was under the command of a 'trierarch' (of whom more later); but the effective skipper of a trireme was its *kybernêtês* or coxswain, and trierarchs were eager to find good men for that centrally important post. As with the land forces, the Athenians left it to the higher commanders to appoint men to positions of subordinate authority and responsibility.

Men who acted as ambassadors or official negotiators with foreign powers were elected from among those deemed qualified. From time to time individuals were elected to oversee special tasks, as Pericles was given overall responsibility for the implementation of the Acropolis building pro-gramme. And, as has already been noted, the fourth century witnessed a growing tendency to elect men with special qualifications to act as secretaries or treasurers of particular boards or funds—already in the fifth century the *Hellênotamiai* had had important responsibilities in connection with the large sums which were collected as 'tribute' (*phoros*) from the member states of the Confederacy of Delos. Any job calling for given technical skills, such as those of an architect, could not be filled by random selection; and a number of appointments connected with the conduct of certain religious activities came into the same net. Such departures from the principle of the equalizing force of the use of the lot did not, however, affect the underlying ethos of the democracy: the posts in question (not all of which, the ambassadorships for instance, were formally termed *archai*) were always filled by the vote of the *ecclêsia*; they were almost always collegiate in nature, so that several men shared the duties and responsibilities; and the officers themselves were subject to regular scrutiny by the *boulê* and exposed to impeachment by any citizen for alleged faults whether of commission or of omission.

Although they were not *archai*, this is a convenient point at which to mention the institution of 'liturgies' (*leitourgiai*), the public services which Athens required of her richer citizens.[79] If anyone alleged that a richer man who was also eligible had

---

[79] On liturgies see Davies, *Wealth*, 9–37.

been passed over, he could challenge him to an exchange of property (*antidosis*). Some men might trim their costs as tightly as possible, while others saw an opportunity to spend generously and put on a lavish show, or even volunteered to undertake a liturgy when not obliged to do so. (On a number of occasions litigants sought to influence the dicasts in their favour by making such claims.) A *chorêgia* involved a man's shouldering the costs and production of a chorus at one of the major festivals which were held every year, and which included the performance of tragedies and comedies as well of purely musical entertainments. (There were also local *chorêgiai* at deme level.) Other liturgies included the *gymnasiarchia*, with responsibility for the teams in certain festival torch-races. But the most significant liturgy was the trierarchy.

A trierarch was obliged not merely to command a trireme, but to defray its running expenses (excluding the pay of its crew) for a year. That was a heavy burden, and by the early fourth century was onerous even when shared between two men; and expenses could vary from one year to another, or between two different triremes in the same year. In the 350s the system was modified to distribute the load between the 1,200 richest citizens, who were grouped into twenty 'partnerships' (*symmoriai*) in which each member was treated on an equal footing, with each vessel the responsibility of a subdivision (*synteleia*). In 354/3 Demosthenes proposed that the number of men called on should be raised to 2,000, each contributing in proportion to his personal means. We do not know if that proposal was accepted; but round about 340 he did succeed in having the obligation restricted to the richest 300 citizens, again contributing in proportion to their resources, but still organized in twenty *symmoriai*.[80]

Of the *archai* which were filled by lot, the oldest and most eminent was the archonship. It was originally a very powerful office which was filled by the election of candidates from the richest classes of *pentakosiomedimnoi* and *hippeis*; direct election was abolished in 487/6 and replaced by

---

[80] For the *symmoriai* see Rhodes, *CAP* 679–82. On the outlay involved in a liturgy, which could range from about 300 drachmai up to as much as one talent, see Davies, *APF*, pp. xxi–xxii.

sortition from amongst (probably one hundred) pre-selected candidates; and from about 460 eligibility was extended to include men of zeugite census as well, that is to say the bulk of the citizen body.[81] Later the appointment process became one of simple double sortition; and, although they were never officially eligible, in practice by the *Ath. Pol.*'s day men of the thetic class were not disqualified, although it seems unlikely that many thetes did actually serve as archons.[82] Under the developed democracy, the office could be held only once in a man's lifetime, and he had to be over thirty to hold it. Archons automatically entered the Areopagus, of which they were members for life, unless later disqualified for some serious misdemeanour.

There were nine archons in all: the (eponymous) archon, whose name was regularly used to date the year in which he held his office; the king-archon; the polemarch; and six *thesmothetai*. Some time between 508/7 and 460 the office of Secretary to the *thesmothetai* was created, making a body of ten men who were selected one from each of the ten tribes, although it seems no system existed to rotate the various individual offices among the tribes in turn.[83] In the developed democracy archons no longer decided cases themselves, but they did retain responsibilities in connection with *anakrisis*, that is to say the receiving of charges, checking that they were in order, and preparing them for hearing and decision by the *dikastêria*, often themselves acting as the presiding officers at the hearing. The eponymous archon had oversight especially of 'family' cases; the king-archon looked after religious crimes, including homicide and arson (the force of tradition and religious sensibilities was such that the most serious cases, premeditated murder and arson, were still tried by the Areopagus even under the fully developed democracy, while the less serious such as unintentional homicide and the killing of a non-citizen, etc., went to a *dikastêrion*); the polemarch looked after those private suits (*dikai* in the narrowest sense) which involved metics and certain other privileged non-citizens such as *proxenoi* (strictly, *proxenoi* represented Athenian interests in their own home states, but

[81] Above, p. 42.   [82] Above, p. 85.   [83] Rhodes, *CAP* 614.

increasingly the title came to be conferred on non-Athenians *honoris causa*). The *thesmothetai* were responsbible for all the court calendars and for allocating courts to the various presiding magistrates; they were also in charge of 'impeachments' (*eisangeliai*), charges of proposing improper decrees or laws, cases where the *boulê* wanted to impose penalties beyond its own level of independent competence, appeals against exclusion from a deme register, personation of citizenship, sycophants, bribery of public officers, private commercial and mining suits, and a mixed bag of other charges including adultery and fornication. In addition, they had the oversight of arrangements for the preliminary scrutiny or *dokimasia* of many of the officers of state.

All ten, including the Secretary of the *thesmothetai*, were in charge of the annual selection of the pool of 6,000 dicasts. The three 'senior' archons also played a leading role in a number of religious rites and ceremonies and festivals; these three each appointed two Assessors or *paredroi* of their own choosing to assist and advise them in the execution of their duties, who were equally required to undergo a *dokimasia* prior to being confirmed in their appointments and subject to *euthynai* in respect of those duties which they discharged under an archon's authority.[84]

The *Ath. Pol.* (55) gives a detailed account of the preliminary scrutiny (*dokimasia*) of the archons as it was in the author's day:

With the exception of the Secretary of the *thesmothetai*, they are first examined in the Council of Five Hundred; the Secretary's examination is conducted only in a *dikastêrion*, like the other officers of state (for all public officers, whether chosen by lot or by election, can enter on their offices only after a preliminary scrutiny). The nine archons, however, are examined both in the Council and then again in a *dikastêrion*. Previously, a candidate rejected by the Council at his *dokimasia* was debarred from appointment; but nowadays there is also referral to a *dikastêrion*, which has the final say. The questions asked are: 'Who is your father, and what is his deme? Who is your father's father, who is your mother and your mother's father, and what are their demes? Next they are asked whether they have a household cult of Ancestral Apollo and

---

[84] *Ath. Pol.* 55–9, with Rhodes's notes and commentary in *CAP*.

Zeus of the Courtyard [two cults very closely connected with the family] and where their shrines are, and whether they have family tombs and where they are, and whether they treat their parents properly and pay their taxes and have fulfilled their required military service. After answering these questions, they are ordered to 'Call witnesses to these statements'; witnesses having been presented, the announcement is made, 'Does anybody wish to object to this candidate and bring an accusation against him?', and if anybody does so both the accusation and the defence to it are heard and a vote then taken, in the Council by a show of hands and in a *dikastêrion* by ballot; but if no objection has been made, a vote is taken straight away. (In previous times only one dicast cast one formal ballot in the *dikastêrion*, but nowadays all the dicasts are required to cast their ballots so that, if a candidate has dishonestly bought off potential accusers, the dicasts still retain the power to disbar him.) When the scrutiny has been completed, they proceed to the stone where the sacrificial victims are cut up . . . and mounting it the new archons take a solemn oath that they will perform their duties with justice and in conformity with the laws, that they will not accept any bribes, and that if they do they will dedicate a golden statue. Having so sworn, they then proceed to the Acropolis, and there repeat the same oath, after which they enter upon their office.

Allowing for casual and trivial variations, the *dokimasia* of other public officers must have followed the same general pattern.

It would be tedious to itemize all the appointments which were made by random sortition. The total number of the *archai* listed in *Ath. Pol.* (42–69), not counting the 500 *bouleutai*, comes to well over 300, and there were something like a further 100 or so the *Ath. Pol.* neglects to mention:[85] the great majority of these offices were held by men chosen at random. (The number was probably not dramatically different a hundred years before the *Ath. Pol.* was written, and down to 404 there had been many more non-domestic posts in connection with Athens' 'imperial' preoccupations.) It must here suffice to indicate the diversity of their responsibilities: an archon to administer Salamis; the Demarch of the Peiraeus (the only demarch who was not appointed at deme level, reflecting the importance of Athens' harbour-town); the

---

[85] For fuller details see Hansen, 'Seven Hundred *Archai* in Classical Athens'.

eleven Police and Prison Commissioners; Superintendents of the Agora, of Weights and Measures, Coinage, Street Cleaning, Roads, Wells and Springs, Grain, Games, Temple Treasures and Furniture, Public Sacrifices, Public Assistance, Public Debts, and assorted Public Purchases; officers to check those attending every *ecclêsia* meeting; Secretaries and Treasurers of this and that and the other . . . Although most of the offices were unpaid, most of them did not take up all that much of a man's time; and generally the multiple-member boards or commissions could have shared a lot of the work out amongst themselves. Non-military *archai* (apart from the *boulê*, where a man might serve two terms) could be held only once in a man's lifetime; but we must allow for a category of active citizens who were ready to let their names 'go in to the hat' for selection for different *archai* in different years. Nevertheless, if we include membership of the *boulê*, round about one thousand posts had to be filled year in and year out from among citizens aged at least thirty in a citizen body which during the period of the developed democracy numbered in all somewhere between thirty and forty thousand or so over the age of eighteen.[86] In comparison with our modern world, the proportion of citizens over the age of thirty who were actively involved in public duties and responsibilities was simply staggering—not to mention the six thousand who every year came forward to register for service as dicasts in the courts.

Of course, given that they were entrusted to a random selection of men serving only for one year and frequently only on a part-time basis, most of the jobs to be done had to be simple and straightforward: checking lists and inventories, ensuring and certifying that specified sums had been duly received or disbursed, that specified tasks had been satisfactorily performed, that certain published rules and regulations had been duly complied with. There was little or no call for individual initiative or innovation: each *archê* had its own clearly defined and usually very narrowly delimited sphere of activity and responsibility, and was simply required to apply

---

[86] The minimum age-limit of thirty is less securely attested than is often implied in modern works; but it seems safe enough on a number of grounds. See, most recently, Hansen, 'Seven Hundred *Archai* in Classical Athens', 167–9.

the rules or discharge the functions which had been laid down either in a general law or by a particular decree of the *ecclêsia.*

Looked at from one point of view, the Athenian system was egregiously inefficient: unprofessional, cumbersome, uncoordinated, time-consuming, and plagued by discontinuity—the despair of any modern time-and-motion-study expert. From another point of view, it was remarkably efficient. It all depends on what one is aiming to effect. In so far as the Athenians were aiming to keep as much control of their affairs as possible in the hands of the whole body of the citizens and to prevent any individuals or groups or 'interests' from exercising power on the basis of birth, wealth, education, or whatever, in so far as they did not need a Lord Acton to tell them that all power has a tendency to corrupt those who wield it, they achieved great success in creating and maintaining a society in which (to fall back on modern terms) the sovereign citizenry exercised a control over the legislative, executive, and judicial branches of their state to a degree unmatched before or since. Whatever was lost in speed, expertise, and continuity was counterbalanced by the constraints which were erected against the emergence of over-powerful ministries and unrepresentative and irresponsive bureaucracies, by the wide pool of practical experience, local knowledge, and common sense that was drawn on, by the provision of a platform for the free expression of every interest, in short by the absence of that 'them-and-us' dichotomy between government and governed which has been so marked a feature of so many other societies. Very few (and those very few very untypical) Athenians wanted their system to be fundamentally changed; all of them knew that every officer of state was carefully watched by those he had to deal with, and could be readily checked and chastised if he misbehaved. There are plenty of grumbles and criticisms in the comic poets and in the orators; but they are concerned with particular and not general defects of the democracy. The Athenian society was an open society, and displayed a remarkable tolerance towards the public expression of criticism and dissent. Aristophanes and the other writers of political comedy were in effect subsidized by the state through the system of liturgies. When we read what they could get away with, and even win prizes for—material which at other times and in other places would have been censored or could have have landed its authors in gaol—we can at once recognize a society which had achieved a generous measure of identification between the state and the citizen. The participation of so high a proportion of its members, not only in the management of their local affairs at deme level and in attendance and voting at the frequent meetings of the *ecclêsia* or in the *dikastêria*, but also in the authority and responsibility of a wide variety of public offices, heightened both that identification and the awareness and involvement, and to some extent even the political expertise, of the mass assemblies which decided national policy.[87]

Personal involvement, participation, and random representation pervaded the taking of public decisions at all levels in democratic Athens. We see everywhere an ingrained suspicion of the corruptive effects of power.[88] At the local level, the *dêmotai* saw to their own local business, with their own officers and regular popular meetings. At the 'national' level, the *dêmos*, the collectivity of the citizens, either reserved such decisions to its own assembly, programmed by a large, constantly changing, and randomly selected cross-section of its own membership so designed as to reflect every part of Attica; or else, where it was clearly impossible for the *ecclêsia* to meet often enough or effectively enough to take all the decisions itself, entrusted them to the equally representative *dikastêria*. Except in the actual conduct of military and naval operations, where the commanders on the spot inevitably had to act to a great extent on their own initiative, and to some extent in the development of a few expert financial offices in the latter part of the fourth century,[89] there was a deep-seated mistrust of the individual—who might well share the view of Polemarchus in Plato's *Republic* that 'the

---

[87] On these general points see further below, pp. 173 ff.
[88] See further below, *ibid.*
[89] Above, p. 53.

right way to act was to do good to one's friends and harm to one's enemies'.[90]

This system of widespread and for the most part random recruitment for short and generally non-repeatable terms of office, coupled as it was with the provision of payment for those public duties which encroached at all seriously upon a citizen's time and energies, worked well enough so far as routine business was concerned. (It must not be forgotten that, throughout the lifetime of the developed democracy, Athens was always either the most powerful state in the Greek world or among the two or three most powerful.) But the formulation of longer-term policies, and the provision of that necessary adaptability and evolution in domestic administration and of those responses both to new domestic challenges and to events in the world outside a state's own boundaries, which other societies associate with 'professional' or 'career' politicians of above average experience, energy, expertise, intelligence, and ambition, were not catered for by arrangements of this nature. Accordingly, we must turn now to look at those of Athens' citizens who chose (whatever their aims or motives) to fill that gap, and to examine how and how far they managed to do so.

[Frequent references have been made in this chapter and elsewhere to the widespread use by the Athenians of sortition, viz. random selection by the drawing of lots, for filling public offices. It must be pointed out that there are a number of uncertainties about exactly how sortition worked. In particular, was the selection made from among all those eligible, or only, at least in some instances, from among those who were not only eligible but also willing to let their names go forward? Obviously, if the latter was true, there would have to have been provision for some element of compulsion if not enough eligible candidates offered themselves; but it makes better sense of some posts if only those both interested in doing the jobs and fitted to do them constituted the pool from which the random selection was made, and sortition would have been an inordinately

---

[90] Plato, *Republic*, I, 332 D.

cumbrous process if the lot had had always to choose between hundreds, and sometimes thousands, of eligible citizens. The German scholar Georg Busolt held that 'sortition from amongst volunteers' was the rule, at least in a number of cases. In default of really hard evidence either way, there is much to be said for his position.[91]]

[91] Busolt, *Griechische Staatskunde*, 1064, where he cites (n. 5) four passages in support of his view: Isocrates 15. 150; Lysias 6. 4 and 31. 33; Harpocration, s.v. *epilachôn*. But these passages are suggestive rather than decisive, and they do not not necessarily entail the practice which they are adduced to attest. In general, see Headlam, *Election by Lot at Athens*.

4

POLITICS AND
POLITICIANS

In a well-known passage of his *Memorabilia* (3. 6) Xenophon
tells of a conversation between Socrates and Plato's brother
Glaucon. Glaucon, though still less than twenty years old,
has his heart set on making a name for himself as a public
speaker and becoming a leading politician, and despite all the
efforts of his family and friends to deter him, persists in
making a laughing-stock of himself and having to be forcibly
removed from the speaker's platform. So Socrates takes him
in hand:

'Are you going to aim at increasing the wealth of our city?'
'Of course!'
'Tell me then, what are the sources of our current public
revenues, and what do they add up to? You've obviously
gone into this question to see whether any of them need
increasing or if any new ones are required.'
'Good Heavens, no!'
'All right, then. But if you've not done that, tell us what
the city spends its money on. Obviously you plan to reduce
any expenditures which are excessive.'
'Good gracious, I haven't had time for that yet either!'
'Well, we'll postpone this question of increasing the city's
wealth—after all, how can anyone control expenditure and
income without knowing the first thing about them?'
'But it's possible to make a city richer at the expense of its
enemies.'
'Most assuredly, provided one is the stronger party; but
otherwise there's a risk of losing what one already has.'
'That's true.'
'So anybody who intends to advise his city about whom it

should fight needs to know its own strength and that of the enemy, so that he can press for war if his city is the stronger but advocate caution if it is the weaker party.'

'Quite right!'

'To start with, then, tell us Athens' military and naval resources, and after that those of her enemies.'

'Good God, how could I carry all that in my head!'

'Oh, but if you've got something written down, please go and fetch your notes. I should very much like to hear you on this.'

Of course, poor Glaucon hasn't 'had time yet' to make any notes on the subject. So Socrates plods on relentlessly, with questions about the strength of the country's forts (which Glaucon has never inspected), the silver-mines (which he has never visited), and the corn supply (which he hasn't thought about). The upshot of it all is that, if Glaucon is to achieve his ambition, he must go away and work very hard at acquiring a really thorough knowledge of facts and figures before he begins to think of getting up on his feet and addressing his fellow citizens on any subject.

It is an amusing little vignette which Xenophon has given us, and the argument, for all its simplicity and obviousness, has rather more pertinence than we might think if we remember how important the art of public speaking was in a society like Athens, and that during the second half of the fifth century a number of professional teachers had begun to make a practice of giving formal instruction in the subject. Clearly, the ability to address and sway large numbers of listeners must have been an important asset before then, especially since the Cleisthenic reforms had ensured a greater independence and authority to the *ecclêsia*; but by Pericles' day the word *rhêtor* ('orator') seems to have been becoming what it remained throughout the fourth century, the regular term for what we would call a 'politician'.[1]

---

[1] On the *rhetores* see Connor, *The New Politicians of Fifth-Century Athens*, 116–7; Hansen, 'Athenian Politicians 403–322 BC', and '*Rhetores* and *Strategoi* in Fourth-Century Athens'. It is interesting to note that the arguments advanced by Xenophon's Socrates are endorsed—indeed, virtually paraphrased—by Aristotle in his *Rhetoric* (1359^b–1360^a).

We have to make a considerable effort to think ourselves back into a society which knew nothing of the newspapers and periodicals (let alone the radio and television programmes) on which we rely nowadays for information and discussion about political issues. Even books were very few and far between, expensively and laboriously copied by hand, and difficult for anyone but an expert to read. To an enormously wider extent than we are accustomed to, men had to rely for information and instruction on the spoken rather than on the written word.[2] It was this that gave oratory its central importance. The orators were the purveyors of facts and arguments, as of misinformation and misrepresentation. Perhaps no single text bears that out more plainly than the last section of the first book of Thucydides' *History*, where we are given a paraphrase of the speech in which Pericles forcefully (and successfully) advocates the rejection of the Spartan demands and in effect secures a war vote from the *ecclêsia*. Here, in the sentence (1. 139. 4) which precedes Pericles' opening words, we are told that 'many other men' got up and addressed the assembled citizenry, some advocating concessions and compromise while others urged rejection and war. It was the *ecclêsia* itself (which we need not doubt was packed full that day) which listened to all that was said and then had to make up its own mind and take the final and effective decision (1. 145. 1): 'The Athenians concluded that Pericles' advice was the best, and passed a decree as he had recommended, and on his motion answered the Spartans' detailed points as he had suggested, viz. to the effect that on the whole question they would do nothing under duress but stood ready to settle any differences by arbitration fairly and justly in accordance with the existing treaty. So the Spartan ambassadors returned home, and no further embassies were sent.'

Classical Athens quite simply had no 'government' as we understand that term. Its constitution made no provision for one. That was not simply the consequence of the system of limited tenure and collegiality so far as concerned her public offices: Republican Rome similarly confined the tenure of

[2] Cf. Andrewes, *The Greeks*, 283–5.

public office within annual limits, and laid great stress on collegiality too. However, Rome's magistrates were neither paid nor chosen at random from the bulk of her citizenry, and appointed by a system of suffrage which was most of the time effectively so controlled and manipulated as to ensure the election of members of the wealthiest class alone, with the result that groups of like-minded men were able to concert their political influence and interests over a period of time so as to ensure that the 'right' men were elected and the 'right' executive actions were taken. Not only that, the authority and powers of Rome's magistrates (especially those of the highest officers like the consuls and the praetors, and the promagistrates who had charge of provinces and armies) were both wide and marked by considerable discretionary independence, and they were immune from prosecution while they were in office. Furthermore, the Roman Senate, which was composed of magistrates and ex-magistrates, was the great council of state to which the annual magistrates turned for guidance and advice, and once admitted its members held their places in it for life; the Senate enjoyed considerable powers in its own right, many of its decrees (in financial matters especially) required no subsequent ratification by any larger body, and it was only rarely that proposals were presented to a popular assembly without their having received the prior approval of the Senate. There was no equivalent of the *boulê* to prepare business for the people. Semi-formal public-meetings (*contiones*) could be summoned by magistrates at which leading men argued the pros and cons of a particular proposal, but the ordinary citizen had no opportunity to get up and address the meeting. The popular assemblies, which were nominally sovereign, could meet only when summoned by a duly qualified magistrate, and could only vote Yes or No to proposals which were presented to them, with no right to debate or amend them. By the late Republic, as its territory extended, at first much and later all of Italy south of the River Po was absorbed within the Roman state, and in consequence most of the ordinary citizens found it impossible to make the long journey to Rome to vote. The various communities of Italy were effectively dominated by their local ruling class. The most senior officers of state were elected by an assembly which was overwhelmingly weighted in favour of the better-off citizens. The courts which sat in judgement on all the most serious cases, including charges of misconduct in public office, were drawn from members of the two highest classes, the Senators themselves and the Knights.

Things were very different at Athens, as we have seen. The *boulê* was chosen by a system of random and broadly proportionate selection from all the citizen inhabitants of Attica of zeugite census or higher, and in due course even thetes were not disqualified if they came forward for selection: it had no corporate continuity, since its membership changed from year to year and no citizen could serve on it more than twice in his lifetime. It was charged with the oversight of the conduct of the officers of state, and with the preparation and implementation of the decisions of the *ecclêsia*, for whose meetings it drew up and published the agenda. But the *ecclêsia* alone had the final and authoritative say in determining the decisions and policies of the state; all adult male citizens (most of whom lived fewer than a dozen miles from the city centre, and none much more than twenty-five) were entitled to attend and address and vote in the *ecclêsia*, which could debate and, if it so decided, reject or amend the proposals which were placed before it, or instruct the *boulê* to put specific items on the agenda for a subsequent meeting. The administration of the 139 local districts into which Attica was divided was firmly in the hands of the collectivities of their registered demesmen. The overwhelming majority of the Athenian officers of state, from the archons down, were likewise chosen by random selection; they held their offices, which were always collegiate in nature, only for one year and for only one term. The state provided payment for those offices which made any substantial call on their holders' time and energies, including service on the *boulê* itself and as a dicast in the popular courts; and, from the end of the fifth century, even attendance at meetings of the *ecclêsia* was remunerated. Only where special expertise was called for which was judged to be beyond the competence of the average citizen were direct election and the possibility of repeated tenure the rule, most notably in the higher military

and naval apppointments and those few other posts which
obviously demanded specific skills or talents; but it was the
ecclêsia itself which decided which of the candidates should be
successful, the discretion and independence of these (as of all)
officers was much more restricted than that of their elected
Roman counterparts, their conduct in office was subject to
regular scrutiny, and the means of penalizing or dismissing
them much readier to hand. In 430 even the 'Olympian'
Pericles himself was censured and fined and (albeit only
temporarily) removed from his office as *stratêgos* by a popular
vote, a decision which probably owed more to a prevalent
mood of disappointment and disillusion about the way the
war was going rather than representing a verdict on a
particular technical offence.[3] The *dikastêria*, the popular
courts, were drawn at random from a pool of 6,000 citizen
dicasts; even a minor 'civil' suit involved at least 200 dicasts,
and major 'political trials' far more than that. The citizenry
evidently regarded the *dikastêria* as a representative microcosm
of themselves, and came to be content to leave them to hear
and decide both major impeachments and charges against
individuals alleged to have proposed decrees or laws which
were technically invalid or otherwise vitiated. In the fourth
century, in their capacity as *nomothetai*, these dicasts also
authorized the rescinding of existing laws or the ratification
of new ones when so empowered by the sovereign *ecclêsia*.

Manifestly, such a system made no formal provision for
what we should call 'political leadership'. But the Athenians
had to have, and did have, their political leaders. For at all
times and in all places there have always been individuals
who, no doubt for a variety of reasons and a range of
motives, have decided to become 'politicians'. Nowadays
they can stand for election to national parliaments or
congresses or assemblies (possibly after an apprenticeship at
local level), and hope to climb the ladder of ministerial office,
as at Rome the young would-be politician Cicero set out to
scale the *cursus honorum* from quaestorship to consulate.
Although those methods and those routes were not available
to the Glaucons of Athens, there were none the less men like

---

[3] Thucydides 2. 65. 2–4. See Gomme, *HCT* ii ad loc. The precise charge and the
amount of the fine are unknown.

Themistocles and Aristides, Cimon and Ephialtes and Pericles, Cleon and Nicias and Alcibiades, Aeschines and Demosthenes, and many more besides, who took similar decisions and applied themselves to work hard to achieve their ambitions, making themselves at least competent public speakers, mastering constitutional, legal, and procedural detail, keeping their ears to the ground, building up circles of associates and supporters, acquiring expert knowledge of public finance, international affairs, military and naval matters, and so on, an example which Socrates advised Glaucon to follow if he wanted to get on. For, as Socrates also observes in Plato's *Protagoras* (319 *b* ff.), a man who does not 'know his stuff' gets short shrift from the *ecclêsia*: 'they simply refuse to listen but jeer and make a din, until the man who is trying to speak either gives up or shuts up or is physically removed by order of the *prytaneis*.'

By the same token, a man might well acquire a reputation for sound advice and judgement in general and for his sure grasp of public business and state policy, and with it a substantial following among his fellow citizens, so that on a number of occasions there would be an expectation or even a demand that he should address the *ecclêsia* on a particular issue, and a considerable number of voters, even if they had reservations or did not fully comprehend the argument, would be ready to follow the line which he advocated because of their confidence in his past performances and proven 'track record'. That was clearly true of Pericles, or so at least Thucydides attests in the famous 'obituary notice' (2. 65) in which he asserts that Pericles had owed his pre-eminence to his

sheer ability and authority and intelligence and manifest incorruptibility, so that he could control the mass of the citizenry in a free spirit, providing them with a lead rather than being led by them, because he did not owe his power to any dishonourable means and so had no need to 'play to the gallery', for such was the force of his character and prestige that he could even oppose and anger them. If he found them in an unwisely elated and arrogant mood, he would lecture them firmly and bring them back to a more circumspect way of thinking; if they were downcast for no sound reason, he would argue with them to restore their confidence.

Cephalus in the following century must have enjoyed a comparable standing, if he was able to claim that he had proposed more decrees than any other man and yet had never once been the subject of an accusation under the *graphê paranomôn*.[4] It may be doubted if anyone could hope to enjoy much political authority unless he was ready continuously to offer a lead based on a fairly consistent policy, as Demosthenes had done in advocating measures for resisting Philip of Macedon in the years before the fall of Elatea. One of Demosthenes' own criticisms of Aeschines had been that the latter was not prepared to give the *ecclêsia* continuous advice (Aeschines 3. 230).

To talk of political 'parties' in fifth- and fourth-century Athens is dangerously misleading and anachronistic. It would of course be arrogant and narrow-minded to claim that our own use of the word is the only correct one, when it derives from the Latin *partes*, and Cicero for instance could write (*De rep.* 1. 31) of the Roman Senate's being dominated in 129 by two rival *partes* with recognized leaders; but our word 'party' carries with it assumptions which would not have been understood or shared even in the days of George III, let alone in Cicero's Rome or Pericles' Athens. First and foremost, we are accustomed to a system of delegated representative government; our democracies are not 'direct' democracies. Neville Chamberlain, unlike Pericles, did not have to address a citizen assembly in September 1939 and seek to persuade it, in face of strenuous arguments on the other side, to vote to send an ultimatum to the Germans; he and his Cabinet took the decision themselves. We are accustomed to fairly tight party organizations each with a durable and recognized leadership and hierarchy for electoral and legislative purposes. At regular intervals we have the right to vote for individual candidates, but much of the time we vote not so much for any one candidate as for the party to which he belongs, in the hope that that party's candidates will win a sufficient number of seats to form a government which will run the country for the next few years. Hence a modern party will publish a programme or manifesto setting out

---

[4] For Cephalus see above, p. 79.

particular proposals which it plans to enact and in general describing the overall tone of its approach to government and administration. Often we may have no option but to vote for the party which we least object to, or at any rate for a party with a programme which we support to some extent but which contains some features or items which are not to our liking; for it can easily happen that there are certain features of each party's programme which we favour or dislike. Even if we cease to favour the party we voted for, there is usually not a lot that we can do until the next General Election comes round.

Such assumptions were alien to an Athenian, who could turn up in the *ecclêsia* one day and raise his hand in favour of something which a given speaker advocated and at the next meeting raise it against another proposal from the same man: he did not have to put all his eggs in any one basket, empower a specific group of men to run Athens and themselves take all decisions even for a single year, and only then have the chance to decide whether or not he wanted them to continue in power for a further term, or to cast his vote for a rival group. Although, naturally enough, individual politicians both could and did collaborate with each other and sometimes accepted the leadership of one amongst themselves, and although various sections among the citizen body itself might more or less regularly support or follow the lead of particular individuals, or share certain common interests and aspirations, it is safest to eschew any mention of 'parties', if only because of the danger that the very use of that word may seduce us into unconscious and misleading or even false assumptions or analogies drawn from our modern usage and experience. A more neutral and harmless word like 'groups' is preferable.

In the sixth century political leadership had been the prerogative of a relatively few wealthy men, above all of the established nobility and gentry of Attica, those who commanded traditional seigneurial influence and prestige (although it is reasonable to suppose that changing economic conditions were already beginning to erode the homogeneity and exclusiveness of that class). Towards the middle of the century we hear of their constituting three broad groupings, whose names ('the men of the plain, the men of the coast, the men beyond the hills') must have reflected at least some regional basis, under recognized leaders. Even when Peisistratus won control and established a tyranny, he needed the help and collaboration of those of them who were prepared to accept his directing authority.[5] And although at the end of the century Cleisthenes' fundamental reforms scrapped many of the former rules of the political game, the old families continued to provide political leadership, for all that their scions had to learn new tricks. Much of the time they were probably in competition with each other for office itself and for the fruits of office as much as over central political issues: the archonships, and with them life membership of a still powerful Areopagus, were filled by direct election for twenty years after Cleisthenes, and thereafter the *stratêgia* continued to be open to competition. Our evidence is meagre, with only the 'biggest' names surviving in the record, and gives us no opportunity to see to what extent 'new men' may have been starting to filter in at lower levels, how far ostracism was affecting the pattern, or how much *boulê* and *ecclêsia* were acquiring self-confidence and flexing their muscles, and the ground was being prepared for the articulation and acceptance of the radical reforms of Ephialtes. Nevertheless, the institution and application of ostracism are a pointer to the highly individualist nature of politics at this time,[6] and blood and marriage connections and personal friendships appear to have been very important.

In treating of the period which followed the Ephialtic reforms, Hignett very aptly cited and exploited Walter Bagehot's observation that 'A new constitution does not produce its full effects as long as its subjects were reared under an old constitution, as long as its statesmen were trained by that old constitution. It is not really tested till it comes to be worked by statesmen and among a people neither of whom are guided by a different experience.'[7] Down to Pericles' death in 429 his most prominent associates

[5] On all this see above, pp. 21 ff. And cf. Meiggs and Lewis, *GHI*, pp. 11–12.

[6] On ostracism see above, p. 33. Connor (*New Politicians*, 73–5) makes this particular point with admirable conciseness.

[7] Hignett, *HAC* 252 (Bagehot, *The English Constitution*, p. ix).

or opponents seem still to have been drawn from the traditional upper class (although it is important again to stress how scanty our evidence is, and that all but the very biggest names are largely lost to us).[8] Themistocles may have been a 'new man',[9] but Ephialtes was probably of good family, and Pericles' antecedents were every bit as aristocratic as Cimon's: his father Xanthippus had been in the forefront of political life in his own day, and his mother Agaristê was the niece of the reformer Cleisthenes and a great-granddaughter of the earlier Cleisthenes who had been tyrant of Sicyon. Nevertheless, Pericles' own career is reported to have marked or reflected a change of approach and methods. Cimon made great use of his personal wealth for largesse and ostentatious display, and paraded his ancestry and connections in the old style:[10] but Plutarch (*Pericles*, 7) records that

Pericles devoted himself to the *dêmos*, choosing the side of the less well-off many rather than the rich few, contrary to his nature, which was anything but populist . . . and seeing that Cimon comported himself in an aristocratic manner and was the darling of all the 'gentlemen' of Athens, he insinuated himself into the good graces of the commons, thereby winning security for himself and power against Cimon. He abruptly changed his own life-style: the only road he was ever to be seen on in Athens was the one which led to the Agora and the Council-House; invitations to dinner and all other such friendly and companionable occasions he declined, and so during all the long period of his political activity the only such gathering which he consented to attend was the wedding of his kinsman Euryptolemus, and even there he immediately got up and left once the formal toasts had been drunk . . . Even with the *dêmos*, he sought to avoid the *ennui* of over-familiarity by spacing out his appearances and not turning up and addressing the people on every issue; to borrow a *bon mot* of Critolaus', he reserved himself like the State Galley for the grandest occasions, content at other times to leave things to his friends and political associates.

In the period which followed the repulse of Xerxes' invasion, Athens established herself as the dominant presence in the Aegean and as easily the wealthiest of all the Greek

[8] Hignett, *HAC* 253–6.
[9] Herodotus' language at 7. 143 can be taken to imply as much, although an alternative interpretation is equally possible.
[10] Cf. Connor, *New Politicians*, 16–20.

states. Her power came increasingly to rest on her navy, and on the thetic rowers who manned her warships, rather than on the zeugite hoplites who had won the Battle of Marathon: as the war of 431–404 was to demonstrate, Athens could afford to avoid confronting the superior armies of Sparta and the Peloponnesian League when they invaded Attica, and withdraw into her forts and above all behind the 'Long Walls' which encircled and conjoined Athens and her port of Piraeus, abandoning her fields to plunder and devastation so long as her sea-lanes were kept open and her control of her 'allies' and of their revenues and resources was not seriously threatened. In consequence, there developed a growing self-confidence among those of her citizens whose property was below the minimum required for service in the heavy infantry, but who manned the triremes on which naval supremacy rested. With that self-confidence came an increasing awareness of their own importance; for, as Aristotle observed (*Politics*, 1321ª5 ff.), in his Greek world which knew nothing of professional standing armies, the durability and character of the government of a *polis* were perforce intimately connected with the nature and composition of the citizen armed forces on which it had to rely for the maintenance of its security from attacks from outside or for the extension of its own power. It was not that Athens' hoplites became unimportant, for they were no less vital to her; the increasing wealth and influence of Athens spread their benefits widely among all her citizens, and any suggestion that the thetes came to dominate Athens is ridiculous, with no basis either in evidence or in probability. Nevertheless, they added their weight to shifting the balance of Athenian politics to the populist side of the scale, as the mass of the ordinary citizens came to assert themselves and their interests.

Pericles was born about 495; and growing to manhood in the years which followed the Persian War, he adapted himself to these changed and changing conditions. Probably the finest orator of his day,[11] he was also intimate with the new

---

[11] The few fragments of Pericles' oratory which survive exemplify his gift for the striking and memorable phrase. In his own lifetime the contemporary comic poet Eupolis (fr. 94) bore vivid testimony to the masterly power and persuasiveness of his eloquence.

and questioning thinkers of this time, one of the most fruitful and innovative periods in the intellectual and cultural history of our world, and on familiar terms with some of its leading theorists and artists.[12] He may also perhaps have been more of a 'professionally' hard-working and full-time politician than his predecessors had had to be. His pre-eminence in his younger days down to and after the death of Ephialtes is often exaggerated by later writers, for we are almost bereft of any good contemporary evidence, and his long and sure ascendancy after the middle 440s has cast a deep shadow behind it, leaving us with only a handful of other names to which we cannot begin to assign their due weight. In the last dozen or so years of his life, Athens was basking in a summer of peace, prosperity, and power, until the skies began to darken with the early disappointments and travails of the long war which broke out in 431, two and a half years before his death. Those golden years of his maturity probably did much to slow the pace of transition to a new style of politics and a new kind of political leader.

It is true that during the fifth century, and especially after the Persian Wars, there was often—but not invariably—a connection between the tenure of the elective office of the *stratêgia* and the performing of a role of political leadership, most notably in men like Miltiades, Themistocles, Xanthippus, Aristides, Cimon, Ephialtes, Pericles, Nicias, Cleon, Alcibiades, and Theramenes, to name the most obvious among them. That is entirely understandable, given the importance to Athens of her 'empire' and of the fleets and armies which enabled her to acquire and maintain it, and given too that *stratêgoi* had often to operate far from Athens and exercise a large degree of independent discretion not only in military but also in diplomatic, administrative, and financial matters. Yet the connection was accidental rather than essential, and probably owed much to a time-honoured 'officer and gentleman' tradition. The question. 'How far did Pericles' long ascendancy depend on his repeated election as a *stratêgos* or vice versa?' may seem the same as 'which came first, the chicken or the egg?' But the answer is clear: his

---

[12] Plutarch, *Pericles*, 4–5, 8, 12–13.

power rested on his ability to command the continuing confidence and hence the votes of the *ecclêsia*, which throughout surrendered none of its own powers to him[13] and whose affirmative vote was required for every plan or proposal which he put forward. Even in his day, we have no good reason to suppose that every prominent politician held the *stratêgia*, that for instance all the many speakers who sought to influence the *ecclêsia* in the 'war debate' in 431 held or had ever held that office. Cleon had been a prominent figure for some years already before he secured the office in 425. In the critical and important debate in 427 on what action should be taken to punish the defeated rebels of Mytilene and to ensure against any such secession in the future, Thucydides (3. 36–48) assigns the leading roles to Cleon and Diodotus, the latter of whom here makes his sole attested appearance on the political stage at Athens! Further, it is clear that in the fourth century, after Athens had lost her 'empire', a fairly sharp division emerged between these two activities. And, even in the fifth century, there were probably quite a number of *stratêgoi* who were elected primarily for their professional skills, or (as with the Nelsonian Phormio) for sheer brilliance.[14]

Plutarch (*Pericles*, 11) tells us an interesting story about Thucydides son of Melesias, who was Pericles' chief and most persistent opponent in the 440s until his ostracism in 443.[15] He was a kinsman (perhaps brother-in-law) of Cimon, but 'more a politician than a military man'. He is said to have induced his upper-class supporters, who had hitherto been scattered anywhere around the Pnyx, to cluster instead in a compact group so as to make a more effective impact on the proceedings of the *ecclêsia*; he thereby incidentally sharpened the division between the 'few' (*oligoi*) and the *dêmos*, and

---

[13] Thucydides 2. 22. 1 may seem *prima facie* an exception; but Hignett's explanation (*HAC* 246–7) that this was an exercise by Pericles of his immense but informal authority and not of any formal power is surely correct.

[14] For Phormio's inspired handling of the vastly outnumbered Athenian squadron at Naupactus in 429 see Thucydides 2. 83–92.

[15] On his background and connections see Wade-Gery, *Essays in Greek History*, 239–70. On his opposition to Pericles see Andrewes, 'The Opposition to Pericles'. Note especially Andrewes's warnings about the reliability of Plutarch, on which cf. below, n. 17.

according to Plutarch this was the time when these words first became political labels. In his account of the abortive oligarchic coup of 411, Thucydides (8. 54. 4) tells how Phrynichus brought together the various close societies (*synômosiai*) 'which already existed at Athens to concert efforts at trials and elections'; the hoard of *ostraka* specially prepared with Themistocles' name already written on them was presumbly the work of one or more such interested bodies.[16] A variety of social and mutual-benefit clubs and comparable organizations were part of the Athenian scene, as often elsewhere, some of them more respectable or less exclusive than others. Even those to which Thucydides refers would not normally have threatened the constitution, although they could be forged into a revolutionary tool in special circumstances such as obtained in 411 and 404. Nicias and Alcibiades are said to have united their supporters (*staseis*) against what they saw as a common danger to themselves to secure the ostracism of Hyperbolus; but it is not clear how safe it is to rely on Plutarch's account here (though his story is at least in part plausible enough), nor how far these *staseis* embraced wider bodies of citizens beyond the active members of particular political clubs.[17] As already noted, leading politicians had their very visible associates and adherents. 'Those around' (*hoi peri*) so-and-so was the regular Greek term for a politician's associates; and thus we find Aristophanes (*Peace*, 756–7) sneering at the 'writhing pack of hangers-on and toadies' who danced attendance on his *bête noire* Cleon.[18]

After Pericles' death in 429 Cleon emerged as an increasingly influential figure in Athenian politics, and in some respects reflected a change in both style and background. Plutarch (*Moralia*, 806–7) preserves a story of how on entering public life Cleon formally renounced his friends and with them any

[16] On this hoard see above, p. 37.

[17] Plutarch was writing 500 years after the events he described. He was not notably critical in handling and evaluating his very varied sources, and was often careless and anachronistically mistaken in his explicit or tacit assumptions about political conditions in earlier times. More often than not we do not know his source on particular points. On his strengths and weaknesses see the excellent discussion in Gomme, *HCT* i. 54–84. (See also Andrewes, above, n. 15.)

[18] On clubs and societies in general see Calhoun, *Athenian Clubs in Politics and Litigation*; Connor, *New Politicians*, 25–32; Gomme, Andrewes, and Dover, *HCT* v. 128–31.

obligation to render them personal services, so as to be able to devote himself fully to the cultivation of the friendship and interests of the *dêmos* as a whole. In so acting, however, he was (as we have seen) merely following a path which had already been marked out by Pericles, who had himself deliberately renounced such entanglements and their concomitant obligations 'to help one's friends and harm one's enemies'. Despite that, however, Cleon did not work in total isolation; he had his own group of associates and what could be pejoratively styled 'toadies' or 'hangers-on'. What Plutarch must be taken to mean is that, like Pericles, he deliberately distanced himself from the vestiges of old-style personal politics and set out instead to identify himself with broader and less individual interests. What chiefly differentiated Cleon from Pericles was, it seems, his abrasive and bullying manner,[19] and—perhaps most importantly—his social origins. Pericles had been born into the traditional 'ruling class'. Cleon's father was well-to-do, sufficiently so to be eligible to perform at least one public liturgy; Cleon did not lack money or education, but the money was 'new money'. The Old Comedy of Athens displays what may seem to a modern reader of liberal persuasion a deplorable streak of class-consciousness and snobbery: men like Cleon, Hyperbolus, Cleophon, Lysicles, and Eucrates were not poor (they could scarcely have enjoyed the education or leisure which they needed to devote themselves to politics if they had been); indeed, Cleophon's father is on record as a *stratêgos* in the year 428, and thus was himself it seems an example of the breakdown of the older pattern of exclusiveness. But their money came from 'trade', and they feature on the comic stage in the guise of vulgarian tanners, sausage-makers, cattle-dealers, lyre-makers, and such, rather than as 'upwardly mobile' and pretentious *nouveaux riches* whose wealth came from large-scale exploitation of such crafts, as petty tradesmen rather than works-owners. Why that was the way of things is not clear; but it was evidently an effective comic device, which one may suspect was intimately connected with the somewhat obscure slapstick tradition from which the Old

---

[19] Thucydides 3. 36. 6 underlines this aspect of Cleon's technique. Note also the picture presented by Aristophanes in his comedies *Wasps* and *Knights*.

Comedy developed, as well as with the efforts which such men probably made to identify themselves with the outlook and interests of the ordinary 'man in the street'.[20] Not that this approach was confined to comedy. The same sort of slanders are found in political debate. The orator-politician Demosthenes inherited a substantial and thriving business from his father (comprising two workshops for making knives and furniture with work-forces of thirty and twenty skilled slaves respectively), yet Aeschines sneered at him as being 'the bastard offspring of a cutler'; not to be outdone, Demosthenes flung back at Aeschines the jibe that he had been employed as a common usher in the school his father had run—'You taught the three Rs, but I was a full fee-paying pupil'. Aeschines calls Demosthenes 'a Scythian', with the implication that his mother was a barbarian slave-woman; Demosthenes hits back with the allegation that Aeschines' own father was an ex-slave.[21] All very childish stuff, we may well think; but it was part of the give-and-take and mud-slinging of Athenian political in-fighting, and not confined to the comic stage.

In the generation which followed Pericles' death there were still some political leaders from the old families, most notably Alcibiades, who after the death of his father Cleinias became the ward of Pericles himself. He set his eyes on the *stratêgia*, and proudly claimed both entitlement to and capacity for political pre-eminence and leadership on the grounds of his birth and the high distinction of his ancestors.[22] At the Olympic festival in 416, in a manner. reminiscent of the golden age of aristocracy, he made a great splash by entering an unprecedented seven teams in the chariot-rate, and won first, second, and fourth places.[23] In the long run he was to fall between two stools: his sheer brilliance and largeness of vision and inventiveness, his superb talent as a public speaker, and his openly populist public stance made him feared and disliked by rival populist politicians, while his irresponsible private life-style, his contempt for convention, and his somethimes blatant opportunism gave his enemies

---

[20] Dover, *Aristophanic Comedy*, 95–100; Davies, *Wealth*, ch. 4.

[21] Demosthenes 18. 129; Aeschines 2. 93, etc.

[22] Thucydides 6. 16. 1.   [23] Ibid. 6. 16. 2.

sticks with which to beat and discredit him, and created ambiguities and vacillations in the attitude of the mass of the citizenry towards him, which led to his final downfall.[24] Nicias was another who does not quite fit the new pattern. He lacked a 'landed gentry' ancestry, but his wealth was enormous, derived not from trade or commerce in the narrow sense but from large-scale mining interests and ownership of a huge slave work-force. He was conscientious and lavish in his performance of public liturgies, rigidly conventional in his private life, and notorious for his piety and religious propriety. All in all, his character and his style of politics, both of which may be loosely termed 'conservative' or 'middle-of-the-road', made him acceptable to a broad spectrum of moderate opinion.[25] Unlike Cleon, Hyperbolus, etc., he did not seek to identify himself with 'Mr Demos of the Pnyx'; but, like Alcibiades, though from the opposite direction and with different policies, he stood with one foot in an older and the other in a newer Athens.

The year 417 was the first time that the weapon of ostracism had been used to get rid of a major political figure since Thucydides son of Melesias had been sent packing a quarter of a century earlier in 443—indeed, there may for all we know have been no ostracisms at all during that period. It was also the last time that it was ever used. Both Alcibiades and Nicias are said to have feared that one or other of them would be ostracized, and so combined their forces to secure their individual safety, and thereby frustrated the resolution of the conflict between their policies. It is tempting to see 417 as marking the demise of a style of politics of which Alcibiades was the final flowering. 'The political class of the fourth and later fifth centuries gradually ceased to be closely linked with the generalship, ceased to be the preserve of men of "good family", ceased to engage in dynastic manœuvring via political marriages, and ceased to be an area within which families could develop long political traditions.'[26]

---

[24] Ibid. 6. 28. 2. Alcibiades' wild and aristocratic irregularities of conduct are documented by Ostwald, *Popular Sovereignty*, 116–18.

[25] Davies, *APF* 403–4; *Wealth*, 117.

[26] Davies, *Wealth*, 125–6. By contrast, Davies shows (122–5) that there continued to exist 'a largely dynastic military caste, closely tied to property'. (On changes in the 420s see now Ostwald, *Popular Sovereignty*, ch. 5.)

The emergence into prominence of a new breed of politicians apparently sharpened internal divisions at Athens and alienated a number of men from the upper class, who felt a distaste for, or a hostility towards, them and their policies and methods. That did not matter much so long as Athens was doing well. But the total disaster which overwhelmed her forces in Sicily in 413 encouraged in the anti-democrats the hope of subverting the democracy—although the oligarchic extremists still recognized that it was essential for them to mask their true objectives if they were to have any chance of acquiring sufficient initial impetus. Their coup failed, but it left in its wake a dangerous legacy of bitterness and suspicion which served to weaken Athens' greatly diminished ability to hold out against the increasing financial and military pressures which were brought to bear by her enemies. The anti-democrats resurfaced as a narrow oligarchic government in 404 in the aftermath of defeat and capitulation to Sparta. Yet, once again, the brevity of the life of 'the Thirty' reveals how little support they enjoyed and how much the great majority of Athenians of all classes and conditions preferred the continuance of their democratic system, which was never again threatened until at the end of the fourth century the city had to yield to the military might and will of Macedon. As the event demonstrated, any fundamental change from democracy could be effected only by defeat in war and the interested intervention of victorious external powers.[27]

Other societies have passed through comparable stages of change. In the United Kingdom the hold of the aristocracy and gentry remained firm enough until after the Third Reform Act of 1884; it was only in the Edwardian period and more especially after 1918 that the social composition of the House of Commons changed its character significantly. Such times of transition are sure to generate strains and stresses, as they did in the United Kingdom. But a system of government which rests securely on the support or at least the acquiescence of the mass of its participating members can weather such temporary squalls without grievous damage, so long as it is not seriously interfered with from outside. After the restoration

---

[27] On 'the Four Hundred' and 'the Thirty' see below, ch. 5.

of the democracy in 403 we enter a century in which the political leadership of Athens is recruited from a far broader spectrum of the citizen body than it had been during most of the fifth century, without that occasioning any special comment, for all that some of the politicians sought to cast aspersions on the competence or respectability of their rivals, or even on their claim to be free-born citizens. Although the loss of imperial revenues meant that there were heavier calls on the wealthier citizens to meet naval expenses, which could lead to considerable controversy,[28] such issues never came near to sparking off a challenge to the constitution.

Precisely what entitles a man to be called a 'politician' is a moot point; but by collecting the names of men attested as proposers of motions, speakers, prosecutors, ambassadors, or generals, Hansen has been able to list not far short of four hundred fourth-century Athenians who may reasonably be so described.[29] The demes in which 240 of them were registered are known; and the distribution of these men—as too of those dicasts whose demes can be identified—between the three main subdivisions of Attica (city, coast, and inland) is remarkably close to the proportions of the represenatation of these areas on the Council of Five Hundred.[30] Some of these men who were registered as members of demes which lay at some distance from Athens may for all we know have no longer been living there and taken up residence in or near the city itself; others may have maintained a residence or at least a *pied-à-terre* in Athens as well as a home in their deme; some may have lodged for regular periods with friends or relatives; some may have been only occasionally active. Nevertheless, we have here a striking indication of how political activity still reflected and represented the whole spectrum of Attica, since we have no good reason to suppose

[28] Jones, *Athenian Democracy*, 3–20; Davies *Wealth*, 88 ff.

[29] Hansen, 'Athenian Politicians 403–322 BC'; '*Rhetores* and *Strategoi* in Fourth-Century Athens'; 'The Number of *Rhetores* in the Athenian *Ecclesia* 355–322 BC'.

[30] Hansen, 'Political Activity and the Organization of Attica in the Fourth Century BC'. His tabulation is set out on p. 229 as follows (figures are percentages):

District	Bouleutai	Rhêtores/Stratêgoi	Dikastai
City	26	26	23
Coast	39	36	42
Inland	35	38	35

that even those who had moved away did not usually maintain fairly close contact with their 'Cleisthenic' demes.[31] As has already been noted, these politicians were not by any means poor.[32] Even so, anything like full-time devotion to political activity cost money, and took up time which could otherwise have been used to look after their own private concerns, which might have been expected to prove more profitable had they directed their energies and talents wholly or largely to that end—and the increased scope and complexity of public business, especially but not exclusively in the field of finance, evidently demanded exceptional skills. Some may have been prepared to make such a selfless sacrifice. But one is bound to suspect that political activity was not always financially unrewarding. Hard evidence is not easy to find; yet the frequent charges that such profiteering went on (regardless of which or how many of these allegations were false or exaggerated) must have been at least plausible, and they attest a contemporary public belief and awareness that men could and did make money out of political activity.[33]

In the early fifth century Themistocles was said to have made a great deal of money out of his public powers and position. The mere fact that it was claimed for both Aristides and Ephialtes that 'their hands were clean' is an indication that such propriety was thought to be somewhat exceptional. In Pericles' day the 'Old Oligarch' (3. 3) was ready to

---

[31] Hansen (ibid. 230 ff.) suggested that the bouleutic quotas may have been 'adjusted, say in 403/2, to fit the existing citizen population which differed both in size and in geographical distribution from that of the age of Kleisthenes'. I am not persuaded by his argument; but, if the suggestion were correct, it would still further underline the involvement in political activity of men from all over Attica.

[32] That Demades, Archedemos, Epicrates, or Aristogeiton were genuinely 'poor', as Davies (*Wealth*, 117) is prepared to accept, I very much doubt. Their 'poverty' was probably relative, not absolute. The fact that Demades had had no formal rhetorical training may point to his having come from a background that was not too well-off, rather than indigent. Demosthenes (18. 108) could even describe all but the very richest 300 among the 1,200 well-to-do citizens eligible to share in undertaking trierarchies as 'poor men' (*penêtes*)! Cf. also above, pp. 8–9.

[33] One may cite *exempli gratia* Lysias (19. 57): 'There are to be sure men who lay out money in order to get it back twice over from the offices which you judge them to merit'; and Demosthenes' reference (21. 189) to 'politicians who have shamelessly enriched themselves at your expense'. For an examination of such material rewards see Sinclair, *Democracy and Participation in Athens*, 179–86.

concede that money oiled many a wheel at Athens, and that
even more wheels could be oiled if more palms were greased;
and the comic poets cheerfully flung such mud in the faces of
office-holders and 'politicians'. Our evidence does not
indicate that things were any different in the fourth century:
the father-and-son 'deme-bosses' Antiphilos and Euboulides
may serve as an illustration.[34] Public office at Athens was
remunerated at a bare subsistence level—and active politicians
did not regularly or often hold such offices: hence it is not
ridiculous to suppose that some men succumbed to the
temptation to solicit or accept payment or favours in return
for employing their discretion, energies, and influence to
support or advance particular interests. Our own society is
very sensitive in such matters; but a Samuel Pepys could
derive much of his income from sources which we would
nowadays condemn as illegal and improper, without expecting
censure from his contemporaries. To glance again at the
trivial matter of the request of some Citian merchants for
leave to establish a shrine to Aphrodite at Athens:[35] the
requisite permission was granted by the *ecclêsia* on the motion
of the highly influential politician Lycurgus, whose support
must have been of no little assistance! One may wonder what
sort of material considerations may have induced him to lend
these merchants his interest and advocacy. Gaius Gracchus
later told the story of how a tragedian once boasted that he
had earned a great deal of money from a play he had written,
to which Demades (a leading figure in later fourth-century
Athens) had replied: 'So you find it marvellous that your
words have earned you a talent? The Great King paid me ten
talents just to keep my mouth shut!'[36]

It is then no surprise to hear Hyperides claiming (*Against
Demosthenes*, 24–5) that the Athenians did not get up in arms
about such practices, so long as they were kept within
accepted bounds: 'There are very heavy fines, even the death
penalty, prescribed for those who take bribes. But you
willingly allow your generals and public speakers to make
large sums of money—not that the laws allow this, but out
of your own kindness and tolerance—with the one strict

---

[34] Above, p. 66.   [35] Above, p. 89.
[36] Aulus Gellius, *Noctes Atticae*, 11. 10.

proviso that the money they get is not taken against your interest. Look at Demosthenes and Demades: from decrees passed here in Athens alone and grants of honour to foreigners they have made, I suppose, upwards of sixty talents, not counting what they have received from the Persian royal treasury and King Alexander.' He goes on to allege, however, that this pair have transgressed the accepted bounds and are greedy for even more, but at the cost of betraying the city's security. Whatever the truth of Hyperides' allegations, we can accept the truth of his dichotomy, and refrain from being shocked at the thought that the average Athenian had enough common sense and realism to appreciate that politicians had to make a living, like everybody else. Without them, what would Athens have done? The mass of the officers of state were selected at random, possessed only average competence, lacked continuity of tenure and experience; they could manage routine business well enough, but that was their limit (as it would be our own). Athens was able to survive and prosper only by grace of the skills and energies of men for whom the constitution made no specific provision and to whom it offered neither a formal position nor a salary. It was to such men that *boulê* and *ecclêsia* perforce turned for guidance and leadership in exercising their own powers: receiving and dispatching embassies, concluding treaties and alliances, 'balancing the budget' and building up reserves and contingency funds, embarking on building programmes, in general outlining and detailing the measures which the city could accept and implement to deal with the ever-changing pattern of domestic and external calls on its energies and resources. The *dêmos* alone could decide which proposals to adopt; but it was the politicians who prepared the various items on the menu from which the *dêmos* selected the dishes of its choice.

Cimon, Pericles, Cleon, Theramenes, and Cleophon, and after them in the fourth century men like Thrasybulus, Callistratus, Cephalus, Lycurgus, and Demosthenes, all enjoyed their periods of pre-eminence, and evidently not just because they were clever and persuasive speakers but also because they had acquired expertise in wide areas of public business and exhibited great capacity in formulating and executing public policies. But politics could be a dangerous game. The very context in which Thucydides (2. 65) expressed his celebrated judgement on Pericles demonstrates that Athens was in fact very far from being a 'one-man show', for he has just told us how Pericles had recently been fined and deposed from office by a disgruntled citizenry! Thucydides overstated the strength of Pericles' position in order to sharpen the contrast he wished to make between Pericles and the politicians who succeeded him.[37] Formal accountability, it is true, existed only for those who held public offices. Nevertheless, even if or when a politician held no such office, he could be held responsible and called to account for the advice which he had given. Not only could politicians lose favour (and, with it, influence), they could be ostracized, impeached or indicted for alleged offences in proposing particular decrees and laws, or otherwise arraigned on formal charges which might be less material or relevant to the outcome of the case than was the attitude of the citizens at large towards the policies which they had advocated or with which they had associated themselves. Thucydides himself tells us (8. 1) that after the news of the Syracusan disaster reached Athens in 413 the Athenians 'were very hard on the politicians who had had a hand in urging the expedition—as if it was not they themselves who had voted to authorize it!' Whatever the rewards, tangible or intangible, of a successful political career, the price to be paid for failure or mistakes could be—and often was—a very high one, not merely a severe or even crippling fine, but exile and even execution.[38]

---

[37] See further below, p. 180.
[38] For a full discussion of the hazards of political life at Athens see Sinclair, *Democracy and Participation in Athens*, 145–161.

5

VIOLENT OPPOSITION

That feelings had run high over the reforms of Ephialtes is clear. What is less easy to determine is whether, or for how long, any considerable number of Athenians continued to cherish hopes of reversing the situation. There were surely those among the richer and better-born citizens who would have preferred a less egalitarian system (the same can be said of modern democracies; and we have noted the continuing existence of upper-class clubs and societies as late as the last decade of the fifth century.) But that is not by any means the same as realistically hoping or actively working for a major change in the constitution.

We learn from Thucydides (1. 107. 4) that only a few years after the reforms, when Sparta had an army in Boeotia in 457, a group of Athenians was prepared to collaborate with this force so as to 'put a stop to the democracy and interrupt the building of the Long Walls which was then in progress'. (It is instructive to have this explicit connection between the radical democracy and the Long Walls linking Athens with her port at the Piraeus, underlining her increasing dependence on sea-power and sea-borne traffic and the 'naval commons', from so authoritative a source; and the 'Old Oligarch' also stresses that link.) Thucydides says nothing of their detailed plans, but his language indicates that those involved were not numerous. An anecdote preserved by Plutarch (*Cimon*, 17. 4–6; *Pericles*, 10. 1–3) about the patriotism displayed by Cimon and his supporters at this time, whether genuine or not, shows that they were not reputed to be the sort of men who were willing to go along with treacherous extremists, for all that Cimon had been Ephialtes' opponent and chief target; and, on his return from ostracism in the late 450s, Cimon himself resumed an active and prominent part in politics and in military and naval command. Nor is there anywhere any hint that Thucydides son of Melesias and his supporters conducted their vigorous opposition to Pericles and his policies in the 440s on other than what may be termed normal political lines.

Despite that, until recently there was a widespread tendency to talk about oligarchs and an 'oligarchic party' in post-Ephialtic Athens—for all that what had been in existence for some forty or so years before those reforms was not any sort of approach to an oligarchy but the broadly based Cleisthenic democracy. Yet our earliest contemporary witness, the 'Old Oligarch' (to use the convenient if misleading nickname given to the unknown author of the pseudo-Xenophontic *Constitution of Athens*), who wrote his brief pamphlet at some indeterminate date in the 430s or 420s, evidently recognized that oligarchy or anything like it was a 'non-starter' in his Athens. It was only in the wake of the massive disaster at Syracuse in 413 that anti-democrats could even begin to envisage the subversion of the democracy as a practicable objective; and even then those extremists had to take care to put down a thick smoke-screen to conceal their true objective so as to have any hope of securing the support of what we may call 'moderate' Athenians. When we see the oligarchic revolutionaries of 411 themselves acknowledging the widespread unpalatability of oligarchy at Athens, who are we to question or contradict them? And the quick demise of their hopes, although they were led by able, well-organized, cunning, ruthless, and unscrupulous men in circumstances which could scarcely have been more favourable to their enterprise, further underlines the strength of the hold which the democracy had over the vast majority of citizens of all classes and conditions. Seven years later, the brief life of the narrow oligarchy of the Thirty, which had been imposed by her enemies on a defeated and helpless Athens, attests that same truth.

As some scholars have rightly insisted, it is misleading to seek to draw over-sharp distinctions between classes and sectional interests at Athens.[1] Thucydides (2. 65. 2) observed

---

[1] See Jones, *Athenian Democracy*, 75 ff.; Forrest, 'Aristophanes' *Acharnians*'. For the 'Old Oligarch' see below, pp. 168 ff. On Athenian 'quietists' see Carter, *The Quiet Athenian*, ch. 5; Lewis, *CR* 25 (1975), 89–90.

that both rich and poor were united in their displeasure with
Pericles in 430: many ordinary Athenians had had little
enough to start with, and had lost what little they had
through the Spartan wasting of the Attic countryside which
had followed the outbreak of the war in 431, while the richer
landowners had suffered severely; all combined to vent their
resentment on the man responsible for their ills, who had
successfully urged a policy of rejection of Sparta's proposals
for a peaceful settlement and who had stubbornly resisted
any move to allow the army to leave the shelter of the Long
Walls and engage the invaders. Nor is there much to support
the superficially plausible view that the country-dwellers
were against the war, in that they suffered more, and more
directly, from the enemy incursions, while the city-dwellers
were in favour of the war because they had no farms or
orchards to abandon to sack, pillage, and neglect, and could
themselves find ready overseas markets for their products or
regular employment in the fleet and so on while enjoying all
the material advantages of the 'empire' which kept Athens
rich and powerful. The country-dwellers constituted a
majority of the citizen body (Thucydides 2. 14.2), and hence
could both influence public policy through their more
numerous representatives on the *boulê* and determine it by
their own personal votes in the *ecclêsia*, especially at the times
when for periods of several weeks on end they were crowded
within the girdle of the Long Walls during the yearly
evacuations when they sought refuge from the enemy
invasions. The reaction of the Acharnians, who lived among
the foothills of Mt. Parnes on the northern edge of the central
plain of Attica, was an eagerness to sally forth and engage the
enemy rather than sit tight and watch while their properties
were being overrun, and thus encourage the Spartans to
continue the same tactics indefinitely without any interference
(ibid. 2. 20. 4); and though during the first invasion Pericles
somehow contrived to prevent any meetings of the *ecclêsia*
itself or other semi-formal gatherings while the enemy army
was in Attica, it was not because he feared that a majority in
the *ecclêsia* would be eager to come to terms but because he
was worried that they might unwisely vote to take the field
against a superior enemy (ibid. 2. 22. 1). Only a few years

later, when Aristophanes wanted to caricature the sort of
Athenians most apt to be upset by his hero Dicaeopolis'
private and personal peace-making activities, he picked these
same Acharnians for the role: this comedy, *Acharnians*, was
staged very early in 425, that is, before the cessation of the
yearly invasions of Attica which followed Athens' capture of
a number of Spartiate hoplites on Sphacteria later that year
and the threat that they would be executed if the invasions
continued. Every Athenian shared in the distress and
privations consequent on the overcrowding within the Long
Walls (*ibid.* 2. 17) and from the Great Plague which carried
off about one-third of Athens' hoplite strength and presumably
at least as high a proportion of the other inhabitants. The
prosperity of Athens was indivisible, with the country
cultivators and craftsmen owing their well-being to the
external power of Athens as much as did the 'townees'.
(Indeed, the five demes which lay physically within the city
walls sent fewer than thirty members to the Council of Five
Hundred, the Peiraeus added a further nine, and three other
demes which we can readily class as genuinely suburban
contributed nine more, a total of forty-five or forty-six
between them. That seems to show that the registered
members of all these demes together constituted well under a
tenth of the whole citizen body.) The rich also derived a
considerable material advantage from the Athenian 'empire'
in that it gave them the opportunity to acquire profitable
property holdings in the wide areas under their city's
control.[2]

In the period of high hopes and nervous excitement which
preceded the sailing of the great expedition to Sicily in 415,
Alcibiades' political rivals seized on the scandals of the
profanation of the sacred Mysteries of Demeter and the
mutilation of the Hermae (pillars topped by a bust of the god
Hermes which stood in the streets and squares of the city)
and inflated them as part of an alleged 'plot to subvert the
democracy'. That can comfortably be dismissed as exaggerated
vilification of an ambitious, opportunistic, and distinctly
'flashy' young aristocrat unwisely disdainful of 'middle-class

---

[2] On such holdings outside Attica see Davies, *Wealth*, 55 ff.

morality' (Thucydides 6. 28. 2). At this time Alcibiades aspired to secure a position of leadership within the democracy comparable to that of his late kinsman and guardian Pericles (ibid. 6. 16. 1).

A serious reaction did, however, set in at Athens in the autumn of 413. The huge losses of men, ships, and materiel at Syracuse sapped the prestige and confidence of the 'naval commons', and their numbers too. A serious naval war flared up in the Aegean, as powerful and strategically important 'allies' broke away from their seemingly fatally wounded mistress. Athens had provoked Sparta into the open renewal of the prosecution of their war, which had been in effect in suspension for several years; and she had affronted the Persian king by the assistance which she had given to his rebel satrap Amorges. To provoke either of those two powers, let alone both at once, was an act of almost incredible rashness. Large numbers of fighting men, and especially of the citizen rowers in the fleet, were required to be abroad for much of the year, a situation which persisted until Athens' naval victory at Cyzicus in April 410. Moreover, early in 413 the Spartans and their allies had seized, fortified, and garrisoned a stronghold at Deceleia, only some twelve miles or so from Athens itself, which they held on to for the remaining nine years of the war, thereby inflicting much more damage on the Attic economy than the relatively brief annual invasions of the early years of the war (the longest of which had lasted 'about forty days' and the shortest as few as sixteen: Thucydides 2. 57. 2; 4. 6).

The first move aimed to constrict the competence of the *boulê*, the Council of Five Hundred which was the microcosm and kingpin of the democracy.[3] The people were persuaded to agree to the appointment of a special commission of ten *probouloi*, made up it seems of men aged at least forty who were to serve for an unspecified period. Aristotle (*Politics*, 1299[b]) refers to *probouloi*, and describes them as being officers characteristic of an oligarchy:

---

[3] Thucydides' account of the events of 411 is to be found in book 8 of his *History*. The *Ath. Pol.* (29–33) is very much briefer. For commentary and discussion and full refs. to recent treatments, see Gomme, *HCT* v, and Rhodes, *CAP* (ad locc.).

not a democratic body, although a *boulê* is. There must be some body of men whose duty it is to prepare business for the people in order that they may not be diverted from their own affairs. When these are few in number, the state inclines to an oligarchy—or rather, *probouloi* must always be few and therefore an oligarchic element. But, when both bodies exist in the same state, the *probouloi* are a check on the *boulê*, for the *bouleutês* is a democratic element but the *probouloi* are oligarchical.

These new Athenian *probouloi* must have superseded the *prytaneis* as the steering committee of the *boulê*, and unlike the latter they were elected and not chosen at random by the lot, nor did they change their composition month by month.

It was also probably at about this time that the *boulê* lost a number of its financial functions to an extraordinary board of *poristai* ('Providers'), which now appears for the first time. Athens was in the grip of a serious financial crisis, and their main job was evidently to overhaul all possible sources of revenue and to cut back on all but the most essential expenditure. (Unlike the *probouloi*, they may have survived the collapse of the Four Hundred, for it is possible that the prominent radical politician Cleophon served as a *poristês* for some years prior to his death in 404.[4])

It was towards the end of 412 that the physical subversion of the democracy was first discussed among some of the trierarchs and hoplites who were serving with the Athenian forces based on Samos. Alcibiades was now in exile and at the court of the Persian satrap (royal governor) of Lydia in western Asia Minor; eager to return to Athens, and well aware that that would be possible only if the existing system and its leading politicians were changed, he quickly got in touch with Peisander, one of the Samian 'activists'. He held out the bait of alliance with and assistance from Persia, provided that Athens eschewed her democracy and replaced it with a system more acceptable to Persia. The bait was taken, and Peisander sailed to Athens, where he secured the consent of a reluctant *ecclêsia* to enter into negotiations with Alcibiades and Tissaphernes. But at this point Tissaphernes had second thoughts, leaving Alcibiades high and dry and reduced to bluffing. By February 411 Peisander and his

[4] Rhodes, *CAP* 356.

associates had lost all faith in him; but they reckoned that they had passed the point of no return and must push ahead with their planned *coup d'état*. Hiding their true objective, and hammering away at the theme of Athens' urgent need for economies in non-naval and non-military expenditure, and deviously emphasizing the vital important of Persian assistance for all that they knew that it was no longer on offer, they enlisted the 'right-wing' political clubs to orchestrate a reign of terror and suspicion and to establish dominance over the *boulê* and the *ecclêsia*. The more prominent and dangerous of the radical politicians were murdered, and 'moderate' support was wooed by the publication of a lying programme to limit full citizen rights to a body of those of zeugite or higher status up to five thousand in number and to abolish state payment for civilian office. (They also meant to oversee the establishment of oligarchic governments in the subject states of the Athenian empire, although this item of their plans was not for public consumption; and at Samos itself some of the leading local politicians secretly undertook to establish an oligarchy there. Their longer-range objective was to secure a peace with Sparta.)

By about mid-May 411 Peisander was again in Athens, where he found things going well. A meeting of the *ecclêsia* was summoned, and a motion pushed through to appoint a board of drafting commissioners (*syngrapheis*), ten in number according to Thucydides, but thirty—including the ten *probouloi*—according to the *Ath. Pol.* The latter source also reports that 'many' Athenians favoured the changes because they hoped for an alliance with Persia; but it does not say that the proposers already knew that such hopes were groundless, and it fails to make any mention either of Alcibiades or of the terrorism employed to cow possible opposition.

To return to Thucydides' account: on the day fixed for receiving the report of the *syngrapheis*, the plotters had the *ecclêsia* summoned to meet, not in its normal meeting-place in the Pnyx in the centre of the city, but at Colonus, which lay just about one mile outside the city walls.[5] There the first

---

[5] The choice of Colonus is nowhere explained. Meetings of the *ecclêsia* could be and sometimes were convened elsewhere than in the Pnyx, notably in the Piraeus. But Colonus is not attested as a venue on any other occasion than this. A modern

proposal advanced was that any citizen should be free to propose any motion whatsoever with impunity, and that any move to use the *graphê paranomôn* against any motion or otherwise seek to impede it should be severely penalized. (The reason for that is clear: everything depended on maintaining the momentum and not giving anybody a chance to pause to consider and examine the proposals in detail; and a *graphê paranomôn* would have imposed a long delay while the proposals were fully examined and argued before a large popular court, which was the last thing the plotters wanted.) That agreed, the revolutionaries now partially unmasked their batteries for the first stage of their take-over: pay for civilian service should cease; five men (*proedroi*) were to be chosen, who should nominate one hundred men, who in their turn should each nominate three others to make up a new Council of Four Hundred, who were to proceed to the Council House, replacing the normal Council of Five Hundred, and rule with full powers (*autokratores*), enrolling the 'Five Thousand' full citizens at their discretion. All these proposals were advanced by Peisander, and when they had been ratified by the *ecclêsia* at Colonus the meeting closed. Thereupon the Four Hundred installed themselves in the Council House; and, although it is not clear exactly when that happened, it was clearly imperative that the old Council should be removed as quickly as possible to scotch any risk that it might constitute a focus for counteraction.

The *Ath. Pol.* (unlike Thucydides) omits to report the

suggestion that it was chosen because its location (about one mile outside the city walls) would discourage thetes from attending is implausible: we have no reason to suppose that the zeugites turned up in full battle armour, and in any case early warning would have been given of any foray by the Spartan troops from Deceleia, and an unencumbered *thês* would have been able to reach the shelter of the walls a lot faster than a panoplied hoplite! There may have been religious associations of which we are ignorant; but I believe that Colonus was chosen in order to unsettle people, to heighten their uncertainty and confusion, and get them away from their customary surroundings, the places where they usually sat, and the friends they sat with or near. A meeting at Colonus was surely bound to have that unsettling effect, and I see no reason to assume that it happened accidentally and was not deliberately intended. (There was a cult of Poseidon Hippios, who was associated with the class of the *hippeis*, located at Colonus. But little is known of this cult, and it is far from clear what connection it had with the choice of Colonus as the venue for the *ecclêsia* on this occasion.)

surely significant oddity that this crucial meeting of the *ecclêsia* was convened at Colonus (the collaboration or at least the acquiescence of a majority of the *probouloi* must have been essential for that). The proposals of the *syngrapheis* are given in some detail, and they are also credited with proposals that the only civilian officers to be paid should be the archons and the *prytaneis* of the new Council; that full citizen rights should for the duration of the war be restricted to a body of not less than five thousand, being 'those most capable of serving the state with their persons and their means'; that only the 'Five Thousand' should have the power to conclude treaties; and that ten men should be chosen from each of the ten tribes to compile the register of the 'Five Thousand'. The *Ath. Pol.* then goes on to say that the 'Five Thousand' (whose existence is now presumed) appointed one hundred men as *anagrapheis* to draw up a new constitution, and presents us with two documents which purport to be (*a*) a permanent constitution for the future, and (*b*) a provisional constitution for the present. These two constitutions are then said to have been ratified by the whole body (*plêthos*) of the Athenian people, with the new Council of Four Hundred superseding the old Council of Five Hundred towards the end of June 411.

That account simply does not hold water. Towards the end, the *Ath. Pol.* (32. 3) notes that the Five Thousand 'were chosen only in name', thereby coming into line with Thucydides (8. 92. 11), who is emphatic that they were always merely a phantom paper body. Evidently such a body cannot have 'appointed' constitutional commissioners, as *Ath. Pol.* has just said they had. Moreover, the two 'constitutions' themselves are highly suspect documents, bitty and scrappy, and have commanded little credence among modern scholars. Some indeed have been inclined to believe that (*a*) may be genuine in the sense that it was ratified by the Five Thousand when the Five Thousand became a reality after the collapse of the Four Hundred in autumn 411: some of its features are then found in existence, but its terms would have made it impossible for anyone to be a *stratêgos* more often than one year in every four, which is something which Alcibiades and his associates on Samos would surely never have accepted, and which makes little practical sense in time of war, when those best fitted for command ought surely not to be disqualified from regular reappointment; even more damning, its provision for a Council of Four Hundred cannot fit that later context, since the restoration of a Council of Five Hundred was emphatically demanded by the forces on Samos, and on top of that the only reasonable inference to be drawn from the decree of Demophantos (Andocides, *De mysteriis*, 96), which was carried shortly after the restoration of the full democracy following the naval victory at Cyzicus and which refers to 'the Council of Five Hundred chosen by lot', is that this long-winded way of referring to the regular Council of Five Hundred was used to differentiate it from an earlier Council of the same number under the régime of the Five Thousand which had been chosen in some other way, not from a Council of Four Hundred. If these two 'constitutions' were ever formally approved—which is extremely doubtful—it can scarcely have been in anything other than some 'hole-and-corner' and distinctly irregular fashion.

Thucydides' statement that the critical meeting took place at Colonus is surely correct; and his ascription of the Colonus proposals to Peisander is not in conflict with the *Ath. Pol.* if we make the easy assumption that Peisander acted as the spokesman for the *syngrapheis*. In general, we have good reason to suppose that what happened at Colonus had been carefully pre-arranged, whatever forms it was dressed up in. In his account Thucydides makes no mention of a proposal to limit full citizen rights to the Five Thousand; but his use of the definite article (8. 67. 3) implies it, and he has already mentioned them as part of the oligarchic programme of deception and misdirection (8. 65. 3). Thucydides had a penchant for cutting through façades to realities: probably the proposal was at least aired at Colonus, but ignored by him because he knew that it was never seriously intended that it should be implemented—for him, it was nothing but a fraud to win support and allay fears, as he makes abundantly plain throughout his account.[6]

---

[6] Aristotle is in complete harmony with Thucydides on this, for he too asserts (*Politics*, 1304[b]) that the Four hundred relied on a programme of deception to hide their true plans and win control.

Meanwhile, on Samos the oligarchs' plans had misfired, thanks in large measure to the energetic action of Thrasylus and Thrasybulus, whose influence over the Athenian servicemen on the island became considerable. There was understandably a strong move to sail to Athens and rectify the situation there before it was too late; but that would have meant abandoning the eastern Aegean to the enemy, who were present in force. The impulse was restrained only with some difficulty, and it was in this tense and confused situation that Thrasybulus persuaded the men to recall Alcibiades, who was a personal friend of his, in the hope that he could detach Tissaphernes from the Spartans and win him over to their side. (Unlike Peisander and his friends, the Athenians on Samos had not been disabused about Alcibiades' ability to influence the satrap.) It was a desperate decision, but it seemed to be the only chance left: the Athenian fleet could not abandon Samos without sacrificing that important base (and much else besides) to the enemy fleet, which was being funded by Tissaphernes; and a Persian fleet which eventually numbered just under 150 ships was itself not far off at Aspendus and believed to be on its way to join the Spartans. So Alcibiades was recalled to Samos, and on his arrival deliberately exaggerated his influence with Tissaphernes for a variety of reasons (some more creditable than others) and to such good effect that he was elected *stratêgos* and given overall command.

Further representatives had reached Samos from the Four Hundred at Athens, but they made no headway; indeed they exacerbated the tension among men who were worried about the safety of their families and fearful that the city itself might be betrayed, disturbed as they were by the rumours they had heard of what was going on there. Alcibiades, however, was in the uniquely fortunate position of having been privy to the plans of the oligarchs before they had at last washed their hands of him; hence he knew that all their talk about the 'Five Thousand' and 'moderate' and 'temporary' adjustments to the constitution was simply a deception to cozen people along until the Four Hundred were securely in control, while concealing the smallness of their support. (Five thousand was a comfortingly large number, and until a list was published nobody knew whether or not his neighbour was in on the secret, which undermined any move to concert resistance.) He was accordingly admirably placed to strike directly at this chink in the oligarchs' armour. In the name of the servicemen on Samos, he declared that they had no objection to the proposed institution of the Five Thousand, but that the Four Hundred must dissolve themselves forthwith, and the Council of Five Hundred be re-established; any economies that could assist the war effort would be welcomed. He thereby grasped the main counters in the game: he was himself the middleman for Persian co-operation (or, at any rate, non-intervention), of which the oligarchs had made so much, and no sensible person could be blind to the urgent need to find money for the armed forces at this critical time; if the inescapable consequence of that need was a temporary suspension of payment for civilian services, it followed that civil offices would have to be restricted to those able to perform them without being paid. The Four Hundred could not reject or resist these demands from Samos without confessing the hollowness and duplicity of their own publicly proclaimed aims, and thereby losing that wider support without which they could not continue in power. Quite simply, a bold and cunning bluff had been called by the one man among their opponents who knew for certain that it was only a bluff.

The resolve of the anti-democrats at once began to crumble, and splits opened in their ranks. The die-hards among them decided that it was time to cut their losses and surrender to Sparta on any terms so long as they could remain in power at Athens; others left the sinking ship, most notably Theramenes and Aristocrates, and flexibly set about making the 'Five Thousand' a reality. The final collapse came in September 411, when many of the extremists sought sanctuary with the Spartans at Deceleia. A 'moderate' administration was set up under the guidance of Theramenes, with full citizen rights restricted to those who were registered as prepared to hold civil office without payment. The Council of Five Hundred was restored, but its (unpaid) members were not appointed by lot.

This 'blend of the many and the few' has acquired

considerable éclat because of the praise given to it by Thucydides (8. 97. 2); but there is disagreement among modern scholars about the precise nature of the system which he commended. His description of it here is no more than summary, and hence open to different interpretations; and, sadly, his *History* breaks off abruptly soon afterwards (at 8. 109), leaving us with no more guidance from his pen. (*Ath. Pol.* 33 contents itself with a curt paraphrase which does no more than clumsily parrot what Thucydides had written.)

It was long accepted without serious challenge that under this administration the 'Five Thousand' alone exercised the public rights of citizenship (most notably those of holding public office and voting in the *ecclêsia*), while the rest of the citizens were left with only the private rights. That consensus was challenged by G. E. M. de Ste Croix in a powerful article published in 1956.[7] After a careful re-examination of the available evidence he concluded that in the period between the collapse of the Four Hundred in autumn 411 and the restoration of the old democracy in early summer 410 all citizens retained the right to vote, but eligibility to hold public offices (*archai*), including membership of the Council, was restricted to a limited number, notionally five thousand, who could afford to serve without remuneration. Despite the objections which have been offered to it, that thesis remains in my view the correct one. From the beginning, the revolutionaries had laid great emphasis on the overriding need to cut back non-essential expenditure, on *euteleia* or 'prudent economy'; and the natural and unique connection of such a programme was with the suspension of state payment for civilian office and not with any limitation of the numbers entitled to vote in the *ecclêsia*, since state payment for attendance at the *ecclêsia* had never been made hitherto and was first introduced only several years later after the end of the war. The emphasis on *euteleia* is found at the start of the whole business (Thucydides 8. 4), and persists right down to the point where the Athenian forces on Samos declared that 'they had no objection to the Five Thousand holding office

---

[7] 'The Constitution of the Five Thousand'. For criticisms of his arguments see Rhodes, 'The Five Thousand in the Athenian Revolutions of 411 BC'; Gomme, *HCT* v. 323–5. For a brief defence see Stockton, *CR* 31 (1981), 182–4.

(*archein*) . . . and were very much in favour of making any financial savings designed to produce more money for the operations of war' (ibid. 8. 86. 6). A parallel emphasis on the urgent need to narrow eligibility for public office is also prominent in Thucydides' account, from Peisander's original proposal to limit offices (*archai*) to the better-off citizens (8. 53. 3) to the cry raised some months later for 'all those who wanted the Five Thousand to hold office (*archein*) instead of the Four Hundred' to rally to overthrow the Four Hundred (8. 92. 11). Whatever the Four Hundred had had in mind, the need for such retrenchment was obvious and urgent: it was not their suggested remedy that was deceptive—in itself it was starkly compelling, which is what the oligarchs were counting on to make the headway they did make; the deception lay quite simply in the fact that they had no intention of applying their advertised remedy, because the system that did emerge when it was actually applied was much too far short of oligarchy and much too close to full democracy for their taste. As Thucydides put it, the overthrow of the Four Hundred and the realization of the Five Thousand marked 'the end of oligarchy and civil conflict (*stasis*) at Athens' (8. 98. 4).

Full democracy was restored towards the end of the archon-year 411/10, soon after the naval victory at Cyzicus in April or May 410 had for the time being restored Athenian supremacy in the Aegean and eased the immediate financial crisis. It was certainly working by the first month of the archon-year 410/9 (July 410), when the securely datable decree carried on the motion of Demophantos required every Athenian to swear loyalty to it.[8] In the third month of this year the two-obol payment (*diôbelia*) was being made, probably a grant to distressed citizens with no other means of support; whatever it was, the provision of public moneys for anything other than active service was contrary to the principle of retrenchment embodied in the 'government of the Five Thousand'.[9]

It is plain that there is a major conflict between our two surviving continuous accounts of the events of 411.

[8] Andocides 1. 96. For the date of this decree see Meiggs and Lewis, *GHI* 258.
[9] *GHI* 260.

Thucydides describes a *coup d'état*, accompanied by thuggery, murder, intimidation, and deceit; but the *Ath. Pol.* presents us with a constitutional reform carried through with every propriety, and achieves that result not so much by misstating or inventing facts as by *suppressio veri* and *suggestio falsi*. To put it in a nutshell, either Thucydides (who was contemporary with these events, although as an exile he was not himself present in Athens or Samos at the time) has invented or swallowed some gross lies, or the author of the *Ath. Pol.* (which was written some eighty years later) has omitted some truths. The choice is obvious: behind the account in the *Ath. Pol.* there must lie a source or sources which produced an apologist and 'white-washing' version; and there are two candidates who stand out, the Atthidographer Androtion and the politician-orator Antiphon.

Androtion had written his *Attic History* (*Atthis*), which now survives only in a few scattered citations, at some time after he was exiled from Athens in 350. His work was certainly known to the author of the *Ath. Pol.* His father, Andron, had been one of the Four Hundred, and hence the son may well have wanted to exculpate him. As for Antiphon, he was a leading member of the Four Hundred, who did not escape to the Spartans at Deceleia but stood trial for treason, was convicted, and executed. The outstanding forensic speaker of his day, his speech in his own defence was renowned in antiquity; Thucydides had read it, and judged that no finer defence to a capital charge had ever been heard before (8. 68. 2). Since Antiphon did not plead guilty, and since he could not possibly deny his prominent involvement in the Four Hundred (which was public knowledge), his only possible defence was to deny that they had been aiming to establish an oligarchic régime at Athens; and that theme is borne out by the handful of broken lines from his speech (fr. B 1) which have survived. Like all ancient orators, he was a master of the art of confusing issues, and far better at it than most. It is attractive to suppose that whoever wrote the *Ath. Pol.* was taken in by a professional illusionist.

The events of 411 are excellent evidence of the strength of the hold which the democracy had at Athens. At a time of acute crisis and with the possibility of defeat staring the

Athenians in the face after their appalling losses in Sicily; with the appearance in the Aegean of a powerful enemy fleet and a number of Athens' more important 'allies' in revolt and affording ships, men, money, supplies, and bases to assist its operations; with the renewed activity of a Persia poised to intervene decisively with ships and subsidies; with a bankrupt treasury (the last 'supreme emergency' special reserve of 1,000 talents had had to be released early in 412, and had been exhausted within one year: Thucydides 8. 15. 1, 8. 76. 6); and with an anti-democratic movement ably led and cunningly and ruthlessly executed—with all that in their favour, the plotters clearly perceived that their only chance of succeeding lay in violence and intimidation, and above all in the lying pretence that they aimed at no more than a limited change designed to concentrate resources on the conduct of the war and to last only for the duration of the emergency. Within a few months the Four Hundred had collapsed, and the moderate régime of the Five Thousand which took their place endured for no more than a further eight months at most.

Nevertheless, 411 bred consequences which were to have a divisive and debilitating effect on Athens' conduct of a war which was not yet irretrievably lost. Knives were unsheathed as scores were settled; men were heavily fined, or wholly or partly deprived of their citizen rights. As Lysias (30. 7) subsequently wryly observed, to judge by the number of those alleged to have been members of the Four Hundred there must have been nearly a thousand of them! Athens was not only divided, she was also pickling a·rod for her own back against the day when Sparta's final victory in 404 was to give frightened and embittered men the opportunity to get their revenge.

Under the command of the brilliant and charismatic Alcibiades, Athens' navy began to pull away from near disaster. The serious defeat which it inflicted on the Spartan fleet at Cyzicus restored confidence and eased the financial crisis a little. But the restoration of the full democracy shortly afterwards and the reintroduction of state payment for civilian services could not but exacerbate the financial difficulties, and Alcibiades' enemies had not been reconciled to him. For the moment he was too popular and successful to be attacked directly, but they could seek to hamper him: they starved him of money and reinforcements to follow up his victory at Cyzicus and secure the Hellespont, the life-line of Athens. [10] Byzantium was not recaptured until the autumn of 408; and in the following spring the Persians at last came down off the fence and committed their vast resources to the whole-hearted support of Sparta. As Alcibiades' string of successes tailed off, the recollection of his erstwhile opportunism and self-centred treachery (he had taken himself off to Sparta when recalled from the early stages of the Sicilian expedition, and given her unstinted and expert help against his mother city, and then worked hand in glove with the Four Hundred in the early stages of their activity) became more vivid. After his failure to capture Andros, and the severe drubbing which his fleet received from the Spartan admiral Lysander in his absence, he was relieved of his command, and once again took himself off into exile. One last naval victory was won by Athens at Arginusae in 406, but the end was near.

Arginusae is a black mark on the Athenian democracy. Losses in ships and men had been heavy, and rightly or wrongly the conviction spread that many of the crews of the twenty-five warships which had gone down could have been rescued if only the *stratêgoi* had shown more energy and efficiency. Feelings ran high, and the eight men who had commanded at Arginusae were arraigned before the *ecclêsia*; two of them had made themselves scarce, but the other six (among them Thrasylus, one of the leaders of the 'counter-revolution' on Samos in 411, and Pericles, son of the great Pericles) were condemned to death and their property escheated to the state. The nastiest feature of the proceedings was a departure from accepted practice which meant that the accused were tried *en bloc* without each being able to present an individual defence. By a curious coincidence, Socrates was one of the *prytaneis* presiding over the *ecclêsia*, and he stoutly

[10] Andrewes, 'The Generals in the Hellespont 410–407 BC'.

objected to this irregularity. But the enraged assembly was not to be denied.[11]

The incident shows the democracy in an ugly light. But sweeping condemnations are out of place. Athens' plight was desperate, and nerves were unstrung as the outlook grew bleaker and defeat more likely. The irregularities were untypical; and those who want to use them to condemn the whole system would do well to remember that instances of cavalier injustice are more frequently encountered under less broadly based systems. The 'trial of the generals' pales into insignificance against the background of the murderous excesses of 'the Thirty', to look no further afield than fifth-century Athens herself.

In the late summer of 405 the Spartan Lysander's doggedly correct strategy of attrition bore fruit when Athens' last fleet, incompetently commanded and dispirited, starved of money and supplies, was surprised and overwhelmed at Aegospotami: of its 180 triremes, a bare twenty managed to escape. As the noose was drawn tighter round the throat of her supply routes, Athens was starved into surrender within a matter of months.

Sparta had no love for democracies, and Lysander himself was all for very narrow oligarchies. Athens was obliged to readmit her exiles. Intimidated by Lysander and an occupying garrison in the Piraeus, the *ecclêsia* was constrained to authorize the establishment of a commission of thirty men to draft new laws. They were in control by about midsummer 404, and appointed a new Council of Five Hundred and a special commission of ten to supervise the dangerously radical port of Piraeus. They also packed the eleven-man 'police commission' with their own sympathizers, headed by the thuggish Satyros. A number of citizens, among them generals and junior officers, had a little earlier formed a plot to try to stave off the extremists; they had been betrayed and arrested, and were now given a trumpery trial before the new Council and executed out of hand.

To begin with the Thirty masked their extremism. Their

[11] For Arginusae and the trial see Xenophon, *Hellenica*, 1. 6–7; Diodorus Siculus 13. 98–103; for discussion and refs. to recent literature see Andrewes, 'The Arginusae Trial'.

early destruction of the laws of Ephialtes can have been little more than symbolic, for it is plain that they would never have been content simply to return to the pre-Ephialtic system. Returned exiles, prominent among them Critias (one of the Four Hundred, who had taken himself off to Thessaly), were well represented among the Thirty; not surprisingly, some of the more active of the professional accusers who had been busy since 411 were put to death. During the autumn of 404, to safeguard their next moves, a Spartan garrison of 700 arrived in Athens; the cost of maintaining it fell on the Thirty, at whose request it had been sent, and was met by further condemnations and confiscations.

Theramenes had negotiated Athens' surrender and the peace treaty. Like Critias, he had been a member of the Four Hundred; but, unlike him, he had got out in time and had then played a prominent part in Athenian politics for the rest of the war. He is not an easy man to fathom; his shifts and changes earned him the sobriquet of 'Mr Facing-both-ways', but whether he was simply a selfish opportunist or a flexible and realistic 'moderate' it is now impossible to determine. Whichever he was, he set out to challenge Critias' dominance among the Thirty. His opposition to the invitation of the Spartan garrison, whose presence in Athens gave Critias and his friends the confidence to step up the tempo of terror and executions, had proved unavailing; and, to his objection that the government was too narrowly based, Critias responded by drawing up a list of three thousand citizens who alone should have full rights, including the right of trial before the Council: anybody not on that list could be executed without trial on the order of the Thirty. Theramenes still stubbornly maintained that three thousand were too few to constitute a secure basis for a lasting oligarchy; Critias countered by calling a general muster and then by a simple ruse separating all but the three thousand from their weapons, which were removed and stored under guard on the Acropolis.

Now free from any constraint; the Thirty extended their *pogrom* of murder and sequestrations yet more widely. Among their projects was one to single out thirty of the richest metics (resident aliens) for execution and give their property to each of themselves. Theramenes refused point-blank to have any part in it, and Critias moved in for the kill. Theramenes was arraigned before the Council of Five Hundred; and when his spirited defence threatened to win them over Critias, backed by a gang of armed men, formally struck his name from the list of the three thousand. The Council was too frightened to resist, and Theramenes was led off to be executed 'by order of the Thirty'. He made a good end: as he drained the fatal cup of hemlock, as if making a toast at a wine-party among friends, he tossed the last drop away saying, 'Here's to the health of our dear Critias!'

All except the three thousand were now debarred from the city itself, and men were expelled from their farms, which were then given to the extremists and their supporters. Many Athenians fled the country, and found refuge in neighbouring Thebes and Megara. Sparta had either instructed or urged her allies not to harbour such refugees, but these two cities along with a number of others had been unhappy about Spartan policy since Athens' surrender, and were probably apprehensive about their own future relations with a reassertively over-confident Sparta. Alcibiades was now dead; but the counter-revolution found a leader in Thrasybulus, who had been prominent in the democratic reaction against the Four Hundred on Samos eight years earlier. With a mere seventy men he crossed the border from Boeotia and seized the small fort at Phylae near the frontier. Bad weather impeded counter-moves, and his forces quickly increased tenfold as more and more volunteers came in. Surprising the opposition, he scattered their troops and marched to the Piraeus, where he fortified the hill of Mounychia. The Thirty took fright, and began to prepare a bolt-hole at Eleusis, many of whose inhabitants were seized and executed. A frontal attack on the Mounychia position was beaten back, and among the dead were Critias himself and Charmides, one of the Piraeus Commission of Ten. (Charmides was an uncle of the philosopher Plato, and Critias a cousin of Plato's mother: both of them were prominent members of the circle which gathered around Socrates.) The Thirty were deposed, but allowed to retire to Eleusis with their supporters; they were replaced by an even smaller executive, 'the Ten', who had the backing of a majority of the three thousand at Athens. But

Thrasybulus' numbers kept on growing, and with money, weapons, and mercenaries supplied by sympathetic states he began an active siege of the city itself.

Lysander managed to secure a large loan from Sparta for the oligarchs to hire mercenaries, together with authority for his own brother, who was currently in command of the Spartan naval forces, to blockade the Piraeus. That should have settled the issue; but internal divisions within Sparta itself, dimly discernible hitherto, finally broke surface. Quite a few Spartans were dubious about Lysander's policies, and also apprehensive about his personal power and pretensions. One of the two kings, Pausanias, secured authority to lead a powerful force to Athens, where he quickly imposed himself on both factions and secured himself a mandate to settle terms for a reconciliation with the assistance of a fifteen-man commission from Sparta.

The details of the settlement are recorded in *Ath. Pol. 39*. Leaving aside some minor puzzles which this and other accounts present,[12] it can be summarized as follows.

Eleusis was recognized as a separate and autonomous entity, except that its temple of Demeter and the associated celebration of the Sacred Mysteries were to be common ground for all the inhabitants of Attica. Any of the men who were holding out in Athens against the Thrasybulan forces could choose to settle at Eleusis, while retaining his private citizenship rights and his private property; a fixed time-limit was set for this, and once settled and registered at Eleusis a man forfeited eligibility to hold any public office at Athens. But undoubtedly the most striking feature of the settlement was its provision for a general amnesty, which covered everybody except (*a*) those who had committed murder by their own hand, (*b*) the Thirty themselves, and the Ten who had succeeded them, (*c*) the Commission of Ten for the Piraeus, and (*d*) the 'police commission' of Eleven; and even those in categories (*b*) to (*d*) were to be covered by the amnesty should they be ready to submit to a full inquiry into their conduct in the office in question, the Piraeus Commissioners before a Piraeus-recruited court, and the rest

---

[12] On these see Rhodes, *CAP* (ad loc.).

before a special court composed of citizens above a given property qualification. Provision was also made for sorting out the tangle of property titles produced by the public confiscations, private pocket-lining, and forced or sham sales of recent months; but that was understandably beset by great or even insuperable difficulties—Thrasybulus himself was one of those who felt constrained generously or resignedly to accept the loss of considerable private property, so Isocrates (18. 23) tells us.

A provisional executive of twenty men took over, and oversaw the institution of a new Council of Five Hundred and the appointment of other public officers: a new eponymous archon, Eukleides, was in office from about October 403. The revision and codification of the laws, which had been begun in 411/10, was resumed and brought to completion within a year or so. But, although the heroes of the counter-revolution or their dependants were variously honoured or rewarded, moves to confer full citizenship on non-citizen loyalists were either rejected or drastically curtailed.[13] Archinus, one of the small band which had first seized and held Phylae, emerged as a leading political figure. When a disgruntled loyalist tried to start a prosecution in breach of the amnesty and of his own oath to observe it, Archinus had him charged before the Council and condemned to death; he also got a law passed that any man who claimed that he was being charged in contravention of the amnesty could have that issue decided first, and that if it were decided in his favour the substantive charge should be disallowed. Such reassurances he reinforced by truncating the time limit for moving to Eleusis, which left quite a number of people with no option but to stay in Athens. A proposal to restrict full citizenship to those above a fairly modest minimum property level was voted down. And two or three years later, in the archon-year 401/400, a combination of military strength and diplomacy, assisted by the execution of the commanders of the Eleusinian forces, effected the reincorporation of Eleusis within the Athenian state, with a solemn undertaking 'to let bygones be bygones'.

---

[13] For details and discussion see Rhodes, *CAP* 474–8.

On top of crippling losses of life in battle against the enemy and in civil war, Athens had suffered terribly from disease and famine, violent disruption and brutal insecurity. Her citizens were stricken with all the despondency and disillusion that are the natural concomitants of losing a long war and a great empire. A yearning to forget the past, to try to pick up the pieces and get back to some sort of regular and reliable normality, was only to be expected. For all that, it is not so much the moderation of the settlement (which owed a great deal to Sparta's moderating influence over all the parties to it) but rather the honesty with which the amnesty was observed in the years that followed which constitutes an achievement of which any society could be justifiably proud. The Athenians were certainly not saints; and for decades to come we find men anxious to win favour or avoid unpopularity by dissociating themselves or their families from any part in the excesses of the anti-democrats.[14] As many as sixty years later, Aeschines is heard insisting that his father, still alive at the age of ninety-four, had left Athens under the Thirty and helped in the restoration of the democracy. Their experiences in 411 and 404/3 had left the overwhelming bulk of the Athenians with a decided taste for their democratic system. Isocrates averred that, while the shortcomings of the earlier democratic politicians had made even the *dêmos* itself favourably inclined towards the ideas of the Four Hundred, the mad excesses of the Thirty had made everyone even more enthusiastic for democracy than the small band who had first seized Phylae. Plato, who was anything but a believer in or apologist for democracy, himself wrote that the rule of the Thirty (among whom two of his own close relatives had been prominent) had had the effect of making the democracy which had preceded it seem in retrospect like a Golden Age.[15] Democracy was never

---

[14] When Socrates was tried and sentenced to death in 399 on a charge of 'introducing strange gods and corrupting young men', his earlier close association with the like of Critias and Charmides can have done him no good.

[15] Aeschines 2. 78, 2. 147; Isocrates 8. 108; Plato, *Letters*, 7, 324 D. Jones (*The Athenian Democracy*, 54) observes, and with justice, that 'When one reads [the] record of the doings of the Thirty, one cannot but be amazed at the steadfast forbearance of the Athenian people.'

again threatened during the next eighty years; and in 321 it
was not any internal movement but the irresistible military
might of Macedon which brought it down.[16]

[16] For an account of Athens after the end of the democracy see Fergusson,
Hellenistic Athens. Rhodes, *AB*, describes the role and functions of the *boulê* in the
post-democratic period.

6

CRITICS AND CHAMPIONS

A. H. M. Jones began his essay on 'The Athenian Democracy and its Critics' with the observation that 'It is curious that in the abundant literature produced in the greatest democracy of Greece there is no statement of democratic political theory'; and he went on to list among its critics the 'Old Oligarch', Socrates, Thucydides, Plato, and Aristotle. Aristotle 'is the most judicial in his attitude, and states the pros and cons, but his ideal was a widely based oligarchy'. For Jones, among the historians

> only Herodotus is a democrat, but his views have not carried much weight, partly because of his reputation for naiveté, and partly because his explicit evidence refers to a period before the full democracy had evolved. Thucydides is hostile: in one of the very few passages in which he reveals his personal views he expresses approval of a régime which disfranchised about two-thirds of the citizens, those who manned the fleet on which the survival of Athens depended.[1]

The last reference is to Thucydides' commendation (8. 97) of the government of the Five Thousand which followed the overthrow of the Four Hundred. But G. E. M. de Ste Croix has argued, contrary to Jones's assumption, that under the Five Thousand all the citizens retained their right to vote in the *ecclêsia*, although eligibility to hold public office was restricted to those among them who were registered as willing and able to serve without remuneration, so as to reduce civil expenditure at a time when the city's funds were desperately low and the fleet and the army had to be given the highest priority in any claim on them. If that is correct (as I believe it is), it places Thucydides' judgement in a very

---

[1] Jones, *The Athenian Democracy*, 41. (Jones takes it that Aristotle wrote the *Ath. Pol.* as well as the undoubtedly genuine *Politics*—on which point see above, p. 2.)

different light.[2] And certainly the account which he gives us in his eighth book of the plans and activities of the Four Hundred themselves is not at all what we should expect from the pen of a man who sympathized with, or approved of, their motives, aims, or methods.

In a famous passage (3. 80–2) Herodotus represented Otanes, Megabyzus, and Darius as debating what would be the best form of government for the Persians (in the end, Darius became the King of Persia in 521). Whatever the historical truth of this supposed discussion, nobody seriously doubts that, in the form in which Herodotus presents it, it reflects Greek thinking of the mid-fifth century or thereabouts. Otanes deplored the arbitrariness, irresponsibility, and inconsistency of monarchy; he favoured the rule of the 'multitude' for its equality for all under the law ('*isonomia*, most beautiful of all words'), for its assigning public offices by lot, for the accountability of those officers, for the fact that all proposals had to be submitted to a general assembly of the people for discussion and decision. Megabyzus agreed with Otanes about the defects of one-man rule, but held that nothing was more foolish and hybristic than a useless mob, which lacks true knowledge; no, what was best was that the best and wisest men should rule, a true aristocracy. Darius agreed with Megabyzus about democracy; but oligarchies breed ambitious rivalries and faction; in the end, both democracy and oligarchy or aristocracy dissolve into chaos, and engender monarchy; nothing is better than that one man, the wisest and best, should rule with justice and firmness, concealing his plans from any enemies.

One would be hard put to it to divine Herodotus' personal position from that. Herodotus was born about 490, and died about 425 or so. His family belonged to the local nobility of Halicarnassus in western Asia Minor, but he early left that

---

[2] See above, p. 153. Andrewes (*HCT* v. 331–9) concludes, rightly in my opinion, that 'what Thucydides was commending here was the actual conduct of Athenian affairs by the Five Thousand rather than any particular constitutional form'. For all that, many people have read into his words here a commendation of oligarchy. Thus Popper (*The Open Society and its Enemies*, i. 155) could write: 'Although [Thucydides] did not belong to the extremist wing of the Athenian oligarchic clubs who conspired *throughout the war* with the enemy, he was *certainly a member* of the oligarchic party' (my italics). For the latter assertion there is no evidence whatsoever.

town for Samos, and thereafter travelled widely, spending
some time in Athens, and then joined the colony which
Athens planted at Thurii in South Italy in 444/3, where most
probably he died and was buried. His own political views are
opaque to us. He was certainly on the side of freedom as
against despotism (5. 78); and in a famous paragraph (7. 139)
he paid a sincere and glowing tribute to the major part which
Athens had played in saving Greece from conquest by Persia.
But his attitude to democracy as such is irrecoverable.
'Herodotus, it would appear, was politically too moderate to
be an idealogue'; and, so far as we can discern, his political
convictions were compatible with a fairly wide spectrum of
Greek polities. Even the arguments adduced for his alleged
admiration of Pericles himself are far from cogent.[3]

Nobody doubts that Thucydides was an admirer of
Pericles, even perhaps in some respects an insufficiently
critical admirer. As a young man, he had lived through the
golden years of Pericles' confident supremacy; and he held a
low opinion of most if not all of the men who emerged as
rivals for leadership after Pericles' death in 429.[4] He held the
view (and who would not agree with him?) that the lack of
firm and capable leadership could bring out weaknesses in a
democratic system. But all through his *History* his analytical
insight identifies with magisterial objectivity the weaknesses
latent in other societies as well. Thucydides was no Plato, he
constructed no ideal system; he very probably did not believe
that any such system could exist. He was explicitly hostile to
the likes of such populist politicians as Cleon and Hyperbolus;
but there is nothing in his work to indicate that he was a
doctrinaire adherent of any system. One may suspect that his
taste was in practice for moderation in such matters; but that
does not make him an anti-democrat or a supporter of
oligarchy. His superb excursus on the civil dissension at

[3] The quotation is from Fornara, *Herodotus: An Interpretative Essay*, 49. Chapter 3
of that book contains excellent criticism of modern efforts to pin political labels on
to Herodotus.
[4] The date of Thucydides' birth is unknown. He must have been at least thirty
when he was a *stratêgos* in 424. He is generally taken to have been born about 460.
For his comments on Pericles' successors see below, p. 180. For instances of specific
and explicit hostility to individual 'demagogues' see Thucydides 3. 36. 6; 4. 21. 3; 4.
28. 5; 4. 39. 3; 5. 16. 1 (Cleon); and 8. 73. 3 (Hyperbolus).

Corcyra (3. 82–4) is impartial in its reprehension of all extremists, whether of the 'left' or of the 'right'. His view of the human condition is bleak and uncomfortable; in the jungle of inter-state relations it is the strong who dictate to the weak, and moral justifications for the actions of states are either absent or irrelevant or hypocritical. In Plato's *Republic* Thrasymachus defined 'justice' as 'the interest of the stronger'; whatever he may have thought 'justice' ought to be, Thucydides would surely have agreed with Thrasymachus (as, again, we all should) at least to this extent, that all too often in the real world in which we live and move and have our being that is the way that 'justice' works, or how its meaning is perverted. He had no time for cant and shallow slogans.[5]

Nevertheless, he does present us with the most famous surviving encomium on the Athenian democracy in the shape of the 'Funeral Oration', the public speech which Pericles gave in honour of the Athenians who had died in the first operations of the war against Sparta and her allies which broke out in 431. It offers us a picture of what we may call the 'positive' face of the democracy. To that we shall return before long. But let us first consider what may be termed its 'negative' face as it is delineated in the pseudo-Xenophontic *Constitution of Athens*.

The 'Old Oligarch', to give the author of this *opusculum* his convenient and now conventional (though misleading) sobriquet, wrote his little essay (it is only just over a dozen pages long) at some date between the late 440s and the late 420s. He was evidently an Athenian, but his identity is unknown; the fact that his work has been transmitted to us as part of the corpus of the works of the well-known Xenophon could suggest that he bore the same name (which would help to explain the confusion), and may even have been a somewhat older member of the same family, an uncle or cousin for instance—the tone and content of his essay indicate that he must have been born

---

[5] Plato, *Republic*, I, 338 C. Aristotle wrote (*Politics*, 1318b): 'Equality and justice are always sought by the weaker party, but those who have power pay no heed to them.' De Ste Croix (*The Origins of the Peloponnesian War*, 5–34) is excellent on this aspect of Thucydides' thinking.

into a comparable upper-class, well-educated, and politically interested milieu.[6]

It is at least debatable whether Jones and others are right in seeing the 'Old Oligarch' as an anti-democrat. It is clear from the variety of views which have been held about him that any reader's reactions are almost bound to be to some extent subjective: our total ignorance of who the writer was and what in particular led him to put pen to paper gives us no marks to steer by, and one reader may see humour or irony where another discerns high seriousness. Nor can we begin to say how much of his argument was original to him, or how far he was merely parroting other people's ideas. To me, his work reads like that of a reasonably clever young man who has sat, not without some profit, at the feet of the sophists, with patches of acuity and insight intermingled with mediocre commonplaces in a somewhat disorganized pattern, concerned rather more with exposing the weaknesses of the arguments of current opponents of the democracy than with excoriating its defects—neither old nor an oligarch.[7]

The main theme of the work is perfectly clear from the start, and can be summarized as follows:

'I am not going to praise the Athenian system as an ideally good system. For my present purpose that is neither here nor there, and any one who starts from that position will get nowhere. What I want to do is simply to show that it is very well designed to do the job which the Athenians wish it to do, that it "delivers the goods". Only if you start by asking what it is that the Athenians themselves want to achieve by their present system, and how effectively they achieve it, will you begin to understand the Athenian democracy. It is not designed or intended to produce an end result which a

---

[6] For recent treatments of these contested points see: Gomme, *More Essays in Greek History and Literature*, 36–89; Frisch, *The Constitution of the Athenians*; Bowersock, 'Pseudo-Xenophon', 33–8.

[7] Popper (*The Open Society and its Enemies*, i. 164) describes the work as 'a ruthless attack on Athens, written no doubt by one of her best brains'! Much nearer the mark is Forrest (*The Emergence of Greek Democracy*, 224–6): 'There is nothing old about this excited, immature undergraduate essayist . . . Far more probably he is not an oligarch at all. He is a young man who is just learning to analyse his society . . . who will, when the time comes to enter political life, accept society as it is.' See further Forrest, 'An Athenian Generation Gap'.

non-democrat would regard as ideal; if it is judged by that standard it is bound to fail—and bound to be misunderstood. The ordinary citizens of Athens, the *dêmos*, man the navy which is the source of her power. Accordingly, the *dêmos* has political control. The democracy is the way in which the *dêmos* exercises and ensures that control.'

He then proceeds to set up a number of 'Aunt Sallies' simply in order to knock them down:

A man might object that they ought not to allow any Tom, Dick, or Harry to have his say and sit on the Council, but only the best and cleverest citizens. But the Athenians are very well advised when they allow even nobodies (*ponêroi*) to have their say. For if only the 'best' people were speakers and councillors, that would be fine for them and their like but bad for the mass of ordinary citizens. As things are, the poor man who chooses to get up to speak is looking for what is good for him and his likes. You might ask: How can a low fellow like that discern what is good for himself or for the *dêmos* as a whole? But they know that this man's 'ignorance' and goodwill profit them more than the 'excellence' (*aretê*) and 'knowledge' and ill will of your 'best' people. A society with such institutions and practices may not be ideally the best, but it is thus that democracy will best be safeguarded. What you term 'lack of good government' (*ouk eunomeisthai*) is the source of the democracy's strength and freedom. If you want 'good government' (*eunomia*), then to start with you will have the best-qualified and ablest men (*dexiôtatoi*) making the laws, and the next thing will be that the 'best' people will discipline the poor, will decide state policy, and will not allow 'madmen' to determine policy or attend or address the *ecclêsia*. So all those 'good things' of yours will quickly bring the *dêmos* down to slavery.[8]

The organization of the remaining sections of this essay is distinctly clumsy, and it is sometimes very difficult to follow the author's train of thought. Various criticisms are stated, and answered: it is hard to distinguish slaves and metics from true citizens on the streets of Athens (but that is because slaves and metics are so valuable to the Athenian economy, and skilled slaves have to be given wider freedom of movement than most slaves elsewhere, who are tied to the

---

[8] 'Old Oligarch', 1. 1–9.

land); the Athenians are hostile to the upper classes in the cities of their Aegean empire (but that is because they are their enemies, while the common people of those cities are better disposed towards Athens and hence to be encouraged and supported against their own upper classes); they compel many allied citizens to come to Athens for the hearing and decision of suits in which they are involved (but that is to counter anti-Athenian bias elsewhere, and there are all the advantages of extra revenues from landing charges at the Piraeus, plus rents to lodging-house keepers and money to be earned by carters and criers—it is rather hard not to see the author as joking here—and on top of that it means that the decisions are taken by the ordinary Athenians and not by high officers of state like *stratêgoi* and envoys operating on their own out of sight of the city); yes, there are long and tedious delays in getting legal and other personal business involving public boards and officials dealt with (but, given the enormous volume of such business, the only way to avoid these delays would be to reduce the numbers of those involved in reaching each decision, and any major reduction would be bound to afford a greater opportunity for bribery and corruption); ordinary people cannot emulate, and even begrudge, the interest and activityof the cultivated classes in gymnastic and cultural pursuits (but at Athens the state makes provision for public gymnasia, shows, performances, and festivals for all to share). Overall, the author displays a sure grasp of the crucial importance of sea power in terms both of the strategic advantages which the city derives from it and of the economic gains which accrue from her secure access to a very wide range of varied and locally specialized resources in other parts of the central and eastern Mediterranean world; and he shows both explicit and implicit awareness of the truth that Athenian power rests at bottom on the broad mass of Athens' citizens. The general thrust of the initial argument is restated thus (2. 20–3. 1)

Democracy is something which, speaking personally, I quite understand the bulk of the people wanting, for everybody must be excused for wanting what is best for himself . . . It is not that I am extolling the way the Athenians order their affairs; but given that they themselves have chosen to live under a democratic system, it is my opinion that they do preserve their democracy efficiently in the way I have described.

To see the 'Old Oligarch' as sharing (as opposed to rehearsing) the objections which he counters is odd: he is answering and, to some extent at least, poking fun at them. The ideal system of the so-called 'best' people is, he points out, ideal not from any truly detached viewpoint but only in the eyes of those who expect to derive material advantage and benefit from it: lift the scales from your eyes, you anti-democrats, and you will see that ordinary people want if they can to safeguard their interests too. In his own admittedly clumsy and ill-articulated fashion, this writer shares that same detached 'amorality' which is so marked a characteristic of his near contemporary Thucydides and of some of the fifth-century sophists. Laws are laid down by those who have the power to enact them (and enforced by those who have the power to enforce them), and in laying down the laws they have regard to their own best interests. In modern times, so long as working people did not have sufficient power to compel alterations in the laws, trade unions were illegal, their agents harried, their funds insecure; once they gained sufficient power, all that changed. It would be hard, even impossible, to dispute the contention that, whatever words they may have spoken or whatever excuses they may have advanced, throughout human history those sections of any society which have enjoyed political power have invariably derived material benefit from it. They may of course pretend that things are otherwise. Cicero is as good an example as any from the ancient world. In his *De legibus* (2. 13–14) he draws a distinction between good laws and bad laws: popular assemblies, he argues, pass many pernicious and pestilential decrees which no more deserve to be called 'laws' than do compacts between bands of brigands; just as one refuses to give the name 'medical advice' to the prescriptions of ignorant quacks which kill rather than cure, so a law cannot be a true law, even if a sovereign assembly has ratified it, if it is in practice harmful. That all sounds very well, but it is quite evidently a one-sided argument.

Over one hundred and fifty years ago, in his first annual message to the Congress of the United States of America,

President Andrew Jackson had this to say in defence of the so-called 'spoils system':

There are, perhaps, few men who can for any length of time enjoy office and power without being more or less under the influence of feelings unfavourable to the faithful discharge of their public duties. Their integrity may be proof against improper considerations immediately addressed to themselves, but they are apt to acquire a habit of looking with indifference upon the public interests and of tolerating conduct from which an unpractised man would revolt. Office is considered as a species of property, and government rather as a means of promoting individual interests than as an instrument created solely for the service of the people. Corruption in some, and in others a perversion of correct feelings, divert government from its legitimate ends and make it an engine for the support of the few at the expense of the many. The duties of all public officers are, or at least admit of being made, so plain and simple that men of intelligence may readily qualify themselves for their performance; and I cannot but believe that more is lost by the long continuance in office than is generally to be gained by their experience.[9]

The 'Old Oligarch' and his fellow Athenians would surely have said Amen to that. Of course, both ancient Athens and Jacksonian America were much simpler societies than we are used to. In both, the central government was primarily concerned with what we may term the 'reserve powers' of government: the maintenance of law and order, the defence of the realm against external attack, the administration of justice, and the raising of sufficient revenue to pay for all that, along with certain other tasks like the maintenance of communications, national religious festivals, or the like. Modern Western governments stretch their tentacles far more widely and deeply—one has only to start to think of departments of education and health, trade and agriculture, energy, industry, and postal services—the list goes on and on. And the speed and efficiency of modern technology enable governments to extend the breadth and detail of their control to an extent unthinkable even a hundred years ago. No longer could a Jackson hold that any ordinary sensible man is equipped, or can readily or easily equip himself, for

---

[9] Cited by Brogan, *An Introduction to American Politics*, 288–9.

the management and oversight of such matters as fall to be managed by a modern administration and its multitudinous hierarchy of expert and experienced public servants.

I believe that the most important theme latent (indeed, sometimes patent) in the 'Old Oligarch', and what most differentiates his approach from that of Pericles in the Funeral Oration, is this: that the Athenian democracy was 'designed' (so to speak) to stop power being abused, to ensure as far as possible that no privileged individuals or groups of whatever nature should be in a position to exercise control or authority in their own interests at the expense of the interests of the majority. It may be doubted whether that was a consciously explicit aim rather than an empirical reaction to the realities of life, an instinctive agreement with Andrew Jackson. The pre-Christian world was free from a wide area of hypocrisy which has long affected later ages, when the governments and governing and possessing classes of Europe have publicly and privately subscribed to the Christian faith, and with it to a set of moral principles and a code of behaviour which put a very high premium on unselfishness and concern for both the spiritual and the material well-being of others. The ancient world was not free from hypocrisy, but it was free from that particularly insidious and widespread variety of it.

Periclean Athens was one state amongst many which shared a common language, a common culture, a common religion. Even if its inhabitants may have retained only an increasingly dim memory of what life had been like a hundred or more years earlier, the increasingly 'international' trade which passed through the Piraeus and the non-Athenian ships' crews who came ashore to eat and drink and even 'see the sights', the overseas voyages of Athenian sailors in merchantmen or men of war, the close involvement of Athens with the affairs of her Aegean 'empire' and the service of many non-Athenian Greeks in her fleets,[10] the thousands of resident aliens who had settle in Athens—all these were quite enough to keep alive the appreciation that in other cities

---

[10] Many of the sailors in the Athenian fleet at Syracuse in 415–413 were non-Athenians whose 'speech and behaviour were Athenian and who were regularly mistaken for Athenians' (Thucydides 7. 63). There is plenty of other evidence that that was a normal state of affairs.

and states of Greece which could be only thirty or forty miles away things were ordered very differently, and the bulk of the population had far less say—or even none at all—in the direction of the affairs of state or in the administration of justice. As late as 428 the government of the allied state of Mytilene which controlled most of the island of Lesbos took Mytilene into a dangerous, arduous, and unsuccessful revolt from Athens without any reference to the bulk of the population, who were not even issued with proper weapons until the situation was desperate, and who then used them to coerce 'the men in power' (*hoi dynatoi*) to share their hoarded food supplies with the large numbers whom the Athenian blockade had brought to near starvation. At that point there was nothing left for the ruling minority to do but to capitulate to the Athenians. There were about one thousand of them, that being the number which the victorious Athenians executed as 'chiefly to blame for the revolt' after Diodotus had successfully argued that the great majority of the Mytileneans bore no responsibility for the revolt and should be spared. When twelve years later the Athenians attacked the island of Melos to compel it to submit to their control, the government there refused to allow the Athenian spokesmen to address the whole people, but only the officers of state and the ruling minority; and they rejected the Athenian demands without any reference to the rest of the island's inhabitants, all of whom were in due course executed or enslaved by the victorious Athenians. More instances could be given, but these two will suffice to exemplify how lively an appreciation the ordinary Athenian (and these same general considerations apply just as much in the fourth century as in the fifth) is bound to have had of the value of that rare freedom from subordination, subservience, and manipulation and that confident sense of equality and participation which his own society guaranteed him but which were so often denied to his neighbours.[11]

Quite often the objections to, or criticisms of, the democracy which we find in the 'Old Oligarch' are found

[11] The whole story of the revolt of Mytilene is in Thucydides 3. 2–50; for the number executed see 3. 50. 1, and for Diodotus' argument 3, 47. 3. For Melos see 5. 84. 3.

repeated later. Thus, in Plato (*Republic*, 8, 563 B) we read that at Athens not only are resident aliens and foreigners on an equal footing with the citizens themselves, even slaves (both male and female) are as free as the owners who paid for them! That ridiculous statement comes in the context of Plato's claim a little earlier (8, 558 C) that democracy is a sort of 'self-indulgent anarchy', a state of affairs which rests at bottom on the false assumption that 'equality means equality for equals and unequals alike', whereas true equality involves assigning different people different shares in accordance with their true worth. Aristotle (*Politics*, 1317^b) also notes the 'anarchic' character of democracies (both he and Plato meant by that an unwillingness on the part of the mass of citizens to take orders from anyone other then themselves); and he agrees (1280^a) that 'justice demands equality, but not for all and sundry but only for those who are in fact equals', although later (1318^a) he honestly faces up to the very serious difficulties involved in determining and agreeing the correct criteria for establishing a practicable distribution of equality.

Plato also echoes the argument that it is quite silly for the Athenians to allow anyone who chooses to get up on his feet and address the *ecclêsia* (*Protagoras*, 319 B–D): true, when some technical business about public construction or shipbuilding is in question, they insist on hearing from architects or shipwrights, and so too with any other matters which call for such professional expertise, and any amateur who tries to speak is booed or jeered or even ejected from the meeting; but when the subject of discussion is the government of the city it is a free-for-all, and nobody worries what credentials the speakers may have to qualify them to give advice on that subject. This line of thought goes back to Socrates himself, who was charged at his trial that he taught that it was folly to appoint the officers of state by lot, 'when nobody would dream of choosing a coxswain or a builder or a flute-player in such a haphazard fashion' (Xenophon, *Memorabilia*, 1. 2. 9).

That the totalitarian Plato was highly critical of democracy is of course not surprising; and his notion of what constituted true 'justice or 'equality' or 'happiness' is itself open to trenchant criticism. His own 'ideal state' is an impracticable (and very unattractive) dream. Aristotle was far less extreme.

As Barker observed, 'He can hardly, perhaps, be called a democrat; but the man who wrote the eleventh chapter of the third book of the *Politics* cannot be called an anti-democrat.'[12]

Aristotle's argument here (*Politics*, 1281ª12 ff.) may be summarized thus:

'A respectable case can be made for popular sovereignty. Collectively, "the many" may have a combination of qualities which is not available to any individual, and which can fit them as a collectivity to weigh proposals sensibly and come to sensible decisions, at any rate in some, although not necessarily in all, democratically organized communities. "The many" may not all be fit themselves to hold high office, but that does not mean that they cannot or should not all have a part in deliberative and judicial activities, elect the higher officers of state, and sit in judgement on their conduct in office. In a number of cases the best judges of a product are not the experts who make it but the people who use it: house-occupiers are better judges of the houses they live in than those who designed or built them, a meal is best judged by those who eat it and not by the chef who cooked it. To exclude any substantial element of a population from participation in government involves the danger of making it actively hostile to the government, with all that that entails. What matters above all else is that the rule of law should be sovereign, and that the laws themselves should be good; the only true safeguard against arbitrary government and the abuse of power is that individuals should be able to make decisions only in particular matters which cannot be covered by the general rules of law.'

Aristotle's own preference was for a 'mixed' constitution, in which a citizen's public rights bore some relation to the level of his wealth, but with stringent checks and restraints on any possible abuse of power. As the above passage clearly indicates, he did not approve of the way in which Athens so indiscriminately opened her highest offices to all and sundry, for he believed that the proper exercise of such offices called for qualities, abilities, and experience not possessed by the poorer citizens in any state. Yet, equally clearly, as Barker

[12] Barker, *The Politics of Aristotle*, p. xxxi.

insisted, he cannot be crudely labelled as an opponent of democracy *tout court*, for there were features of the Athenian system which he held to be either desirable or at any rate defendable.

Aristophanes, whose earliest and latest surviving comic dramas, *Acharnians* and *Plutus* (*Wealth*), were staged in 425 and 388 respectively, tells us a great deal about the Athens of his day. It was for a long time almost *de rigeur* to represent him in books and essays and commentaries, many of which are still read and still valuable in other respects, as an 'oligarch' or a 'fanatical conservative', a man in constant outspoken and vituperative opposition to democratic politics and all new ideas—or at the least as a 'moderate democrat', an enemy of demagogues and imperialism alike. Happily, that approach is now generally recognized as quite unjustifiable. Certainly, Aristophanes is forever poking fun at many of the features of contemporary Athenian society: self-seeking and dishonest politicians 'on the make'; pompously self-satisfied 'brass-hats'; ineffectual diplomatic envoys spinning out their missions and living luxuriously on their over-lavish per diem allowances; dilatory *prytaneis* who loiter in late to open important meetings of the *ecclêsia*; raffish young men-about-town, fire-breathing blood thirsty war-mongering old charcoal-burners, busybody and senile jurors; imperial agents (*episkopoi*), decree-purveyors, public informers, oracle-mongers, philosophers like Socrates and town-planners like Meton, even gullible old 'Mr Demos of the Pnyx' himself, the ordinary Athenian voter. He joyously contrasts the delights of peace and the happy pre-war days of security and prosperity with the travails, hardships, discomforts, and uncertainties of war. He was, after all, a writer of comedies, and the 'Old Comedy' of Athens by tradition contained a large element of exaggerated and topical political satire of a kind which is familiar to modern radio and television audiences. The criticism was by and large indiscriminate: not one of the men known to have been prominent in Athenian public life in the second half of the fifth century and the first quarter of the fourth (the heyday of the Old Comedy) escaped ridicule or scurrilous and sometimes scabrous character assassination at the hands of Aristophanes and his fellow comic dramatists; Pericles himself, the 'uncrowned king of Athens' in the 430s, was sometimes savaged during his lifetime (and got scant respect from Aristophanes after his death).[13]

Aristophanes was not out to preach a political gospel, but to amuse his audience, the groundlings of the Athenian citizenry, and win the first prize against his competitors at this or that comic festival. For all the comparative smallness of scale and participatory nature of the Athenian political system, the timeless distinction between 'them' and 'us' could be exploited to raise a belly-laugh. The ordinary Athenian, just like ourselves, took his system for granted, and only on very rare occasions (as in 411 and 404/3) had any cause to worry that it ran any risk of being subverted.[14] He did not go to see a comedy to have the virtues of that system dinned into his ears, or be lectured on its theoretical deficiencies by somebody anxious to undermine it. He went to enjoy himself, and a not inconsiderable part of his enjoyment came from watching 'them' being caricatured and lampooned in hilarious situations ('them' being active politicians and officials, 'advanced' thinkers and 'fancy' theorists, etc.); he was also evidently happy enough to guffaw at the comical quirks and quiddities, gullibility, petty-mindedness, and short-sightedness, of his next-door neighbour as well. Most of us today enjoy witty cartoons and skits and satires which exaggeratedly 'send up' politicians or parties or positions, regardless of whether we ourselves have voted for or against them or share them; if we have any humour, we can also enjoy laughing at caricatures of ourselves too. Nobody with a grain of common sense can doubt that Aristophanes had his own political views, that—just as we do—he disliked some politicians more than others (notaby Cleon, against whom he had a personal grudge), and approved of some proposals and policies more than others (no contentious proposal was ever carried by a unanimous

[13] On all this see Gomme's splendid article 'Aristophanes and Politics'. For a good recent study of Aristophanes, and analyses of all his plays, see Dover, *Aristophanic Comedy*. Although Aristophanes is the only representative of the Old Comedy any of whose plays survive intact, we possess relatively numerous citations from the lost works of the other practitioners of the craft.

[14] See above, ch. 5.

vote in the *ecclêsia*, any more than any modern government is elected by 100 per cent of the electorate, or each of its actions approved of even by everyone who has voted for it). From time to time his likes and dislikes are actually or potentially discernible, and there can be much instruction and amusement in arguing such points. But he is the last person to go to for either a pro- or an anti-democratic ideology. In truth, the most remarkable thing about Aristophanes and his fellow comic dramatists (all of whom were subsidized out of the public purse through the system of liturgies, which paid for their productions) is the virtually unlimited licence which they were allowed, and seized with both hands, to say whatever they wanted to say without fear of being either muzzled or punished. Cleon's attempt to get Aristophanes convicted on a charge of 'bringing Athens into disrepute' (in his lost comedy of 426, *The Babylonians*) failed, and Aristophanes continued thereafter to poke fun at and abuse both Cleon and whoever or whatever else took his fancy.

The long war between Athens and the Peloponnesian League headed by Sparta broke out in the spring of 431. Pericles died two and a half years later, and Thucydides appended to the notice of his death a brief 'obituary' of Athens' great leader (2.65), which may be summarized as follows:

'Pericles maintained that, provided Athens observed caution and held on to her naval supremacy and abjured any physical expansion of her empire while the war was in progress and declined to court any unnecessary risks, she would come through the war safely. But the political leaders who came after him stood all that on its head, advocating policies seemingly unconnected with the war in pursuit of their personal ambition and private gain, with damaging effects both for Athens herself and for the cities of her alliance— policies which, when they came off, brought prestige and advantage more to them as individuals than to the city itself, but, when they went awry, weakened the city's war effort. Why was that? Pericles' ability, and experience, and manifest incorruptibility had won for him the freely given and unchallenged confidence of his fellow citizens to such an extent that he dominated the formulation and execution of

Athens' policies. Thus Athens, although a democracy, began to all intents and purposes to operate as if it had an uncrowned king! Unfortunately, nobody proved big enough to fill his shoes. His successors were much more on a level with one another, and in their eagerness each to become the first man at Athens turned to currying favour with the citizenry and surrendering control to them. This preoccupation with political "in-fighting" diverted Athens from a proper conduct of the war, and was the source of the major political and military mistakes which in the end led to her capitulation in 404.'

Leaving on one side the many other important and absorbing issues which are raised by this passage, and in particular the suspicion that Thucydides may have been guilty here of some 'telescoping' of events, we must at once scotch the idea that it represents the enunciation of an 'anti-democratic ideology'. Looking back, it made a great deal of sense to conclude that Athens had lost the war by her own ill-judged policies, and that that was at least in some large part the result of division and contention among her leading politicians and of internal schisms, that an assured and prudent leader like Pericles might have presided over a very different outcome. But we have no reason to suppose that Thucydides did not accept that the same sort of defects could affect other forms of government just as seriously. The major Athenian blunder was to overstretch the city's resources in Sicily in 415–413. But Napoleon and Hitler were guilty of comparable misjudgements when they each invaded Russia; and plenty of other despotisms or quasi-despotisms, aristocracies and oligarchies, or even 'moderate democracies', have come to grief through lack of capable leadership and/or intestine rivalries and squabbling ambitions. Democratic systems have certain potential weaknesses which other systems do not share; by the same token, they have certain strengths which other systems lack, and are free from certain weaknesses which other systems are exposed to. (The major defects of the Spartan system of government were pretty rapidly exposed in the years which followed her total victory over Athens in 404.) In short, there never has been nor ever will be any perfect system of government this side of heaven;

and to point out the various essentially or accidentally latent or patent shortcomings of any one existing system does not inescapably mark the critic as the advocate of any other variety. If that is accepted, we are not required to see Thucydides here as doing anything other than pin-pointing what he perceived to be the basic reasons why Athens lost a war which she might otherwise not have lost.

For all that, it is hard not to agree with those scholars who have detected in Thucydides' attitude towards, and judgements on, the leading politicians of post Periclean Athens a subjective and personal (although we may wish to allow also an unconscious) bias.[15] Down to and including Pericles, Athens' political leaders had been for the most part drawn from what we might term the traditional ruling class. Men like Cleon, who came to the forefront after Pericles' death, were of a very different stamp. It is as plain as can be that Thucydides disapproved of, indeed detested, Cleon. He may possibly have had a personal grudge against him as having had a hand in his own banishment on a charge of incompetence in his handling of his command in the northern Aegean in the latter part of 424 (although that is only speculative). Cleon was educated and well-to-do, but he and his like were not 'gentlemen'. Thucydides was unquestionably a 'gentleman', and closely related to earlier 'gentlemanly' politicians like his namesake, Thucydides son of Melesias, and the illustrious Cimon himself.[16] Pericles, although a genuine radical, was a cultivated aristocrat of venerable lineage: the admiration which the young Thucydides clearly felt and expressed for him was not perhaps readily transferred to men like Cleon and Hyperbolus. The same sort of reaction is well attested in other places and in other ages in men who have not, however, necessarily been moved on that account to favour the subversion or overthrow of their constitutions.

Thucydides was in his middle to late twenties when the

---

[15] For some representative recent views on this issue see Gomme 'Four Passages in Thucydides', 74 ff.; *More Essays in Greek History and Literature*, 112 ff.; Hignett, *HAC* 252–68; Westlake, 'Athenian Aims in Sicily'; Brunt, *CR* 75 (1961), 143–4; Andrewes, 'The Mytilene Debate'; Finley, 'Athenian Demagogues'.

[16] On Thucydides' exile see Gomme, *HCT* iii. 584–8. On his family see Wade-Gery, *Essays in Greek History*, 239–70.

Peloponnesian War broke out; and he tells us (1. 1) that he at once began taking careful notes and scrupulously cross-checking evidence and informants with a view to one day writing an account of it. We have every reason to suppose that he was himself one of the large concourse which assembled to hear Pericles deliver the formal address in honour of those Athenians who had fallen in the first year of that war. The Funeral Oration (2. 35–46), although presented in oratio recta, does not purport—any more than do the other speeches in his *History*—to be an exact verbatim record of the words which Pericles actually used; and it is written in Thucydides' own highly idiosyncratic style.[17] But we can safely take it that he has here accurately condensed and represented the essence of one of the most memorable speeches of the finest orator of his generation, and very probably exploited or adapted some of its most striking or characteristic images and turns of phrase. Of itself, the Funeral Oration contributes nothing to the narrative of the war; its sole purpose is to give the reader an eloquent, moving, and unforgettable picture of a society the defence and preservation of which Pericles declared to be worthy of the supreme sacrifice of self or sons, husbands or brothers, fathers or friends. It is a highly idealized picture, as was fitting to the occasion. But, given that Thucydides reworked the speech with such painstaking care and skill, and accorded it so prominent a position in his *History*, it is very difficult not to believe that he himself shared some measure of respect for the ideals which it celebrated.

One may paraphrase the main thrust of the speech as follows:

'We Athenians have lived in Attica since time immemorial, and ever preserved its integrity. More recently, we have greatly increased its power and extended its dominion, and made our city unmatched in its self-sufficient independence both in peace and for war. Let us then consider what underlies that great achievement, and remind ourselves not only of the political ordering of our society but also of the spirit and character and culture which made that achievement possible.

---

[17] On the speeches in Thucydides' *History* see Gomme, *HCT* v. 393–9.

'Our society is unique in Greece, and an example to every other. We call our system a "democracy", because it subserves the interests not of a privileged few but of the majority. [It is significant that Pericles does not say 'because it is *governed* by the majority'.[18] Like the 'Old Oligarch', he looks to the end which has been achieved; he is not concerned with the mechanics of the constitution, but rather with what we nowadays call its 'cash value'.] Every private citizen is guaranteed complete equality under the laws; and public life is open not solely to some privileged few but to everybody, rich or poor, humble or eminent, who has the ability to serve Athens. That same spirit of tolerance pervades our everyday life, with its friendly readiness to "live and let live". We are a law-abiding people: we respect those who hold positions of public authority, and above all those laws which safeguard the individual against injustice, and those unwritten laws which all decent men accept that they must abide by.

'We are a civilized society. No other city provides so many recreations for the spirit, plays, concerts, spectacles, and religious festivals throughout the year, so many buildings to delight the eye. [It is tempting to guess that Pericles is here deriding the sort of sneering criticisms reported by the 'Old Oligarch' of the supposed inability of any but the 'best' people to care for culture, just as he claims that Athens offers the ordinary man an opportunity to display his innate *aretê* in the service of his city—*aretê*, a word denoting high personal gifts and qualities which the Old Oligarch's 'best' people liked to believe exclusive to themselves.] The greatness of our city draws to itself all that the rest of the world has to offer, so that we are not insular but truly international in our tastes and our receptiveness.

'In our military preparations too we are unlike our enemies. The gates of Athens stand open to the world. Unlike Sparta, we conduct no periodical deportations of aliens to keep them from seeing too much; we put our trust, not in materiel or equipment, but in our courage and confidence in the test. Their young men are trained from childhood in a hard and narrow school for war; ours are

---

[18] On this see Gomme, *HCT* ii. 107–10.

relaxed and free, yet trusting in our native courage we face the same dangers no less bravely. Our forces are not concentrated, for they are stationed far and wide; yet in their totality they are a match for the world.

'We love beauty, but eschew extravagance; we cultivate the things of the mind, but with no effeteness. We value wealth for the uses to which it can be put and not for vainglorious ostentation; for us poverty is no disgrace—the only disgrace lies in tamely accepting it. We are all of us at once private individuals and public servants; for us, the man who shuns involvement in public business is not simply somebody who minds his own business, he is a useless citizen. If few of us are capable of originating policies, we are all sound judges of them. [A similar note is struck by the Syracusan democratic leader Athenagoras at Thucydides 6. 39. 1: 'The rich are the best guardians of public moneys, the wise the best advisers, and the many, when they have heard an issue discussed, the best judges of what to do.'] We are not the sort of people who are frightened or suspicious of open debate; we think it essential to correct action. Others may be unreflectingly bold; our courage rests on a careful appraisal of the chances of success or failure, and we go open-eyed into danger. We would rather give favours than receive them, which makes us the more steadfast in our loyalty to the beneficiaries; our yardstick is not self-interest but a fearless trust in freedom.

'All in all, I maintain that Athens is the centre of Greek civilization. "the school of Hellas" (*paideusis tês Hellados*), and her individual citizens the most versatile, independent, and self-reliant of all Greeks; a city worth dying for, as these men did.'

It must be recognized that Pericles' praise of democracy in this speech lays great emphasis on the fact that it subserves, or at least does not detract from, the imperial strength of Athens. The power of the city is the dominant theme. Although, as already remarked, the revenue from her empire did not contribute directly to the costs of the democracy, the surpluses which were accumulated during the mid-fifth century from this and other 'imperial' sources (booty,

ransom, and sale of prisoners of war, etc.) were exploited to
meet heavy public expenditures, most notably on the lavish
and expensive Acropolis building programme; and large
numbers of citizens were furnished with grants of land in the
areas under Athenian control. Much of the cultural primacy
of the city which Pericles makes so much of was made
possible only by that imperial might in which he also takes
such evident pride. Again, despite his dismissal of those who
shunned involvement in public affairs as 'useless' and
untypically selfish, some Athenians could claim it as being to
their credit that they 'minded their own business'. Nevertheless, however much allowance we make for hyperbole and
selection, he does depict the ideal of the open society which
Athens represented (however imperfectly) in scarcely veiled
contrast with the illiberal, stunting and repressive closed
society which Sparta exemplified. If the 'Old Oligarch'
shows us the 'freedom from' or reverse side of the coin,
Pericles presents us with its 'freedom to' or obverse face. For
the Greeks, in their to modern eyes tiny states, a *polis* was
more than a collection of fields and buildings, a *politeia* more
than just a 'constitution'. A *polis* was a self-standing society
with its own individual and in some respects unique
character; *politeia* was an abstract noun which in different
contexts could mean any or all of our words 'constitution',
'society', 'culture', or even 'citizenship'. When Pericles says
in the Funeral Oration that Athens 'enjoys a *politeia* which
provides an example for the rest of Greece to follow', he is
not so much talking of his city's constitution as singling out
those qualities which make Athens characteristically and
uniquely Athens, and so very different from the other *poleis*
of the Greek world in the assumptions which its citizens
hold, their attitude to life, the very air of individuality, open-
mindedness, and independence which they breathe, the
excitement and novelty (and, implictly, the fragility) of this
great experiment in participation and equality. It may not be
that 'statement of democratic political theory' for which
Jones looked in vain; but in its eloquent advocacy of the
virtues of 'government of the people, by the people, and for
the people' it was the earliest, and for many readers remains
the finest, statement of what a democracy should aspire to

be.[19] As Dr Johnson said of eighteenth-century Oxford: 'That the rules are sometimes ill observed may be true; but is nothing against the system.'

[19] What Pericles had to say about the place and proper comportment of Athenian women is illiberal and unacceptable to modern readers (of both sexes); and, even granted that quite a few of the slaves had a better life at Athens than in many other places, not all did (especially in the mines), and slavery is an abominable institution. But to make too much of either issue is to be guilty of anachronism.

BIBLIOGRAPHY

This is not intended to serve as a comprehensive guide to the learned literature on the subject. It is simply a list of the full titles of the books and articles which have been cited in the notes to this book.

ANDREWES, A., *The Greeks* (London, 1967).
—— 'The Generals in the Hellespont 410–407 BC', *JHS* 73 (1953), 2–9.
—— 'The Mytilene Debate', *Phoenix*, 16 (1962), 64–82.
—— 'The Arginusae Trial', *Phoenix*, 28 (1974), 112–22.
—— 'Kleisthenes' Reform Bill', *CQ* 27 (1977), 241–8.
—— 'The Opposition to Pericles', *JHS* 98 (1978), 1–8.
BAGEHOT, W., *The English Constitution* (edn. of Oxford, 1949).
BARKER, E., *The Politics of Aristotle* (Oxford, 1946).
BOWERSOCK, G. W., 'Pseudo-Xenophon', *HSCP* 71 (1966), 33–55.
BROGAN, D. W., *An Introduction to American Politics* (London, 1954).
BRUNT, P. A., *Social Conflicts in the Roman Republic* (London, 1971).
—— Review of Ehrenberg, *The Greek State*, in *CR* 75 (1961), 143–4.
BUSOLT, G., *Griechische Staatskunde*, 3rd edn. (Munich, 1920).
CALHOUN, G. M., *Athenian Clubs in Politics and Litigation* (Bulletin of the University of Texas, 1913).
CARTER, L. B., *The Quiet Athenian* (Oxford, 1986).
CAWKWELL, G. L. '*Nomophylakia* and the Areopagus', *JHS* 108 (1988), 1–12.
CONNOR, W. R., *The New Politicians of Fifth-Century Athens* (Princeton, 1971).
DAVIES, J. K., *Athenian Propertied Families 600–300 BC* (Oxford, 1971).
—— *Democracy and Classical Greece* (Hassocks, Sussex, and Atlantic Highlands, NJ, 1978).
—— *Wealth and the Power of Wealth in Classical Athens* (Salem, NH, 1984).
DE STE CROIX, G. E. M., 'Greek and Roman Accounting', in A. C. Littleton and B. S. Yamey (eds.), *Studies in the History of Accounting* (London, 1956), 14–74.
—— 'The Constitution of the Five Thousand', *Historia*, 5 (1956), 1–33.

DE STE CROIX, G. E. M., *The Origins of the Peloponnesian War* (London, 1972).
DOVER, K. J., *Aristophanic Comedy* (London, 1972).
FERGUSSON, W. S., *Hellenistic Athens* (London, 1911).
FINLEY, M. I., *Studies in Land and Credit in Ancient Athens* (Rutgers, NJ, 1951).
—— 'Athenian Demagogues', *Past & Present*, 21 (1962), 3–24.
—— *Politics in the Ancient World* (Cambridge, 1983).
FORNARA, C. W., *Translated Documents of Greece and Rome*, i. *Archaic Times to the End of the Peloponnesian War* (Baltimore and London, 1977).
—— *Herodotus: An Interpretative Essay* (Oxford, 1971).
FORREST, W. G., *The Emergence of Greek Democracy* (London, 1966).
—— 'Aristophanes' *Acharnians*', *Phoenix*, 17 (1963), 1–12.
—— 'An Athenian Generation Gap', *Yale Class. St.* 24 (1975), 37–52.
—— and STOCKTON, D. L. 'The Athenian Archons: A Note', *Historia*, 36 (1987), 235–40.
FOXHALL, L., and FORBES, H. A. 'Σιτομετρεία: The Role of Grain as a Staple Food in Classical Antiquity', *Chiron*, 12 (1982), 41–90.
FRENCH, A. *The Growth of the Athenian Economy* (London, 1964).
FRISCH, H., *The Constitution of the Athenians* (Copenhagen, 1942).
GLOTZ, G., *Ancient Greece at Work* (London, 1926).
GOMME, A. W., *The Population of Athens in the Fifth and Fourth Centuries BC* (Oxford, 1933).
—— *More Essays in Greek History and Literature* (Oxford, 1962).
—— 'Aristophanes and Politics', *CR* 52 (1938), 97–109 [= *More Essays*, 70–91].
—— 'Four Passages in Thucydides', *JHS* 71 (1951), 70–80.
—— ANDREWES, A., and DOVER, K. J., *A Historical Commentary on Thucydides*, 5 vols. (Oxford, 1945–81).
HANSEN, M. H., *Demography and Democracy: The Number of Athenian Citizens in the Fourth Century BC* (Herning, 1985).
—— *The Athenian Ecclesia* (Copenhagen, 1983).
—— *The Athenian Assembly in the Age of Demosthenes* (Oxford, 1987).
—— *Eisangelia: The Sovereignty of the People's Court in Athens in the Fourth Century BC* (Odense U. Classical Studies, 4; 1974).
—— 'Eisangelia in Athens: A Reply', *JHS* 100 (1980), 83–95.
—— 'Seven Hundred *Archai* in Classical Athens', *GRBS* 21 (1980), 151–73.
—— 'Athenian Politicians 403–322 BC', *GRBS* 24 (1983), 33–55.
—— '*Rhetores* and *Strategoi* in Fourth-Century Athens', *GRBS* 24 (1983), 151–80.

—— 'Political Activity and the Organization of Attica in the Fourth Century BC', *GRBS* 24 (1983), 227–38.

—— 'The Number of *Rhetores* in the Athenian *Ecclesia* 355–322 BC', *GRBS* 25 (1984), 123–55.

HARDING, P., *Translated Documents of Greece and Rome*, ii. *From the End of the Peloponnesian War to the Battle of Ipsus* (Cambridge, 1985).

HARRIS, E. M., 'How often did the Athenian Assembly Meet?', *CR* 36 (1986) 363–77.

HARRISON, A. R. W., *The Law of Athens*, 2 vols. (Oxford, 1968–71).

HARVEY, F. D., 'Literacy in the Athenian Democracy', *REG* 79 (1966), 585–635.

HEADLAM, J. W., *Election by Lot at Athens*, 2nd edn. (Cambridge, 1933).

HICKS, SIR JOHN, *A Theory of Economic History* (Oxford, 1969).

HIGNETT, C., *A History of the Athenian Constitution to the End of the Fifth Century BC* (Oxford, 1951).

JACOBY, F., *Atthis: The Local Chronicles of Ancient Athens* (Oxford, 1949).

—— *Die Fragmente der griechischen Historiker* (Berlin and Leiden, 1923–57).

JONES, A. H. M., *Athenian Democracy* (Oxford, 1957).

KRAAY, C. M., *Archaic and Classical Greek Coinage* (Berkeley, 1976).

LEWIS, D. M., 'Cleisthenes and Attica', *Historia*, 12 (1963), 22–40.

—— 'Themistocles' Archonship', *Historia*, 22 (1973), 757–8.

—— Review of Connor, *New Politicians*, in *CR* 25 (1975), 87–90.

MACDOWELL, D.M., *The Law in Classical Athens* (London, 1978).

MEIGGS, R., *The Athenian Empire* (Oxford, 1972).

—— and LEWIS, D. M., *A Selection of Greek Historical Inscriptions to the End of the Fifth Century BC* (Oxford, 1969).

MERITT, B. D., *Epigraphica Attica* (Harvard, 1940).

OSBORNE, R. G., *Demos: The Discovery of Classical Attika* (Cambridge, 1985).

—— 'Law in Action in Classical Athens', *JHS* 105 (1985), 40–58.

OSTWALD, M., *Nomos and the Beginnings of the Athenian Democracy* (Oxford, 1969).

—— *From Popular Sovereignty to the Sovereignty of Law* (Berkeley, Los Angeles, and London, 1986).

PATON, J. M., *The Erechtheum* (Cambridge, Mass., 1927).

PEARSON, L., *The Local Historians of Attica* (Philadelphia, 1942).

POPPER, K. R., *The Open Society and its Enemies* (London, 1945).

RHODES, P. J., *The Athenian Boule* (Oxford, 1972).

—— 'The Five Thousand in the Athenian Revolutions of 411 BC', *JHS* 92 (1972), 115–27.

—— *A Commentary on the Aristotelian Athenaion Politieia* (Oxford, 1981).

—— 'Eisangelia in Athens', *JHS* 99 (1979), 103–14.

—— 'Athenian Democracy after 403 BC', *CJ* (1979–80), 305–23.

—— 'Ephebai, Bouleutai, and the Population of Athens', *ZPE* 38 (1980), 191–201.

ROBINSON, E. S. G., 'The Coins from the Ephesian Artemision Reconsidered', *JHS* 71 (1951), 156–7.

SEALEY, R., 'Ephialtes', *CP* 59 (1964), 11–22.

SHERWIN-WHITE, A. N., 'Violence in Roman Politics', *JRS* 46 (1956), 1–9.

SIEWERT, P., *Die Trittyen Attikas und die Heeresreform des Kleisthenes* (Vestigia, 33; Munich, 1982).

SINCLAIR, R. K., *Democracy and Participation in Athens* (Cambridge, 1988).

STAVELEY, E. S., *Greek and Roman Voting and Elections* (London, 1972).

STOCKTON, D. L., 'The Death of Ephialtes', *CQ* 32 (1982), 227–8.

—— Review of Gomme, *A Historical Commentary on Thucydides*, vol. v, in *CR* 31 (1981), 182–4.

THOMAS, K., 'The United Kingdom', in R. Grew (ed.), *Crises of Political Development in Europe and the United States*, (Princeton, 1978), 41–97.

THOMSEN, R., *The Origins of Ostracism* (Copenhagen, 1972).

TOD, M. N., *A Selection of Greek Historical Inscriptions*, 2 vols. (Oxford 1946–8).

TRAILL, J. S., *The Political Organization of Attica* (*Hesperia*, suppl. 14; 1975).

WADE-GERY, H. T., *Essays in Greek History* (Oxford, 1958).

WESTLAKE, H. D., 'Athenian Aims in Sicily', *Historia*, 9 (1960), 385–402.

WHITEHEAD, D., *The Demes of Attica 508/7–ca.250 B.C.* (Princeton, 1986).

ZIMMERN, A., *The Greek Commonwealth: Politics and Economics in Fifth-Century Athens*, 5th edn. (Oxford, 1931).

GENERAL INDEX

INDEX OF PASSAGES CITED